The
EVERYTHING.
Mafia Book

Dear Reader:

When John Gotti died in June 2002, his death and the events surrounding his funeral made the New York City newspaper headlines for several days. Much ballyhoo was made of the stylish suit the "Dapper Don" wore in his coffin and of his elaborate wake and the motorcade that escorted his remains to the cemetery. Columnists hailed him as a man of panache and class, a New York original. His daughter eulogized him as the man who "taught her to dream."

Hello?!? John Gotti was a murderer. He made his living stealing things from honest, hard-working people and killing those who got in his way. There was nothing heroic or swashbuckling about him. Yet the Mafia continues to fascinate so many of us. Why?

Americans have always had romantic and unrealistic notions about the "outlaw." The Wild West was nothing like it is in the movies. The "bad boy" actor or athlete is often a self-absorbed doofus. There is nothing praiseworthy about a crook and a killer. But people continue to get vicarious kicks from following the unsavory antics of the Mafia, both in real life and on *The Sopranos*. These people do the things we would not dare, and usually get away with it. And if they occasionally get whacked, well, that goes with the territory.

We follow the activities of the Mafia the same way that drivers slow down to view an accident—with visceral dread and lurid fascination. However, we must always remember that they are anything but "goodfellas." Any claims to the contrary we can easily refute.

James Mannion

The EVERYTHING® Series

Editorial

Publishing Director	Gary M. Krebs
Managing Editor	Kate McBride
Copy Chief	Laura MacLaughlin
Acquisitions Editor	Bethany Brown
Development Editor	Karen Johnson Jacot
Production Editor	Khrysti Nazzaro

Production

Production Director	Susan Beale
Production Manager	Michelle Roy Kelly
Series Designers	Daria Perreault
	Colleen Cunningham
Cover Design	Paul Beatrice
	Frank Rivera
Layout and Graphics	Colleen Cunningham
	Rachael Eiben
	Michelle Roy Kelly
	Daria Perreault
	Erin Ring
Series Cover Artist	Barry Littmann
Interior Photographs	AP/Wide World Photos

THE
EVERYTHING®
MAFIA
BOOK

True-life accounts of legendary
figures, infamous crime families,
and chilling events

James Mannion

Adams Media Corporation
Avon, Massachusetts

An Everything® Series Book.
Everything® is a registered trademark of Adams Media Corporation.

Published by Adams Media Corporation
57 Littlefield Street, Avon, MA 02322 U.S.A.
www.adamsmedia.com

ISBN: 1-58062-864-8
Printed in the United States of America.

J I H G F E D C B A

Library of Congress Cataloging-in-Publication Data
Mannion, James.
The everything mafia book / James Mannion.
p.   cm.   --(Everything series book)
ISBN 1-58062-864-8
1. Mafia—Italy. 2. Mafia—United States. 3. Organized crime—Italy.
4. Organized crime—United States. I. Title. II. Series: Everything series

HV6453.I83 M358353 2003
364.1'06'0945–dc21

2002152395

This publication is designed to provide accurate and authoritative information with
regard to the subject matter covered. It is sold with the understanding that the pub-
lisher is not engaged in rendering legal, accounting, or other professional advice.
If legal advice or other expert assistance is required, the services of a competent
professional person should be sought.
    —From a *Declaration of Principles* jointly adopted by a Committee of the
American Bar Association and a Committee of Publishers and Associations

Many of the designations used by manufacturers and sellers to distinguish their
products are claimed as trademarks. Where those designations appear in this book
and Adams Media was aware of a trademark claim, the designations have been
printed with initial capital letters.

This book is available at quantity discounts for bulk purchases.
For information, call 1-800-872-5627.

Contents

Organization of a Mafia Family

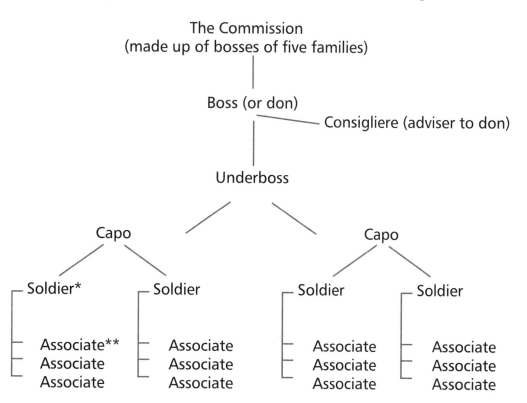

The Commission
(made up of bosses of five families)

Boss (or don) ── Consigliere (adviser to don)

Underboss

Capo

Capo

Soldier*

Soldier

Soldier

Soldier

Associate**
Associate
Associate

Associate
Associate
Associate

Associate
Associate
Associate

Associate
Associate
Associate

*There may be as many as ten soldiers under one capo.
**There can be any number of associates under a soldier.

Top Ten Gangsters You Will Get to Know
After Reading This Book

1. **Salvatore Maranzano**—an Old World Mafioso who was the leader of the organization of the major crime families in the United States
2. **Dutch Schultz**—who was killed by his own crime family when he made it known that he intended to kill (against Mafia rules) a politician who was after him
3. **Al "Scarface" Capone**—who made and sold bootlegged alcohol during Prohibition in Chicago in the 1920s
4. **Lucky Luciano**—the powerful mobster who took over as "Boss of Bosses" after having Salvatore Maranzano murdered by hit men posing as IRS agents; later exiled to Italy
5. **Louis "Lepke" Buchalter**—the founder of the elite group of killers known as Murder, Inc.
6. **John Gotti**—mobster who took power after ordering a hit on the previous boss, which took place on a crowded Manhattan sidewalk during the Christmas shopping season
7. **Albert Anastasia, alias the "Mad Hatter"**—mobster who was shot in a barbershop while getting a haircut as a result of a power struggle between Mafia men
8. **Sam Giancana**—the mob boss who was good friends with singer Frank Sinatra
9. **Joe Valachi**—mobster who rose through the crime family ranks until he was sent to prison on a drug charge, where he decided to become an informant to the police, revealing details of the inner workings of the Mafia never before known
10. **Henry Hill**—the mobster-turned-informant who now runs his own Web site (though he remains in hiding from the Mafia)

Introduction

▶ WHO ISN'T FASCINATED BY THE IDEA OF THE MAFIA? You may not think you have much involvement with the Mafia. You probably think of them as the Sopranos or the Corleone family, characters that you can watch from the comfort and safety of your home.

Have you ever bought electronics at a super savings that in your heart you knew "fell off the back of the truck"? Have you ever had a cheese pizza at a neighborhood pizzeria in a major metropolitan center? Played a pinball machine in your neighborhood gin mill?

If you answered "yes" to any of these questions, you may have had dealings with the Mafia. The Mafia is entrenched in our culture, and its tentacles extend into every area of society, from politics to entertainment to unions and beyond. It is as American as a pizza pie, and its operators are as smooth as extra-virgin olive oil.

The Mafia goes by other names, the most well-known being "La Cosa Nostra," which is translated as "Our Thing." Their very name is the first indication of a recurring Mafia theme—insularity and silence. "Never let anyone outside the family know what you're thinking," as Don Corleone tells Sonny.

The American Mafia has its roots in Sicily. For centuries intrepid entrepreneurs made a living offering protection from invaders, bandits, and other bad apples. There was a time when they were regarded as local heroes, Sicilian Robin Hoods who protected the peasant class from its enemies. Or at least that's what their press agents would like you to believe. Eventually, they offered protection from themselves. For regular payments they themselves would not kill you. The local Mafia chieftains became more powerful than any of the princes, priests, or politicians.

The Mafia came to the New World along with the millions of huddled masses yearning to breathe free. The mobsters wanted a little more than breathing room, however. They wanted their version of the American Dream, and set about setting up shop in the major urban centers. All ethnic groups have their criminal element, but for our purposes this book will focus on the Italian and some Jewish gangsters who came to America and established "families." Their family values are a little different than what we perceive as good-old-fashioned American family values.

From even before the "golden age" of Al Capone and the Chicago mob to the "Dapper Don" John Gotti, the mob became as American an institution as baseball. There are still those who are inclined to romanticize them as modern day mavericks like the cowboy outlaws of the Wild West. It is worth noting that Billy the Kid was a psychotic punk and cold-blooded killer. Bonnie and Clyde did not look like Warren Beatty and Faye Dunaway. And the Corleones are more akin to Macbeth and King Lear than their real-life counterparts.

The Mafia is comprised of ruthless hoodlums who sought and seek to make an easy buck and don't fret much about who gets hurt in the process. They purport to be Old World family men but inevitably have mistresses on the side. They go to Mass on Sunday yet regularly employ violence and murder as the tools of their trade. Yes, there was a certain code they lived by in the "good old days." They kept the women and children out of it—though the Sicilian Mafia resembled their Colombian drug cartel counterparts in their penchant to wipe out entire families.

The Mafia is an intriguing tale of colorful characters with colorful nicknames. From the speakeasies and bootleg booze of the 1920s to the glitz and glamour of Las Vegas in the 1950s and 1960s up to the flamboyant conduct of John Gotti in the 1980s and 1990s, the story of the Mafia is the story of America. For every yin, there's a yang. For everything up-front and in the light of day, there is darkness lurking in the shadows. The Mafia embodies the dark side of the American Dream. Everyone is fascinated by an intriguing villain, from Shakespeare's Richard III to Batman's grinning nemesis, the Joker. That simple fact of human nature makes the Mafia a perennially fascinating sociocultural phenomenon.

Chapter 1

The Second-Oldest Profession

Crime has been around since the dawn of humankind, and organized crime has been around almost as long. Ever since humans, social animals by nature, banded together in primitive tribal associations, there have always been rogue elements that banded together in the shadows to prey on the rest of the pack. This chapter is a brief history of that tendency.

A Brief History of Crime

As long as there have been societies, there have been secret societies within them. Many of these had a criminal element that thought it was a better arrangement to steal from the hard-working members of the culture than to work for a living. For much of ancient history, the predominant criminal was the bandit. Gangs of bandits terrorized the countryside of every land. The organization of these crime families was for the most part fairly simple. One alpha male ruled the roost. The less macho types followed him, and occasionally an up-and-coming bandit challenged and defeated the leader. If he bested the bandit leader, he was then the top dog.

FACT

Organized crime needs collaborators to thrive. As long as there has been political and governmental structure, there has been corruption. The underworld needs, and always finds, help from the "overworld" to pursue its illegal endeavors.

The goals of the bandit gangs were also rather simple. Raid any vulnerable town or village and rape and pillage. There was no code to live by, no notion of honor. Fear and control were the only methods employed by the bandit leaders. It was essential for the bandit leader to instill fear in the rest of the bandit gang. Through fear the leader maintained control. Intimidation and the threat of bodily harm and/or death were the ways that a bandit leader stayed in power. Of course the communities the bandits preyed upon lived in a constant state of fear.

One Man's Bandit . . .

There is a popular argument that has been made over the years that "one man's bandit is another man's freedom fighter." It is true that there have been many tyrannical governments over the millennia and that people have taken up arms against their oppressors many times in the history of the world. Legends like Robin Hood and the movie and television adventures of Zorro always capture the imagination of people. These are archetypes of the crusading hero against social injustices.

The Mafia has tried to use this argument as a public relations tool on occasion. The Sicilian Mafia is said to have begun as a ragtag band of freedom fighters who took refuge in the rocky hills, often swooping down to attack the many conquerors in that island's long history. Al Capone tried to paint himself as a maverick rebel who was providing a service that an oppressive government tried to deny the people (a drink during Prohibition). He said he was simply giving the people what they wanted.

Al Capone

Courtesy of AP/Wide World Photos

▲ Al Capone photographed at a football game in Chicago on January 19, 1931. Everywhere he went, people recognized him. Capone always wore a loud tie, a bent-brim fedora hat, and a camel's hair polo coat and always had an entourage of bodyguards.

Some things never change. The alleged recent efforts of the Russian Mafia to influence the judges at the 2002 Winter Olympics is nothing new. Similar corruption occurred at the ancient Greek Olympics. In those days it was considered "impiety," a crime against the gods, and punishable by death.

There is a big difference, however, between criminals and freedom fighters. Criminal organizations are not altruistic outfits that have the good of the people as their prime directive. They do not want to work to accumulate goods or currency. They want something for nothing and do not hesitate to use violence to achieve their goals.

Early Organized Crime Groups

One of the earliest organized crime groups originated in China. The contemporary Chinese criminal groups all trace their roots back to this old tradition. The origin of this gang is generally regarded as a fanciful legend with little basis in historical accuracy. In fact, it sounds a lot like *Kung Fu*, the popular television show from the 1970s.

The Triads

The alleged genesis of the crime gangs that have come to be called the Triads is the story of a Shaolin temple full of peaceful monks who meditated and practiced the form of martial arts called kung fu. When their kingdom was under assault by barbarian invaders, the monks left the sanctuary of their monastery to do battle with the brigands. They defeated them handily and sent them on their way. The emperor offered them great riches as a reward, but humble guys that they were, they returned to the quiet and contemplative life in their temple.

The emperor's advisers convinced him that these men could someday pose a threat to his position. They were so powerful that if they chose to, they could depose him from the throne. The emperor and his men visited the monastery, ostensibly to throw the monks a party in gratitude for their service. They spiked the rice wine and murdered the monks as they lounged in a drunken stupor. Then the villains set fire to the temple. Five monks escaped and wandered the land, eventually finding a talisman that they interpreted as a sign from God to fight for truth, justice, and the Chinese way. The called themselves the Heaven and Earth Association, and their symbol was a triangle. Hence future incarnations became known as the Triads. There were many Chinese criminal groups that evolved over the centuries, some of which remain active today. They all like to claim the legend as their own.

Like the Mafia, the successors of the ancient Chinese Triads came to the New World. They usually make large urban "Chinatowns" their home base and engage in both low-level and high-profile crimes. A favorite these days is assisting illegal immigrants across America's borders (for a hefty fee, of course).

However, historians believe this story bears little resemblance to reality. In reality the germ of the Triad gang was roving bands of vagabonds who banded together and preyed on the hapless villagers. It is a sad and repetitive story.

Thugs, Not Hugs

For an unknown period of time, probably thousands of years, the subcontinent of India was plagued by a secret society of criminals called the Thuggees. If the word sounds familiar, that is because their name entered the English language as the word *thug*.

The earliest reports of the Thuggees date back to the 1300s, but the group is believed to be much older than that. The modus operandi of the Thuggees was to join a caravan of travelers. Caravans were a common method of transportation in ancient times. Long journeys took many months, often through desolate terrain where travelers were subjected to marauding bandits. Caravans were similar to the wagon trains that traversed the American West in the nineteenth century.

While it is true that the British occupation of India was not based on altruism, the Brits did help rid the country of the Thuggees, a vicious and ancient criminal society.

The Thuggees would infiltrate the caravan posing as fellow traveling merchants. They would ride with the group for a while and ingratiate themselves to their fellow travelers. One night they would ritually strangle the merchants, bury their remains, and steal their loot. The weapon of strangulation was an orange scarf. The Thuggees worshipped the Hindu goddess Kali, who had many arms and wore a necklace made from the heads of her male victims.

The British Get Involved

In the seventeenth century, the British Empire went into India with designs to exploit the natural resources. They wished to control resources and run the government. One particular man who came to India from Britain took a strong interest in the Thuggees.

FACT

Like the Mafia, in which only "made men" (those who have committed murder) are invited into the inner sanctum, so too the Thuggees made murder a prerequisite for membership. However, the Thuggees insisted on a minimum of one murder a year to remain in good standing.

William Henry Sleeman came to India as a military man. He was fascinated by the stories of this mysterious society of bandits and murderers and learned as much as he could about them. Originally the British did not believe that such a society could exist. Sleeman believed and made it his life's work to wipe the scourge of the Thuggees from the Indian landscape.

He became a judge and was given the title General Superintendent for the Suppression of Thuggees. Through his research and eventual prosecution of the Thuggees, many of their secrets became public. They are similar to the modern Mafia in several ways. They committed both common crimes and cruel murders but created a myth of nobility around themselves. They had established an elaborate underground network and struck fear into the hearts of their fellow citizens. Like the Mafia, everyone in the community knew about the Thuggees, but the people remained silent out of fear of reprisal. That is, until the Thuggees began to be arrested by the British. Some individual Thuggees turned into "rats" and "sang" for the authorities, naming associates and revealing the society's secrets. Their motives were not to avoid punishment, however. The Thuggee believed that being caught must have been God's will.

FACT

The Al Capone of the Thuggees was a fellow called Thug Burham. He strangled 931 victims in his fifty-year career. Ironically, he met his end at the end of a hangman's rope in 1840.

The Thuggees also had an elaborate form of slang. Underworld crime groups often have a very colorful vernacular of slang expressions. We will examine the modern Mafia's "slanguage" in depth in Chapter 18. Sleeman researched and catalogued the "slanguage" of the Thuggees, eventually publishing a dictionary of Thuggee slang.

The Thuggees were eventually smoked out, hunted down, and brought to justice. They became extinct as a criminal entity. The most famous portrayal of Thuggees in the movies is in the classic 1939 film *Gunga Din*. They are depicted as insane and murderous zealots whose leader whips them into a frenzy by raving "Kill for the love of Kali! Kill for the love of killing!"

Crime Busters of Antiquity

Society has always tried to curb its criminal members. In the old days the law cracked down ruthlessly upon lawbreakers. There were early attempts to create a system of laws to bring civility to an out-of-control society. An early example was the ancient Mesopotamian Code of Hammurabi. This code included 282 "rules" for society that established a uniform rule of law for the empire of the ruler Hammurabi. It is the first-known attempt to create a set of uniform laws that were then made available to citizens so they could read them and know what was expected of them. It was enlightened for the time but did not deal kindly with the criminal element. The ancients did not waste breath debating the pros and cons of the death penalty. Death was the prescription for breaking many of the laws.

The Code of Hammurabi dealt with criminals in the spirit of "an eye for an eye." If a house collapsed and killed its owner, the builder of the house would be put to death. Some less final but equally brutal punishments included cutting off a slave's ear if he disobeyed his master (as the organ of hearing was a symbol of obedience).

Perhaps the most famous effort to instill a code of decency is the Ten Commandments, handed down by God to Moses on Mount Sinai. Humankind was still in a barbaric state 5,000 years ago. The Ten Commandments may seem like basic rules to live by, but it was a revolutionary document at the time. These rules provided guidelines to be followed by every individual, not just by the society as a whole.

Where There's a Will . . .

The rogue element of society has always existed, even before there were official "laws" declaring anything "illegal." Groups have organized for as long as we can look back in history for the purpose of satisfying their greed and need for power. Criminals in both India and China found ways to get what they wanted using threats, violence, and the fear of death.

The Ten Commandments and the Code of Hammurabi were early attempts to curb the lawless and immoral nature of humankind. They were not entirely successful then or now. There has always been a criminal element in every society and among every subgroup of society, and it's possible there always will be.

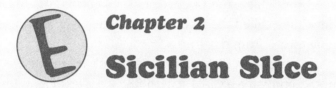

Chapter 2

Sicilian Slice

The America Mafia has its origins on the island of Sicily, which is off the coast of Italy in the Mediterranean Sea. The island has had a tumultuous and turbulent history that proved to be fertile soil for an underworld crime structure to take root. This chapter examines the emergence of the Mafia from Sicily.

Strange Invaders

Sicily's history is one of occupation. The native inhabitants were called Siculi, and it is believed that they came over to the island from southern Italy. This was in the mists of prehistory, before the time when written records were chiseled into stone or scratched onto papyrus. Hence we do not know the exact date this band of travelers set sail from the mainland. These Siculi, sometimes called the Sicani, were subject to the whims and fancies of invading forces from day one.

First it was the Greeks and Phoenicians who took up residence on the island, from approximately 734 B.C. to 580 B.C. Next came the Carthaginians, who arrived on the island and waged war with the Greeks for supremacy. They battled it out for many decades, and control changed hands more than once.

As an island-nation, Sicily did much more than give birth to the Mafia. Frank Sinatra, Al Pacino, Robert De Niro, baseball great Joe DiMaggio, and former New York City Mayor Rudolph Giuliani can all trace their roots back to Sicily.

The mighty Romans came, saw, and conquered the Carthaginians, seizing control in 210 B.C. The Roman reign was the longest, lasting several hundred years until the Roman Empire fell. In A.D. 440 the barbarian tribe called the Vandals conquered Sicily. They did more than scrawl graffiti on the walls. These invaders killed many citizens and enslaved the rest. Then it was the Byzantine Empire's turn. The Saracens, a group of Arabs who practiced the newly established religion of Islam, attacked and occupied the island in 827.

The Norman French ousted the Arabs after a thirty-year war that ended in 1091. In 1194, the House of Hohenstaufen, part of the Holy Roman Empire, invaded, conquered, and occupied Sicily for a time. In the late Middle Ages and the Renaissance, the Spanish and French were in control of the island for various periods of time.

The native Sicilians, who came over from Italy before recorded history, never had control of their island homeland. It was conquered by one invader after another. Millennia of subjugation made the people insular, clannish, and suspicious. This climate allowed the secret society that became the Mafia to germinate and grow.

Vive La France

The French were in control of the island when the Mafia as we know it came to be. It is natural for oppressed peoples to form secret societies. In Sicily, the native men banded together in groups to discuss their situation and their plans to fight their oppressors. In all tyrannies, freedom of assembly is forbidden and punishable by imprisonment or worse. The oppressors know that, as the old saying goes, "in unity there is strength," and therefore they cannot safely allow the oppressed to join together for fear of losing their power over them. But the oppressed population often *does* manage to come together in a covert and clandestine manner.

FACT

The Sicilian dialect, while basically an offshoot of Italian, also has a strong Greek and Arabic influence, since these cultures dropped by and stayed a while in Sicily, usually as unwelcome guests.

One of the theories about how the word *Mafia* entered the language is that it started as an acronym for the rallying cry of the Sicilian resistance forces. *Morte alla Francia Italia anelia!* is translated as "Death to the French is Italy's cry." As you can see, the first letter of each Italian word spells *Mafia*. There is another opinion that *Mafia* is a corruption of an Arabic word meaning "refuge." In Sicily's violent history, people regularly ran for the hills to seek refuge from the current invader. When the Saracens took over their land, many ran for the rocky hills to hide out and make plans.

FACT

In *The Godfather, Part II*, Vito Corleone's older brother heads for the hills when a Mafia chieftain is intent on his murder. The hills were always a favorite hiding place in reality and in Mafia movies. "Head for the hills" is an old expression meaning to make a hasty escape.

The secret societies that formed against the oppressive invaders also battled pirates, bandits, and assorted outlaws that plagued the peasants. Some of these men were brave and patriotic and became heroes of the people. The legend is that they became real-life Robin Hoods and Zorros, battling the French invaders and instilling a national pride in a conquered people. They had gained power by fighting for the oppressed peoples of the island against a common enemy—the French.

Talk to the Hand

By the 1700s, the Mafia had begun to extort money from the very people they purported to protect. People would receive courtly and politely written letters "requesting" money for protection. The gimmick was that the money was protection from the group that sent the letter. If the recipient did not pay up, they could expect a violent response. Family members might be kidnapped and held for ransom. Their house could be set ablaze and destroyed. They might even be killed. People lived in terror that one of these notes would be slipped under their door.

The "Black Hand" was another name for the Sicilian Mafia. It was called that because of the Mafia's penchant for slipping a politely written note under people's doors asking them in a nice way to pay a fee to avoid getting killed. The note was not signed, but instead was stamped with an inked image of the caller's hand.

The Sicilian Mafia continued to gain power, prestige, and influence in all aspects of the island's culture and political establishment. By 1876 the Mafia chieftain Don Raffaele Palizzolo was elected to the Sicilian Parliament. He arranged for his hand-picked men to become prime minister and director of the National Bank. This commingling of Mafia and politics is a tradition that never stopped. As we shall see in Chapter 10, the American Mafia has been a behind-the-scenes player in American politics, allegedly influencing at least one presidential election.

The Omerta Code

The Mafia ritual called "Omerta" originated in Sicily. It is translated as "manhood" but has evolved into the Mafia's "code of silence." Rituals of initiation into manhood have existed in every culture going back to ancient and primitive cultures. There are rites of passage into manhood that in primitive cultures involve elaborate ceremonies. The Mafia shrouds its activities with ritual and ceremony to give themselves an air of dignity. These rituals are an amalgam of the traditions of Roman Catholicism and Freemasonry and native Sicilian rituals.

FACT

You have probably heard the expression "the fish rots from the head down," meaning that corruption starts at the top of any organization. But you may not have known that it is a Sicilian expression: *U pesci fet d'a testa*.

Omerta was the tradition in which young men were initiated into the secret society of the Mafia. It evolved into the modern Mafia tradition of Mafiosi being "made," that is, they are allowed into the inner sanctum of the Mafia family. One of the requirements for membership in the modern Mafia family is to have killed someone, or to have participated in a murder, even if the initiate isn't the one who pulls the trigger.

The code of the modern Mafia harks back to the Old World traditions of the ancient Sicilian culture. In addition to the vow of Omerta, a second element of the Mafia code is a vow of total devotion and loyalty to the head of the family, or don. This comes from the ancient traditions of royalty and the divine right of kings. Among royalty, the clever kings determined that there could be no dissent or challenging of the monarch because it was God's will that the king was on the throne.

Another source of the Mafia tradition of total obedience to the don was the feudal system. This medieval social structure had a feudal lord in his castle lording over the peasant class. Serfs, as the peasants were called, worked the land and delivered the majority of the produce to the castle while they kept just enough for themselves to eat. This medieval tradition is carried on in the modern Mafia, where the people on the lower rungs of the hierarchy work for the good of those above them.

A third code of the Sicilian Mafia was the duty to offer help to anyone "in the family" that was in need and any person or group with close ties to the Mafia that needs assistance. The fierce loyalty to friends and equally fierce hostility to any outsiders is a cornerstone of both the Old World and New World Mafia.

FACT

The Sicilians are not the only branch of the Mafia. On mainland Italy, the "Camorra" emerged in Naples as a criminal organization that also came to America, as did the Calabrian Mafia that originated in the province of Calabria.

The fourth code followed by the Mafia is the obligation to seek vengeance against anyone who attacks a member of the family. In its very insular unity, the Sicilian Mafia took an assault on one member of the family as an attack on the family as a whole. The Old World term for this is *vendetta*. The Sicilians took it to an extreme that the American Mafia did not. The Sicilian Mafia would slaughter the entire families of anyone who offended them.

This is something the American Mafia did not do. In fact, they prided themselves as "only killing their own," and anyone who violated that rule would be killed. The Sicilian Mafia of the nineteenth century are akin to the vicious Colombian drug cartels of the later twentieth century who routinely and ruthlessly wiped out the entire families, including the small children and babies, of their enemies.

The fifth code of the Sicilian Mafia is that its members must avoid interaction with the authorities. They could bribe corrupt policemen and crooked politicians, even intimidate and kill them, but they were not allowed to socialize with them. A Mafioso should not join the PTA or the Elks club.

The Culture of Crime

What kind of culture produced so powerful and insidious a criminal underground? We have seen how Sicily was always under the thumb of invaders, whether the majesty of Rome or barbarian hordes. This climate created a clannishness and insularity and suspicion of outsiders. These are characteristics of Sicilian culture, and certainly elements of the Mafia.

People in Sicily have always had a tendency to assume the worst. It is a given that politicians are out to fleece you, that cops and judges are corrupt, that governments come and go and do not have the best interests of the citizenry at heart. Exchanges of power had happened so many times over the millennia that the Sicilians saw no constancy in government. The "powers that be" would not be there for very long. The only constant is the land and the simple people who work the land. And the hand—the Black Hand.

QUESTION?

Why would such a barren island appeal to so many conquerors?
Sicily was not always the arid rocky landscape that we see in the *Godfather* movies. In fact it had dense forests and rich wheat fields, all of which were exploited and squandered by the Romans and other interlopers.

As a result of their turbulent history, Sicilians assume there will be corruption in business and politics and even infidelity in relationships and marriage. The Sicilian language reflects the fact that bribery is the rule and not the exception in Sicilian culture. The language includes words to describe people who have a Mafia-esque approach to life but are not members of the Mafia. *Mafiosità* describes a corrupt politician or businessman who acts like a Mafioso without actually being one. A woman who is ruthless about getting her way is called a *Mafiosetta*. The island of Sicily is permeated with an atmosphere from which an entity like the Mafia would naturally emerge.

The Influence of the Mafia Spreads

In the 1860s there was a wave of immigration to America from Italy and Sicily, and an even larger one in the 1890s. In the first wave many thousands of Italians and Sicilians settled in New Orleans, Louisiana. It was in this Southern port city that the first official Mafiosi took up where they left off in their native land. Though most people associate Mafia activity with big cities in the North, New Orleans was the birthplace of the modern American Mafia.

The Mafia continued to be a powerful and dangerous force in Sicily after it branched off to set up shop in America. The Sicilian and American Mafia families formed alliances, had feuds, and did business together. The younger, Americanized Mafiosi, who were known as the "Young Turks," fought a series of violent gangland battles to wrest control from the old guard, who they referred to as the "Mustache Petes." This was a slang expression for a conservative old coot that refused to adapt to the New Underworld Order.

Il Duce

Benito Mussolini was the fascist dictator of Italy from 1922 until his assassination during World War II. It was to be expected that a totalitarian dictator and an organized crime family would not get along together. Like rivals in a Wild West town, the island of Sicily was not big enough for both of them.

FACT

Sicily, roughly the size of the state of New Jersey (home to *The Sopranos*), has continued to entrance both conqueror and tourist alike. German literary giant Goethe said of the island, "To have seen Italy without having seen Sicily is to not have seen Italy at all, for Sicily is the clue to everything."

During one of Mussolini's many parades, this one through a Sicilian town, the local don, who felt this dictator was unworthy of respect, ordered the townspeople not to come out and line the parade route in tribute. To add to the flagrant disrespect, he had several bedraggled homeless men amble into the square to hear the dictator's bombastic and bellicose ranting. This was just one example of the lack of respect that the Mafia had for politicians. The bullet-headed Mussolini went ballistic and launched a crackdown on the Mafia. When he was done, many were dead and most of the major dons were behind bars. Ultimately, however, the Mafia would have the last laugh, with a little help from Uncle Sam.

Mussolini did not have a chance to fully rid Sicily of the Mafia. His alliance with Adolf Hitler and Nazi Germany launched Italy into World War II. The feud between the Sicilian Mafia and the dictator Mussolini inspired the Americans to side with the Mafia. Sicilian Mafiosi spied for the Americans during the Allied invasion of Sicily, and after they kicked the Germans off the island, they allowed the Mafiosi to come into positions of authority.

Strange Bedfellows

The American government formed an alliance with the Mafia during the war (for more on this, see Chapter 7). They prevailed upon the jailed American gangster Lucky Luciano to use his connections with the Sicilian Mafia to monitor German troop movements as the Allied forces prepared for the invasion of Sicily. The Allies took control of the island, and this led to the fall of Italy and the end of Benito Mussolini's reign. Italy switched sides and joined the Allies, and Mussolini was assassinated.

The American forces released the Mafiosi from the prisons and put them in charge of reorganizing the social and political structure of the country. To give the United States the benefit of the doubt, one can say that the military was not aware of the criminal tendencies of these men. If they were looking at the situation in straightforward terms of black and white, they may have assumed that anyone who was clearly not a "common" criminal that was imprisoned by Mussolini must be there because they were political prisoners and part of an organized opposition of freedom fighters.

Given the fact that the Americans helped Nazi scientists escape from the clutches of the Russians in the days right before the end of and immediately after World War II, one could make the case that the American leadership may have known that these prisoners were Mafiosi. The Nazi scientists helped America in the Cold War and during the space race to the moon in the 1960s, so it is not out of character for the American government to work with unsavory characters to further its goals. In either case, the Mafia benefited from the Allied liberation of Sicily and returned to prominence in Sicilian society.

The Postwar Era

One hoodlum who benefited from Allied assistance was Calogero Vizzini. The Allies made him the mayor of his community. He and other Mafia men were given political offices because they were known in the communities and clearly commanded respect. This was more fear than respect. The citizenry knew them well as Mafiosi and would not dare oppose them. Vizzini ultimately became the "Boss of Bosses" of the Sicilian Mafia. The whole Mafia made out like Sicilian bandits during the post–World War II era. They became more powerful than ever and solidified their stranglehold on the island.

When Vizzini died in 1954, the Mafia went through a metamorphosis. Gone were even the pretensions of Old World civility and honor. The younger generation were called "gangsters," a common and generic term in America. In Sicily, however, the dignified, albeit deadly Mafia had disdain for this low class criminal element and its coarse manners and tactics. The Mafia descended to this level of "gangsterism" in the 1950s.

Unholy Alliance

It was during the 1950s that fences were mended and relations reestablished between the Sicilian Mafia and its American brethren. Lucky Luciano (about whom much more later) was the hoodlum who extended the olive branch. The American Mafia's "Commission" (an organization of the bosses of the biggest crime families) and the Sicilian "Cupola" joined forces in the lucrative drug trade. Both factions claimed they regretted having to get into the drug business. As enterprising gangsters, they would have been remiss not to become involved in the narcotics industry. Other criminal forces were entrenched in the trade, and the Mafia wanted a piece of the action.

The Sicilians were even more bloodthirsty than the Americans when it came to their business practices. They committed more murders, including the brazen assassinations of judges, police, and politicians, than did their American counterparts. The Sicilians were more intertwined with the political sphere than the American Mafia. Business, politics, and even the Catholic Church interact seamlessly in Sicily, working together to achieve their goals. The Archbishop of Palermo issued a press release saying that an organized crime group called the Mafia did not exist. But of course we know this to be untrue now, and many believe that the people knew it wasn't true at the time, either. It is indicative of how deeply entrenched the Mafia was in every aspect of Sicilian culture.

According to Greek mythology, the goddess of love, Venus, was born on Sicily. Unfortunately the island's tumultuous history would lead one to believe that Mars, the god of war, was more influential in Sicilian affairs.

The Mafia is not as integral in American culture, but its underworld empire does affect Americans in many ways that they are not even aware of. In the next chapter we will look at the genesis of the Sicilian Mafia in America, and a scandal that shook the young nation.

Chapter 3

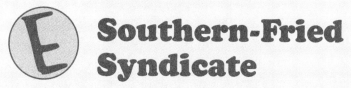

Southern-Fried Syndicate

People usually associate the Mafia with the Roaring Twenties and the rat-a-tat-tat of Tommy guns in Chicago or New York. But the word *Mafia* came into national consciousness in 1891 in the Deep South. This is the shocking story of the first Mafia scandal.

Coming to New Orleans

Italian immigrants came to America in great numbers in the last decades of the nineteenth century. From 1860 to 1890 thousands of Sicilians came to New Orleans, Louisiana. Perhaps they liked the climate. It is similar to their homeland. Both criminal and non-criminal alike encountered racism from the locals, as new immigrants often do. The Mafia element went into the shadows. This was their comfort zone, functioning in the nooks and crann-ies of the culture. In the periphery they banded together and made plans.

New Orleans was the first foothold of the Mafia in America. The families that formed later in New York, Chicago, and other big and small cities have become very well known. The Mafia is usually associated with Northern urban types, but the Southern Mafia family was here first. The port city was an ideal place to begin its crooked business dealings. A port city was ideal for its penchant for muscling in on trade and commerce, demanding "protection money" that was nothing more than protection from themselves.

Every major American city has its "Little Italy." The Little Italy of New Orleans was pretty big. In the late nineteenth century, Italians were arriving in town by the thousands every year. Ninety percent of those were from Sicily.

The Mafia gangs were using the "Black Hand" technique to extort money from their own kinsmen. A politely written note would be left for the merchant or businessman stating that money was expected at a certain date/time or they would be brutally killed. The bizarre Old World gentility of the letter's wording contrasted with the threats of violence. This was no bluff. People were beaten, businesses trashed, and families killed if they did not make a prompt payment to the sender. The signature of the letter was a black palm print, hence the name "Black Hand." Numerous clans had committed more than 100 killings since their arrival in New Orleans.

Shakespeare's Not in Love

The mayor of New Orleans was a man named Shakespeare. He did not like the wave of Sicilian immigration and spoke against his new neighbors in no uncertain terms. He called them "vicious and worthless," adding, "They are without courage, honor, truth, pride, religion, or any quality that goes to make good citizens." He went even further by making the threat, "I intend to put an end to these infernal Dago disturbances, even if it proves necessary to wipe out every one of you from the face of the earth." Strong stuff indeed, but the actions of the Mafia were tarnishing the image of all Sicilians, including those who had nothing to do with the Mafia. The New Orleans Mafia was particularly vicious.

FACT

New Orleans served as a port of entry for many Sicilians, and many of the early mobsters got their start here before moving on to cities like Chicago and New York.

Band of Brothers

From day one Italian gangsters had a penchant for the waterfront. In 1890 the earliest Mafiosi in America quickly muscled in on the docks. New Orleans has been an active port city since its inception. Ships from all over the world docked on its waterfront.

Two enterprising brothers, Antonio and Carlo Matranga, formerly of Palermo, Sicily, were making a nice living shaking down and intimidating skippers and ship owners, who were obliged to pay extortion money or else end up shot, stabbed, or beaten to a pulp and tossed into one of the many canals. It was a reign of terror that the chief of police was determined to stop.

A rival group of brothers was vying for control of the New Orleans waterfronts. The Provenzanos were Italians, and they were gangsters, but they were not Mafiosi. The underworld was well aware of such delineations and distinctions, while to the untrained eye they were all just thugs. Savage hits were commonplace. One gangster's head was stuck into a burning stove, many were shot, some hits were near misses that only succeeded in grisly mutilation and the amputation of various body parts.

FACT

In addition to having a climate similar to their homeland, one of the reasons Sicilians found New Orleans appealing was the fact that it had a Catholic culture. New Orleans did and still does retain its French flavor. In the North and elsewhere, Catholics were in the minority and often subject to discrimination.

Crusading Cop

New Orleans police chief David Peter Hennessey was determined to put an end to this endless slaughter. He spoke to some of the Sicilian immigrants and learned that even the non-gangsters were inclined to be insular and clannish. They had the Old World innate distrust of authority. Most would not talk to him, but those who did whispered an alien phrase not uttered before on American soil—*La Mafia*. That was when Hennessey discovered the existence of a secret organized collective of criminals. He was dealing with something deeper and more menacing than mere street hoodlums.

ESSENTIAL

Police chief David Hennessey had a hard time getting anyone on his staff to work with him in his crusade against the Mafia. They had all received threats, and they didn't doubt that the Mafia would follow through on those threats.

Desperate to break the cycle of violence, he took sides. He supported the Provenzano brothers over the Matranga brothers. Hennessey had members of his police force vouch for the Provenzano gang after a vicious attack on the Matranga clan. He rigged the subsequent trial and got them acquitted. Hennessey was now a marked man. He was being followed by the Mafia and his routine was being noted. A hit was in the works.

Hennessey was brave but foolish. He could not be bribed and he was unfazed by the many death threats he received. He meticulously built a case against the Matranga siblings. He was ready to present his airtight case to a grand jury when he was surrounded on a darkened street by four men. All four men brandished shotguns and fired at close range.

Even though he was cut to ribbons, Hennessey fired in vain at his murderers and then dragged himself back to the police station. He was discovered by his friend, Captain Billy O'Connor, and another policeman. He was asked if he knew who shot him and he uttered a sentence that unleashed a wave of violence and retribution that achieved national attention: "The Dagos did it." (*Dago* is an ethnic slur for an Italian—it is not very common today but was a popular slur for many decades.)

National Scandal

America was outraged at the police captain's murder at the hands of these foreign hoodlums. An anti-Italian furor swept the nation. Demonstrations were held in all the major cities that had large Italian populations. Mayor Shakespeare ordered a crackdown on *La Mafia*. More than 100 men were arrested, many simply because they were Italian. The media made things worse with sensational and racist editorials. The word *Mafia* became nationally known.

FACT

Although it is highly likely that Police Chief Hennessey was murdered by the Mafia, the fiasco of the trial and subsequent chaos and carnage overshadowed the quest for justice. The case is still officially listed as unsolved.

Among the men rounded up in the dragnet were the actual culprits in addition to innocent parties. An informant in the jail got cozy with one of the accused, who spilled the beans about the conspiracy against Hennessey. The loose-lipped prisoner implicated high-level members of the Matranga clan, including Charles Matranga, Joe Macheca, and numerous others. The trial divided the country along racial lines. The Mafia exploited ethnic pride to collect money for a defense fund for the accused.

Nineteen Sicilian men were brought to trial for the murder of Police Chief Hennessey, but in a story that quickly became an old Mafia trick, the local gangsters bribed and intimidated the witnesses and the jury. The frightened jurors found sixteen of the accused not guilty, and couldn't come to a verdict on the other three, including the two kingpins, Matranga and Macheca, who would have to stand trial again.

Lynch Mob

The jury verdicts created an uproar in the city of New Orleans. The aftermath of the verdict coincided with an Italian holiday. The leader of Italy, King Umberto the First, was a hero who had unified the country. The Italians in New Orleans flew flags and were engaged in a festive celebration. Many of the non-Italians in the city were incensed. Whether they thought the party atmosphere was a celebration of the verdict or they simply did not like the pomp and parades immediately after their police chief's killers did not meet the justice they felt was their due, protests broke out.

QUESTION?

"Who killa da chief?"
This question was derisively asked of Italian immigrants for many years after the murder of Police Chief Hennessey. It was a rhetorical question designed to let the Italian people know that they were disliked and unwelcome.

Eight thousand people assembled at City Hall. They listened to a lot of inflammatory rhetoric from several notable citizens, one of whom flat out exhorted the throng to take the law into their own hands. The crowd raided the city armory and proceeded to the prison where the Mafiosi were being held. The prison warden let the Italians out of their cells so the rioters could get to them.

The angry mob barreled into the prison looking for the Mafiosi. Top man Joseph Macheca was shot dead. Six other men were also rounded up and shot. Manuel Polizzi was dragged from the prison and lynched. Several members of the lynch mob shot him as he writhed at the end of the rope. A total of sixteen men were killed that day. Two of them had no mob connections at all. They were executed simply for being Sicilian. In a stroke of luck for the Mafia, its leader, Charles Matranga, the man who had orchestrated the murder of the police chief, survived the mob's bloodlust. He had been able to successfully hide during the carnage.

FACT

We will never be sure whether it was a less-than-airtight case by the prosecution or Mafia intimidation that resulted in the charges against the accused being dismissed or mistrials declared and defendants found not guilty. No matter which side you take in these tragic events, justice was not served.

Aftermath to the Slaughter

The newspapers ran editorials in support of the vigilante murders. One paper lauded the crazed mob for its self-control in that only the Mafiosi were killed, which was not true. The episode became an international incident. The Italian ambassador lodged a complaint with the president, as did the Italian government. Rumors of a potential war between the United States and Italy filled the newspapers. The President of the United States, Benjamin Harrison, denounced the incident, and the government paid settlements to the families of the murder victims. None of the vigilante mob or the men who incited them were brought to trial.

Mafia kingpin Charles Matranga ultimately had all charges dismissed, and he laid low after that. The lion's share of the $25,000 sent to the families of the victims ended up in the Mafia's coffers. After the massacre, the newspapers announced that the Mafia was dead and buried. But the press was dead wrong. The New Orleans Mafia continued to do quite well in its illegal enterprises. The man who guided the New Orleans crime family through most of the twentieth century, Carlos Marcello, will be discussed at length in Chapter 13.

Chapter 4

The Roaring Twenties

America's experiment with Prohibition in the 1920s opened the door for the Mafia to make a bundle in the trafficking of illegal booze, resulting in the heyday of the mob, as most people think of it. This chapter also explores the life and career of perhaps the most famous gangster of them all, Al Capone.

Demon Rum

Alcohol has been consumed by humankind since the first caveman left grape juice lying around too long and got a pleasant buzz when he drank it. The abuse of alcohol probably began almost immediately thereafter, and addictive personalities could not get enough of that euphoric high until it destroyed their lives and the lives of their loved ones.

There have been many attempts to deal with the problem of alcoholism. These were called temperance movements, an antiquated phrase meaning moderation in one's indulgence in the so-called vices. Most temperance movements in history have been initiated by religious folks who felt that only a spiritual conversion could combat the deleterious effects of "demon rum." And there were many who wanted to ban all alcoholic beverages from the American landscape.

FACT

Carrie Nation was one early leader of the temperance movement. She led militant crusades against the scourge of alcohol and the damage it caused families and society as a whole when it was abused. She regularly brandished a hatchet to personally smash casks and kegs of whiskey and beer.

In the late nineteenth century, the temperance movement in America became increasingly popular and influential. It was sometimes called the "Women's War," since most of its members were women who were fed up with their drunken fathers, husbands, and sons. The Anti-Saloon League (ASL) gained popularity in many states. The ASL endorsed candidates and tried to influence state and local governments, and its dream was to have an impact at the national level.

Prohibition Passes

The movement was gaining momentum, and twenty-three states had prohibition laws by 1916. There was enough support for an amendment to the Constitution. An amendment requires two-thirds of the states to vote in favor of it, and in 1919 the Eighteenth Amendment to the Constitution was ratified, outlawing the manufacture, sale, or exportation of alcohol by anyone in the United States.

Bootlegging was not exclusively an enterprise of the Mafia. Many immigrant families made their own wine and beer in the privacy of their own homes and for their personal consumption. This was as illegal as operating a speakeasy after Prohibition, but most private citizens did not cease and desist their clandestine fermentation.

It became the law of the land in 1920. It was called Prohibition for short, and it lasted until the early 1930s. Ironically, the 1920s was, for many Americans, one big party that preceded the Great Depression of the 1930s. The booze never stopped flowing during Prohibition, thanks to the friendly neighborhood Mafia family.

Getting Around It

The National Prohibition Act was passed to enforce the Eighteenth Amendment. It was also known as the Volstead Act, named for the congressman who introduced the law. There were some exceptions to the rule. Alcohol could be used for medicinal purposes, and priests could perform Mass with sacramental wine. It was generally accepted that it would be difficult to enforce, and that law enforcement officials were not necessarily going to aggressively enforce the law. Many of them liked to drink and were not eager to deny themselves the pleasure.

The demand for alcohol was there, and someone who could supply the demand was more than welcome. At first it was the Irish saloon owners who had brothers and cousins on "the force." But soon the Italian and the Jewish mobsters muscled in on their turf. Prohibition was counterproductive. It spurred the increase of organized crime.

Cast of Characters

Prohibition and bootleg whiskey and the sputtering of Tommy guns and the splattering of blood is associated with Al Capone, but there were other gangsters who made a name for themselves and made their fortunes in the Roaring Twenties. The first bootleggers were Irish. They constituted most of the saloon owners, and after Prohibition was enacted they immediately became criminals if they continued to do business.

The Irish Players

Two Irishmen were the big-time bootleggers in the Northeast. Owney Madden was New York's main bootlegger until the Mafia demolished the Irish mob. And Boston's premier rumrunner was a man named Joseph P. Kennedy. Yes, the patriarch of the Kennedy clan was considered to be a major league player in the illegal booze trade and an associate of many a more overt gangster. (See Chapter 10 for more about him.) Suffice it to say, alcohol was not merely the drug of choice of the lower classes. In 1922 Kennedy provided the booze that was served at the tenth anniversary reunion of his Harvard graduating class. Many a Boston Brahmin and scion of the ruling class partook that night of alcohol that had landed on Plymouth Rock under cloak of darkness, about 300 years after the Pilgrims.

The Jewish Players

Among the Jewish bootleggers, the most famous was Arnold Rothstein, the man who for years legend told us fixed the 1919 World Series. It is now believed that the legend is questionable. Rothstein learned of the fix and bet a bundle to make even more, but he did not orchestrate the biggest scandal in American sports history. Rothstein's protégé was a young man named Meyer Lansky, who went on to be one of the men who made the modern Mafia.

The Players in Philly

Bootleggers loved the "City of Brotherly Love" as well. The main man in Philadelphia was Maxie "Boo Boo" Hoff. He also owned boxers and was chummy with many policemen and politicians. The Philadelphia Republican political machine was in cahoots with the gangsters. In other cities, including New York and Chicago, the machine was Democratic. Political corruption has always transcended ideology. Greed is a nonpartisan vice.

Ships with bootleg booze lingered in international waters, and small boats went out to meet them to collect the booty. It was all done in the open. The Coast Guard was not immune to bribery, and enterprising small craft owners even took tourists out to watch the bootleggers at work. The booze that came off the boats was quality vintage from Europe, Canada, and elsewhere, but "Boo Boo" Hoff was involved in making local moonshine, with sometimes fatal results. He got involved with a couple of industrial alcohol companies and had alcohol redistilled for human consumption. The process was less than perfect, and sometimes the product was more poisonous than rubbing alcohol. People suffering blindness and death from drinking "bathtub gin" was becoming all too common. The rationalization of many moonshiners was that all they did was sell it. What people did with it was their business.

ALERT!

Today, taking after the term "bootlegging," the term "buttlegging" has come into use. It refers to the Mafia's traffic in the black market cigarette business. At $7 a pack in New York City, many honest citizens will purchase their smokes at a discount and not ask where they came from.

The new mayor of Philadelphia brought in a former Marine with the Dickensian name of Smedley Darlington Butler to clean up the town. After two years and little cooperation, he called the city a cesspool, was unable to oust "Boo Boo" Hoff, and left in a huff.

The Jazz Age

When saloons became illegal, they went underground and became "speakeasies." Now there was an illicit element that made drinking more attractive. People did not stop drinking during Prohibition. They just had to pay more money (a shot of booze went up from ten cents to $3 in some places) and they had to do it in secret. But it was the worst-kept secret in the nation that people still drank, and drank plenty. Some made their own alcohol, and others went to speakeasies.

The new and uniquely American form of music called jazz was heard in many of the speakeasies. Many performers who went on to great fame got their start in the Mafia-owned nightclubs. Harlem's famous Cotton Club was owned by Irishman Owney Madden and regularly featured the likes of Duke Ellington and Cab Calloway. Ellington was threatened with death when he tried to perform at a rival gangster's Philadelphia club. Breaking a contract with the mob was not a smart move.

Irish versus Italian

Irish gangs controlled the Brooklyn waterfront after World War I. They took protection money for keeping the ships and the merchandise therein safe and sound. The Irish called themselves the "White Hand," in counterpoint to the notorious Italian "Black Hand." The leader of the White Hand was a man named Wild Bill Lovett. The Italians' leader was Frankie Yale. Both were brutal and ruthless killers. Yale had a protégé who was rising through the ranks as a bouncer and bartender in his speakeasies. This outspoken chubby tough guy once told a female patron of a speakeasy, "You got a beautiful ass." This prompted her brother to try to cut the bouncer's throat. The man missed and sliced the bouncer's cheek. And that is how the bouncer, destined to become the most famous Mafioso ever, got the name Al "Scarface" Capone.

FACT

"Medicinal purposes" became a euphemism and a loophole around the Prohibition laws. Pharmacists were allowed to dispense alcohol in some circumstances. Just as the use of "medical marijuana" is a controversial and sometimes abused practice today, so were the instances when the pharmacist doubled as bartender.

Scarface

Alfonse Capone was one of the first American-born Italian gangsters. His parents came from Italy like so many other immigrants seeking the

American Dream. His father was a barber who wanted to open his own shop. They settled in Brooklyn near the Navy Yard. The family later moved to a more ethnically diverse neighborhood. He mingled with kids who were Irish, German, Jewish, and Asian. This exposed young Al to the American "melting pot" experience, making him less insular than his Old World relatives.

Al left school at the age of fourteen after hitting a teacher who had struck him. He was expelled and never looked back. There were bigger things on the horizon for young Al Capone. He would soon take his first adolescent steps into the underworld.

Al Capone

Courtesy of AP/Wide World Photos

◀ Al Capone, called before a grand jury, talks to an unidentified man in Chicago, Illinois, on March 21, 1929. Capone was charged with tax evasion in 1931 and sentenced to 11 years in prison.

Johnny Torrio

The Capone family moved to another neighborhood, and their new residence was a few blocks away from the headquarters of Mafioso Johnny Torrio, who was one of the first of the modern hoodlums. Torrio took a primitive organization and turned it into a structure resembling a modern corporation. Capone began running errands for Torrio, who took a liking to the pugnacious street urchin and gave him more and more responsibilities. Capone watched the older men conduct business, and they served as role models to the impressionable boy.

Capone also became involved in the teenage street gangs of the day. They were usually divided along ethnic lines and were territorial about their "turf." At various times in his misspent youth, Capone belonged to the South Brooklyn Rippers, Forty Thieves Juniors, and the Five Point Juniors.

Yale Grad

The next mentor Al Capone had in the life of crime was the aforementioned Frankie Yale (born Francesco Ioele). Yale owned a bar ironically called the Harvard Inn, and he hired the eighteen-year-old Capone as a bartender. It is in this gin mill that he made the inappropriate remark that changed his life.

FACT

The "Noble Experiment," as Prohibition was sometimes called, seemed to have made a dent in alcohol consumption in the early years of the 1920s, but with the Mafia's help, the experiment was doomed to failure, as bootleg booze flowed freely.

Yale continued to serve as Capone's coach and mentor even after the faux pas in the bar went all the way to Lucky Luciano for mediation. Capone was forced to apologize for his remark. The man who left three permanent scars on Capone's face was not obliged to say he was sorry.

Capone learned about business finesse from his first mentor, Johnny Torrio; Yale schooled him in the more brutal arts of the Mafia. Capone became proficient at both in his notorious career. During this time Capone met and married (after their first child was born) an Irish-American girl named Mae Coughlin. The poor baby had inherited syphilis from Big Al, who had caught a dose somewhere in his travels and neglected to mention it to Miss Coughlin.

Shortly after his wedding, Capone flirted with respectability by taking a regular job, but this phase did not last long. His former boss, Johnny

Torrio, invited him to "Go West, Young Hoodlum." Torrio had left New York City for the heartland. Capone accepted his pal's invitation, and Capone and Chicago soon became inextricably linked in American history.

His Kind of Town

The Windy City was already known for vice and corruption when Capone got off the train in 1920. It was known as a slaughterhouse in more than one way. Neighbors could hear the feral squeals from the meat-packing district, and the pitter patter of Tommy guns punctuated the night.

The "Mr. Big" at the time was a man named "Big Jim" Colosimo. His wife was also Chicago's most celebrated madam, Victoria Moresco. Prostitution was the big business of the Chicago Mafia. (This would, of course, change with the advent of Prohibition.) Johnny Torrio had become Colosimo's right-hand man when he got to Chicago with Capone. Torrio was a stable gangster who did not indulge in the vices from which he profited. The same could not be said of Colosimo, who was spiraling out of control. He became wrapped around the little finger of a singer named Dale Winter. The call of the siren distracted him from more important matters, such as survival. All the way from New York City, Frankie Yale graduated him to the Great Beyond with a violent rub out, in an effort to take over Colosimo's business interests. This coup d'état did not succeed, however. Yale was arrested, avoided a trial (no witness would testify, a familiar story in mob prosecutions), and Johnny Torrio assumed control of the multimillion-dollar empire.

Capone started out managing the many brothels in Chicago, but he was not very comfortable in the role of pimp. When Prohibition roared into the 1920s, he got into the speakeasy end of the business and quickly became Torrio's business partner.

Equal-Opportunity Mafioso

Capone, being American-born and exposed to many other ethnic groups growing up, was not as clannish as other Mafiosi. He married an Irish girl and met his new best friend in Chicago, an Orthodox Jewish family man named Jake Guzik. Like superheroes Batman and Superman,

Capone put on the façade of a mild-mannered used furniture dealer for his neighbors while he was a true "dark knight" in his other life. Like many Mafiosi, he strived for respectability while making a living in illegal enterprises and using terror and murder as tools of his trade.

For many years Capone had a free ride in Chicago. The politicians and police were shamelessly corrupt. The people wanted their vices, and Capone was more than happy to provide them. Cries of outrage and calls for reform from the political machine were nothing more than lip service. It was a wide open town where the mob ruled. Mayor "Big Bill" Thompson is considered to be one of the most corrupt men in the pantheon of American politicians. And that's no small accomplishment.

In the nineteenth century, the temperance movement and the women's suffrage movements were linked. One of the most influential women of her day was Frances E. Willard. She fought to get women the vote and to get their husbands out of the saloons. There is a statue of Willard in the United States Capitol.

However, real reform was slowly making inroads into the Windy City. A man named William E. Deaver succeeded Thompson as mayor, and he promised to crack down on the vice and corruption on his town. The Mafia took it in stride. A reformer at the top was a minor inconvenience when the rest of the team was more than eager to play ball.

The 'Burbs

The Capone outfit moved down the road apiece to the small town of Cicero, Illinois. They simply bought the town lock and stock with the smoking barrels of their machine guns, using bribery as needed. In short order Capone controlled all the prostitution, gambling, and bootlegging in the town. He even took over the racetrack. Capone's brother Frank acted as liaison with the corrupt local government.

Freedom of the Press

A maverick journalist named Robert St. John openly opposed the Capone invasion in his newspaper. It looked like Capone's hand-picked politicos might lose the election of 1924. Capone used muscle to try to sway the voting public. His goons loomed around polling places making it clear which candidate would be the "healthiest" choice. The cops were called in response, and Frank Capone was gunned down. He allegedly pulled his revolver when he found himself surrounded. A dumb move, if indeed it's true. It was deemed that the police acted in self-defense when they killed him. And the end of the day, Al Capone owned Cicero, but at a terrible price, a brother's blood.

Capone vented his frustration by shooting a small-time hood who dared to call the little big man an ethnic slur. He was brought to trial for the first time in his life, but he beat the murder rap. Witnesses were hard to come by, as was always the case with Mafia trials. The highly public trial made him something most mobsters did not want to be—famous.

Master of the Universe

Few twenty-five-year olds achieve the power and wealth that Al Capone had at that young age. And few people have to deal with murderous rivals and regular assassination attempts. Such is the price one pays for being King of the Underworld. Capone knocked off opponents, and they in turn were out to get him. One attempt on his partner Johnny Torrio was almost successful. The volatile hoodlum Bugs Moran pumped several shots into Torrio as he was entering his apartment building, but Torrio survived. Capone stayed with him at the hospital, even sleeping on a cot at the bedside of his friend and mentor.

Torrio got out of the business after being shot. He decided to retire and move to Europe. He turned over his share of the massive empire to Capone. Success spoiled Capone. He moved into the palatial Metropole Hotel and lived a very public life of a media darling and national celebrity. He was a showman gangster, attempting to cultivate a Robin Hood image. He was a regular Joe who provided a service that the public wanted, a man who was misunderstood and being harassed by the authorities. Or so he wanted people to believe.

Death of the Party

Capone continued to cement his position as über-thug when he orchestrated a flamboyant hit on an old rival. He was back in New York attending a Christmas party and got wind that an old enemy, Richard "Peg-Leg" Lonergan, was going to crash the bash with some of his boys. The boisterous blowhards did not get very far before the Capone mob wished them a very bloody Christmas.

Al Capone was not averse to being a true "hands-on" murderer. He personally killed many men in his time, and ordered the hits of many more. The notorious scene in the movie *The Untouchables* when Capone bashes the man to death with a baseball bat is based on a true story. In reality, however, Capone cracked the skulls of three men in the same session.

Capone faced another legal dilemma when his men machine-gunned a gang of Irish bootleggers. He did not know that partying with the Irishmen was Billy McSwiggin, the prosecutor who had unsuccessfully tried Capone for murder. Capone had not intended to hit McSwiggin, but nevertheless he took the heat from the otherwise indifferent police force. Cops, like the Mafia, look out for their own, and Capone had inadvertently broken the Mafia's "we only kill our own" code. His gambling joints and bordellos began to be raided. Capone went into hiding. He surrendered after three months on the lam, but faced no charges. There was not enough evidence for an indictment. The frustrated authorities could not get this slippery gangster.

Peacemaker?

Capone fancied himself a peacemaker. Since he did not skulk in the shadows and everyone knew who and what he was, he called a public peace conference asking his fellow gangsters to put an end to the violence. Many felt his calls for peace were insincere. While he spoke publicly for an end to violence, he ordered the murder of a former friend. Capone had come into conflict with old crony Frankie Yale. There was evidence that Yale was responsible for the numerous liquor truck hijackings plaguing their joint operation. These amounted to theft on Yale's part while pinning the blame on anonymous hijackers. Yale was blasted to kingdom come while in his car. His riddled remains revealed that there was more than one hit man with more than one type of firearm.

Happy Valentine's Day

Bugs Moran had attempted to kill Capone's good friend Johnny Torrio, and Capone was not a man who forgot such things. Moran was still operating in Chicago, and Capone's plans for revenge culminated in the single most famous incident in the annals of Mafia lore.

FACT

According to the FBI, Capone's gang fired 200 bullets in a mere eight minutes during the Valentine's Day Massacre.

In addition to almost whacking Torrio, Moran had twice tried to hit another Capone pal with the colorful name "Machine Gun" McGurn. Capone ordered a hit on Moran as revenge.

Capone had bought a lavish estate in Florida and spent the winters there, so he left the hit in McGurn's murderously capable hands. McGurn hired out-of-town talent and planned to lure Moran to a garage on the morning of February 14. The bait was a stash of quality booze at a good price. The hit team would be dressed as cops. Moran and company would think it was a raid, not an assassination. The phony cops burst into the garage simulating a police bust, made the hoods line up against the wall, and mowed them down. There was good news and bad news. The good news was that the hit went off without a hitch. The bad news was that Bugs Moran did not show up that day. The target of the hit had a guardian angel on his shoulder that Valentine's Day. Or perhaps a cherubic Cupid.

NYC prohibition
is repealed

▲ A crowd gathers as kegs of beer are unloaded in front of a restaurant on Broadway in New York City on the morning of April 7, 1933.

For an entertaining look at this infamous shooting, check out the 1967 movie *The St. Valentine's Day Massacre*, starring Jason Robards as Al Capone.

Capone was out of town, and McGurn had checked into a hotel across town with his girlfriend, so he had witnesses who could place him at the hotel and not at the scene of the crime. Everyone knew who ordered the hit but no one could prove it. The murders captured the fascination of the nation and has become as mythical an event as the Gunfight at the O.K. Corral. In addition to the sensational media attention, the powers-that-be in Washington began to take a closer look at the shenanigans taking place in Chicago. President Herbert Hoover announced that he wanted to see Capone behind bars.

Al Capone was eventually convicted of income tax evasion and sent to prison for an eleven-year stretch.

The Last Years

Capone was first sent to a federal prison in Atlanta, where he lived in relative comfort and used his influence to enjoy special privileges. Unfortunately for Al, he was transferred to the infamous island prison of Alcatraz. Here Capone enjoyed no creature comforts. On Alcatraz he was just another number. He had minimal contact with the outside. All letters were censored, and he was not allowed to read the daily newspapers.

Capone's health deteriorated during his prison stretch. The syphilis he had contracted in his youth grew progressively worse. He served six and a half years of his sentence. He retired to his Florida estate and continued a slow but steady mental and physical decline until his death in 1947.

Long Lost Brother

A fascinating subplot in the life of Al Capone involves his long lost brother. Al Capone had an older brother James, who left home at age sixteen never to return. Young Al was eight at the time. James went west, joined a circus, mingled with Native Americans, and, like many Italian-Americans of the day, changed his name. He became Richard Hart.

Hart fought bravely in World War I. After the war he went back to the Midwest, married a local girl, started a family, and made Homer, Nebraska, his home. Ironically, he became a law enforcement officer and made a name for himself chasing moonshiners and keeping alcohol off Indian reservations. He even had a nickname: Two-Gun Hart.

Al Capone's brother was a frontier lawman in the modern Wild West who spoke several Indian languages. He even served as a bodyguard for President Calvin Coolidge. Capone had a few other brothers who worked for him, but all had lost touch with the elder sibling.

In the 1940s Hart contacted his family and had a series of reunions with his brothers and his elderly mother. His wife and family were stunned to learn that he was the brother of Scarface Capone. Ⓔ

Chapter 5

The Real Untouchables

The Mafia felt they were above the law, but there was no shortage of crime fighters eager to put a stop to the illegal activities that were going on. In this chapter we look at some of the famous crime busters who battled the Mafia.

Federal Case

We have all heard the expression "Don't make a federal case out of it." This originated in Al Capone's Chicago. The Mafia did not want to tangle with the federal government. It shined too much light on them, and the power of federal law enforcement was formidable. Local cops were more easily bribed and intimidated. It was against the Mafia code to kill a cop and a very big no-no to whack a federal agent.

As discussed in the previous chapter, Capone's growing celebrity status and his increasing willingness to revel in the attention put the spotlight on his organization and activities.

The president had declared that he wanted Scarface behind bars, and a young man came to Chicago with the mandate to get Al Capone. Television and the movies later made Eliot Ness and his story part of the fabric of American folklore. Unfortunately, he did not live to see his name become a household name.

FACT

Eliot Ness died before his memoir *The Untouchables* was sold to television and became a hit series starring Robert Stack. Kevin Costner played Ness in the award-winning 1987 feature film that costarred Sean Connery and Robert De Niro.

Ness assembled a hand-picked team of agents. He wanted his agents to be under thirty and unmarried. It was a dangerous business, and he did not want to be a widow-maker. After extensive interviews, he settled on nine men. For the record, these were the real "Untouchables": Marty Lahart, Sam Seager, Barney Cloonan, Lyle Chapman, Tom Friel, Joe Leeson, Paul Robsky, Mike King, and Bill Gardner.

The Taxman Cometh

It may seem like a strange strategy to prosecute a murderer for not paying his taxes. Capone was always able to slip out of any murder indictment against him. Taxation was another matter altogether. Compliance and/or noncompliance with tax laws is kept on record.

Most people have heard of Eliot Ness, but fewer folks probably know the name of Elmer Irey. While Ness went to Chicago to try to nail Capone on Prohibition violations, it was Irey who did the paper shuffling and bean counting to catch Capone on income tax fraud. Ness had recruited a team of intrepid fellow agents who could not be intimidated or bribed. They could not be swayed or stopped by the seductive nature of sin or the potential violence against them.

The word *untouchable* when applied to Eliot Ness and his crime fighters has nothing to do with its more familiar usage, the lowest rung in India's rigid caste system. To be an Untouchable in Al Capone's Chicago meant that you could not be bribed or intimidated out of performing your duty.

When the Rat's Away

Al Capone was arrested in Philadelphia for carrying a concealed weapon. He did a little time behind bars. In his absence he left the business in the hands of his brother Ralph and one of his henchmen, Frank Nitti. Nitti took over the administrative duties while Capone was in jail, and he eventually ran things after Capone was sent away for good. Ralph Capone did not have the intelligence, caginess, or business acumen of his brother. He found himself charged with tax evasion. The dogged Elmer Irey had been trying to nail Ralph for a long time. And Eliot Ness had been listening in on Ralph's business dealings courtesy of hidden wiretaps. Ralph was not adept at covering his financial tracks and he was an easier target for the feds than his brother Al was.

Ness did more than simply listen in to private conversations. He began to raid Capone's breweries, which were often "hidden" in plain sight. Distilleries were also raided, but most of the hard liquor consumed in Chicago was imported from elsewhere. The Capone mob made its own beer, and there were hundreds of breweries in the greater Chicagoland area. As Sean Connery's character tells Kevin Costner's Eliot Ness in the 1987 movie *The Untouchables*, "Everybody knows where the booze is. The problem isn't finding it. The problem is, who wants to cross Capone?" Ness was willing to cross Capone. It is estimated that Ness cost Capone over $1 million in spilled beer by seizing and destroying illegal breweries run by Capone. Capone probably would not have cried over spilled milk, but that was a lot of lost loot in spilled brewski. Gangsters do not cry, however. They kill you. Capone's response was to first try to bribe, and later try to kill Ness and the Untouchables.

FACT

The further adventures of Eliot Ness made their way into pulp fiction. He became a character in a series of hardboiled novels by Max Allan Collins that chronicled his post-Untouchable years as Cleveland, Ohio's director of public safety.

America's Most Wanted

When Capone got out of jail (he was released early for good behavior) he was surprised to learn that he and several of his underlings were now on FBI boss J. Edgar Hoover's Most Wanted list. Capone was stunned and outraged. It seemed that he was in denial about his invulnerability and the bad publicity that his criminal activities inspired. He was popular with the populace but not quite beloved.

The feds decided they needed an agent in place within the enemy camp in order to get a better handle on Capone's strengths and weaknesses. An Irishman named Malone passed himself off as a Brooklyn hoodlum eager to join the Capone organization. Malone was what is called "black Irish." He had a Mediterranean look that could pass for Italian. He was also an accomplished actor and good with dialects. He earned the trust of Capone's henchmen, even met the Big Boy himself, and got a job in one of the many gambling joints.

Malone and another undercover agent provided valuable intelligence. Their information thwarted an attempted hit on a federal agent and found out the names of a couple of accountants who had cooked Capone's books.

Deal with the Devil

Capone, stone-cold killer that he was, preferred to reason with Ness than to kill him. Bumping off Ness would make it a "federal case" and create myriad problems. Instead, Capone offered Ness $2,000 a week to look the other way. He turned down the bribe. Ness was making about $2,800 a year at the time. Ness, never shy of publicity and often accused of egomania, held a press conference to announce that he had turned down the bribe. It was one of the newspapermen who covered the press conference who coined the term "the Untouchables."

ALERT!

In one of life's ironies, the man who battled the bootleggers eventually developed an alcohol problem. Eliot Ness's public career ended after a drunken driving accident that he tried to cover up. He was compelled to resign from his post shortly thereafter.

Eventually there were attempts on his life. He discovered a bomb under the hood of his car at one point. On another occasion gunshots were fired at him as he escorted a date back to her home, and he was almost the victim of a hit-and-run. However, none of the attempts were successful.

Psychological Warfare

Eliot Ness wanted to up the ante with his nemesis after the murder of one of Ness's associates. One of the best ways to psych out one's opponent is to force him to lose his cool. Michael Corleone counseled his volatile nephew Vincent not to hate his enemies because it clouds one's judgment. Ness figured if Capone got really riled he would act impulsively and slip up.

Ness led a parade of the various trucks and other vehicles that had been used in raids on Capone's bootleg operations down the street outside of Capone's office, in an attempt to mock Capone. Ness even called Capone and told him to look out the window. Capone went ballistic and trashed his own office in a rage. The trucks were also a painful reminder of the millions of dollars Capone lost in Ness's relentless raids.

What ultimately brought the big man down, however, was his long history as a tax scofflaw. An investigation that was years in the making culminated with an indictment against Capone in 1931. He faced twenty-two counts of tax evasion, on top of the evidence Ness had gathered of several thousand violations of the Prohibition law. The tax case was judged the easiest to win, and Capone went to trial.

Twelve Crooked Men

Capone had a couple of months before his trial began, but the jury had already been selected. His henchmen took that time to locate and bribe the jurors-to-be. Big Al walked into the courtroom quite confident. He got the shock of his life when the judge switched juries, bringing in twelve men from another trial. Capone was found guilty, fined $50,000, and sentenced to eleven years. The reign of Al Capone was over.

The Untouchables have entered the popular mythology, but have you ever heard of the Secret Six? This was the crime-fighting team established by Eliot Ness when he was Cleveland's director of public safety.

Eliot Ness and the feds brought down Al Capone, but the Mafia, like the Energizer Bunny, goes on and on. Capone's henchman Frank Nitti took over, and he got right down to the nitty-gritty of maintaining the mob's influence in Chicago. Prohibition ended a couple of years later, but the Mafia had plenty of other rackets in its repertoire.

Locked Out Ness

Eliot Ness never became a law enforcement superstar after his success in Chicago. He bounced around in other assignments that were not as high profile. It is generally believed that another federal official, J. Edgar Hoover, was envious of Ness's successes and did his best to sabotage his career. Eliot Ness was largely forgotten when he wrote his memoirs in the 1950s. He died soon thereafter at the young age of 54 and did not live to see his autobiography turned into a hit television series and later an Academy Award–winning feature film.

J. Edgar Hoover

Hoover became director of the FBI and remained there for almost fifty years. In that time he amassed detailed files on thousands of politicians, entertainers, and ordinary citizens. It is believed that the dirt he had on the revolving door residents of the White House was sometimes used as blackmail, and was one of the ways he maintained job security.

Hoover worked for the Library of Congress and later the Justice Department. He tracked down illegal aliens on the home front during World War I. There was a fear that many Germans were potential spies and saboteurs. After the war it was a fear of the communists. Although there was hysteria among paranoid Americans, it's also true that there were and always are spies and saboteurs in our midst, especially during wartime.

The FBI Story

Hoover was placed in charge of the newly formed General Intelligence Division of the Justice Department, and his career as a lawman had begun. It was here that Hoover began his lifetime obsession of amassing files on people. In these early days it was mostly files on suspected "radical" groups. A necessary endeavor, but over the decades Hoover fancied himself the final arbiter of what was considered radical and "anti-American." The Hoover Files eventually included people like Bing Crosby and Rock Hudson, hardly rabid anarchists bent on toppling the government.

Hoover rose within the ranks of the Justice Department seeking out and destroying communists and other radicals both real and imagined. His eyes were on his prize, his personal Holy Grail—directorship of the Bureau of Investigation, later called the Federal Bureau of Investigation. He achieved that goal in 1924 and remained in the position until his death in 1972.

Hoover dressed in white linen suits and had an avid interest in collectibles. He was never seen in the company of women and had a longtime male companion, fellow FBI agent Clyde Tolson. They worked together and lived together. Naturally, rumors about Hoover's sexual tastes were dished for decades. One mobster claimed to have seen a photograph of Hoover in women's clothing, dressed as a 1920s "flapper." The photo has never surfaced.

FACT

There have been many movies glorifying the Federal Bureau of Investigation. James Cagney starred in the 1935 movie *G-Men* and James Stewart put on the badge in the 1959 movie *The FBI Story*. These were done in Hoover's lifetime and with his approval, as was the long-running television show from the 1960s called *The FBI*. Another long-running show, *The X-Files*, takes a darker view of the bureau.

Melvin and Hoover

Hoover was a man full of righteous indignation and by all accounts not blessed with a sense of humor or healthy self-deprecation. He was outraged by gangsters being romanticized in the Roaring Twenties. He achieved national attention in the Depression-ravaged 1930s, when a different breed of gangster terrorized America's heartland. These were not the slick and well-oiled cogs of elaborate La Cosa Nostra machinery. These were oddballs and outcasts and misfits with colorful names like Machine Gun Kelly, Pretty Boy Floyd, Baby Face Nelson, Ma Barker, and Bonnie and Clyde.

As with the Mafia, the media often treated these cold-blooded killers as romantic modern-day Robin Hoods. Hoover was indignant and set the FBI on their trail. The spectacular shoot-'em-ups that ensued made the FBI the Wyatt Earps of the day. James Cagney took a break from his usual gangster roles to star in a movie called *G-Men* (gangster-ese for the FBI, the *G* stands for *government*).

One of Hoover's star agents in the bureau was the flamboyant Melvin Purvis. He is the agent who hunted down and killed the ruthless bank robber John Dillinger, with a little help from a shady dame who has gone down in history as the "Lady in Red."

Purvis went on to corner and kill Pretty Boy Floyd and Baby Face Nelson shortly after that. He was outshining Hoover, and J. Edgar deeply resented it. Hoover made life in the FBI so miserable for Purvis that he finally resigned. Not satisfied with that, Hoover followed Purvis's career with malevolent interest, often using his influence to prevent him from getting jobs in law enforcement. In 1960 Purvis shot himself with the same gun he had used to shoot down John Dillinger. He was a victim of the egotism and hubris of J. Edgar Hoover.

Hoover has been portrayed unfavorably in Hollywood after his death, either mentioned for his misdeeds or as a character. He is the evil force who unfairly imprisoned Sean Connery's character in *The Rock,* and in Oliver Stone's *Nixon,* Hoover and Tolson are depicted as a catty, campy gay couple.

Hoover and the Mafia

Hoover, the intrepid lawman, keeper of the national dish and dirt, did not have an exemplary record as an antagonist of the Mafia. In fact, he repeatedly denied that an organized crime network existed in the United States. His reason for this stubborn denial could have been his titanic ego. Conspiracy theorists may find more sinister reasons for his refusal to acknowledge the mob's existence. Whatever the reasons for his belief, it made Hoover either a willing or unintentional accomplice in the Mafia's rapid growth and increased influence on the American landscape.

FACT

Data- and dirt-obsessed Hoover hounded Eliot Ness even after the latter's death. Not content with keeping a file on Ness in his lifetime, Hoover assigned FBI agents to watch the television series *The Untouchables* and report on the activities of the fictional Ness!

The theory that gives J. Edgar Hoover the benefit of the doubt is that he was afraid that corruption would spread through the bureau if his agents had close contact with the Mafia. The Mafia would not have become as powerful as it did if not for the greed of law enforcement officials at the local and state levels. Hoover's rationale may have been to steer clear of the Mafia's seductive allure and concentrate on his favorite pursuit, tracking down real and suspected communists. Skeptics suggest that Hoover focused on the easy targets to increase his crime-busting statistics, which would enhance his personal quest for acclaim and his ability to go to Congress to make the case for higher and higher funding for his bureau.

Kindred Spirits

There is a line in *The Godfather* spoken by Don Barzini, a rival of Don Corleone. He wants Corleone to be generous in sharing the influence he has upon the many politicians and judges on his payroll. He tells Corleone he may present a bill for his services, adding, "After all, we are not communists." In a twisted manner, the Mafia's leaders were participants in and advocates of the free enterprise system. Just like the CEOs of any big corporation, they were enthusiastic capitalists. There are those who suggest that Hoover saw them as ideological soul mates. The Mafia did not advocate the overthrow of the government and the American way of life. They were no threat to the status quo—in fact they thrived in the status quo.

It is reported that Hoover mingled with the Mafia. They were often at the same parties and social functions. Hoover loved gambling, especially on the horses, and this was, as we know, a main source of the Mafia's income. Hoover was often at the racetrack with his pal Clyde Tolson. He was publicly seen betting at the $2 window, a seemingly innocuous pastime. But he had agents placing bets for him at the $100 window. It would have ruined his reputation as Mr. Law and Order if the public found out he was a high-stakes gambler.

Or were the stakes really that high? Hoover got his betting "tips" from the notorious syndicated columnist Walter Winchell, who in turn got them from Mafia boss Frank Costello. In other words, Hoover was, whether he knew it or not, betting on fixed races. Hence he was a big winner. If he did not know it then, he was being manipulated by the Mafia. If he did know about it then, Mr. FBI was engaging in behavior punishable by imprisonment.

FACT

While his track record on dealing with the Mafia is lackluster at best, Hoover was aggressive in his war against communism, called the "Red Menace" in those days. The FBI even published a pamphlet called *Red Channels*, which listed prominent men and women suspected of having communist affiliations.

The Truth Is Out There

Eventually it was impossible even for Hoover to deny the existence of the Mafia. The New York State Police raided a gathering of the Commission in upstate New York in 1957. Sixty mobsters were arrested. It was the largest single arrest of a group of Mafiosi. It was proof that they existed, proof that they had an organized, hierarchal structure. The Mafia that J. Edgar Hoover steadfastly maintained did not exist was on the front page of every newspaper in the country. Hoover was, to say the least, embarrassed.

The press and the public wanted to know why the FBI's track record on battling the Mafia was nonexistent. Everyone in the nation except Hoover was acutely aware of the Mafia's integral influence in everyday affairs. He shook up his bureau in a frenetic effort to appease an outraged public. He had agents reading everything they could find on the Mafia. They reported back to the "the Boss," as Hoover was known, that there was indeed a Mafia, and it had existed longer than the FBI itself. With the election of a new president and a new attorney general in 1960, Hoover not only had to acknowledge that the Mafia was out there, he also had to aggressively take them on.

Hoover and the Kennedys

When John F. Kennedy appointed his brother Robert to the position of attorney general, Hoover was not a happy camper. The aging Hoover hated the younger men he thought of as arrogant young aristocrats. Given his mania for accumulating data, he had plenty of dirt on these two Boston Irish rascals, whose FBI files would make Jackie Collins blush. This was the trump card that Hoover had used on everyone in Washington, including presidents and their senior advisers.

Hoover ostensibly reported to Robert Kennedy. At least that is how the chain of command was supposed to be structured. Hoover had been in place since 1924, and he knew the politicians would be gone with the wind in short order. Many a president would have loved to give Hoover his walking papers, but he was like a Sword of Damocles precariously perched above their coiffures.

J. Edgar Hoover

Courtesy of AP/Wide World Photos

▲ This photo shows FBI director J. Edgar Hoover speaking to the Senate Crime Investigating Committee, urging them to continue its exposure of organized crime in Washington D.C., on March 26, 1951.

Robert Kennedy had a history of taking on the Mafia, and he wanted to continue the crusade as attorney general. As we will see in Chapter 10, this is not without irony, because there is strong evidence that John Kennedy might not have been elected without the Mafia's help.

ALERT!

What goes around comes around. Hoover, who often salivated at uncovering salacious scandal, was not immune to vicious gossip. Anonymous FBI agents nicknamed Hoover and his pal Clyde Tolson "J. Edna and Mother Tolson," and tart-tongued writer Truman Capote called them "Johnny and Clyde."

Robert Kennedy was not afraid of Hoover, and Hoover was livid that this cocky young man did not defer to him. He forced Hoover to ratchet up his efforts against organized crime. However, the arrogance and recklessness of the Kennedys worked against them, and when Hoover saw an opportunity to remind them who had the power, he did not hesitate.

Judy, Judy, Judy!

John Kennedy had a presidential libido that was unrivaled at the time. One of his many conquests was a party girl named Judy Campbell. Frank Sinatra had introduced her to him. Old Blue Eyes had also introduced the alluring Ms. Campbell to Chicago Mafioso Sam Giancana. The president and the Mafia don essentially were "dating" the same woman at the same time.

And J. Edgar Hoover had evidence of this live on tape. He made the attorney general aware of this, who then informed his brother. Hoover let them know what he knew, framing it as if his goal was to protect the president, but of course he was putting the Kennedy boys on notice.

After John Kennedy's assassination in 1963, Robert Kennedy resigned as attorney general to run for the United States Senate. For the remainder of his tenure, Hoover resumed his lackadaisical attitude toward the Mafia. When Hoover died in 1972, the Mafia was sorry to see him go. In the post-Hoover years, the FBI has been considerably more aggressive in its efforts to arrest and prosecute Mafia leaders. Ⓔ

Chapter 6

The Mustache Petes

The 1920s Mafia legends may center around Al Capone and Chicago, but of course the Mafia was active in other cities, too. There were considerable Mafia doings and dealings in the city that never sleeps. One of the first major gang wars occurred in New York City in the 1920s. The young usurped the old, and the modern Mafia was born.

Old Boy Network

The term "Mustache Pete" was an old slang expression for a conservative and cautious fellow. It had nothing to do with facial hair and everything to do with attitude. The earliest American mobsters were given this moniker by their rivals and the young tyros who sought to seize power from the old guard. The old boys were believed to be too traditional and Old World to make the Mafia a viable enterprise in the New World. Tending to their olives and tomatoes or leisurely sipping a cappuccino or some vintage wine while business got done at a leisurely clip was their style. They had one speed, and it was not fast forward. The younger breed of mobster was lean and hungry, and very dangerous. The most powerful and influential of the Mustache Petes were Joe "the Boss" Masseria and Salvatore Maranzano.

FACT

Don Vito Cascio Ferro was the Sicilian crime kingpin who sent Salvatore Maranzano to make criminal inroads into the New World. He had spent a few years in America in the nineteenth century before returning home and acting as liaison between the U.S. and Sicilian Mafias.

Boss of Bosses

Salvatore Maranzano originally studied for the priesthood in his native Sicily, but by the time he came to the United States in 1918, he had been seduced by the Dark Side, so to speak, and was one of the first of the American Mafiosi. He was not inclined to think outside the criminal box, and that made him a target for the up-and-coming next generation of more Americanized gangster.

Maranzano was sent as the emissary of the head of the Sicilian Mafia, Don Vito Cascio Ferro, to oversee his interests in the New World. Maranzano's hometown was Castellemmare del Gulfo, so naturally he hooked up with some people from the old neighborhood. Joseph Bonanno, Joseph Profaci, and Stefano Magaddino were all ruthless Mafiosi in their own right and future bigwigs in the New Underworld Order. Maranzano's mandate was to solidify power for his Sicilian master. This compelled him to butt heads with the Mafia "mainlanders," as they were called. His main nemesis among the mainlanders was Joe "the Boss" Masseria.

Who's the Boss?

Joe "the Boss" was New York's answer to Al Capone during the 1920s. He left his native Sicily with a price on his head, first seeing Lady Liberty in New York harbor in 1903. He went to work for the Morello gang on Manhattan's Lower East Side, where his singular talents as an enforcer were in great demand.

Future Mafia dons are nothing if not ambitious. It was not long before he grew tired of being somebody else's leg breaker. The Mustache Pete syndrome got its first kick in the pants when Masseria and a few loyal confederates attacked the Morello Gang's headquarters and killed several loyalists. He carried out additional hits until the hoods decided it was better to switch than fight and consolidated under his leadership. Masseria was then the Boss of Bosses of New York City. If he could make it there, he could make it anywhere.

Unbreakable

Masseria gained a reputation as something of a super-gangster by his ability to survive multiple assassination attempts during his reign. One of the first hits was ordered by a certain Signor Morello, the guy who had his gang shot out from under him. In this legendary near hit, Masseria's two bodyguards were shot dead as they flanked him on the sidewalks of New York, but hit man Umberto Valenti missed Mr. Big. He chased him into a shop, firing ten shots that the Boss successfully dodged. This earned Masseria a reputation as being "bulletproof." No bad deed went unpunished, and Valenti was later whacked on the orders of Masseria.

Salvatore Maranzano's killers, who shot and stabbed him to death in his New York City office, were never found. It is believed that they were recruited by Meyer Lansky, and two of them were named Sammy Levine and Abe Weinberg.

A pragmatic hood, Masseria accepted the olive branch from Morello and even made him one of his lieutenants.

Racial Intolerance

One of Masseria's protégés was the man who went on to become known by the moniker "Lucky Luciano." As we will see in Chapter 7, he was not averse to mingling with the Jewish and even Irish criminal element in New York City. Masseria, an insular Mustache Pete, did not approve. He wanted to keep things in the ethnic family.

Masseria was, for the most part, unopposed until 1928, when Maranzano blew into town. The rivalry between the two Mafia dons would be the first big mob war on American soil. There would be much "going to the mattresses" as they prepared for a long battle. During this gang war they would be ensconced in a secret location that is structured like a military barracks. They slept on mattresses on the floor when not battling their rivals and would live in these conditions until the war was over. This bloody conflict began when Maranzano began hijacking Masseria's truckloads of bootleg moonshine and muscling in on his other varied rackets. The conflict was named for the town in Sicily that gave the United States so many Mafia hoodlums.

The Castellemmarese War

The feature bout of Maranzano versus Masseria was a brutal free-for-all that went the distance and left fifty known dead, though that number is probably much higher, since the Mafia is not known for reporting its homicide statistics to the public at large. Masseria thought it was going to be a breeze. He had more men and means than the younger upstart and his Sicilian sidekicks. But the ruthless and determined Sicilian underdogs gradually wrested more and more power in the violent struggle.

The two Mustache Petes battled it out for supremacy of New York City, but the real machinations were going on among the ambitious young hoods who were coming to the conclusion that they did not want to serve the winner of the war, no matter which one it may be. And the leader of the pack of wolves in waiting was a young Charlie Luciano, who would prove to be very "lucky" indeed when the dust settled and the Tommy guns were silenced.

One of the four gunmen who shot Joe "the Boss" Masseria in a Coney Island restaurant (while Lucky Luciano hid in the men's room) was Albert Anastasia, the man who would later make a name for himself as the head of Murder Incorporated.

Lucky Luciano was, in a twisted sort of way, an insightful man of vision. He believed that Masseria and the other Mustache Petes were squandering great opportunities out of Old World prejudices and their reticence to adapt to changing times. He wanted to do business with the other ethnic crime organizations, and Masseria would have none of it. Masseria, though slow to act, was not stupid. When he learned of Luciano's grumblings, he knew the younger man was a threat, and he took decisive action.

Luciano was kidnapped at gunpoint by three goons and hustled into the back of a limousine, where he was bound, gagged, beaten, and stabbed.

FACT

Lieutenant Joseph Petrosino was a heroic Italian-American policeman who doggedly drove Don Vito Ferro out of the United States and back to Sicily. Sadly, when he left his home turf to pursue Ferro in Sicily, he was murdered.

Luciano regained consciousness on a desolate beach. He was surprised to find himself still alive. He wandered off the beach and walked for about a mile before offering a policeman $50 to call him a cab. The cop took him to the hospital instead, and Luciano was subjected to interrogation from law enforcement officials. He kept mum. The code of Omerta forbids squealing upon threat of a painful demise. Luciano assured the police that he would take care of the problem himself.

THE EVERYTHING MAFIA BOOK

It was Luciano's pal Meyer Lansky who offered the theory that it was Masseria who orchestrated the hit. They could only assume that the bumbling thugs had intended to kill him, leaving him for dead without making sure he was indeed deceased. Together, Lansky and Luciano devised the plan that would end the reign of the Mustache Petes and bring the Mafia into the twentieth century.

Both Sides Now

Luciano took a look at the warring factions and decided to play the two sides against each other to his own advantage. Luciano dreamed of establishing a "commission" of crime syndicates on a national level with—who else?—himself as its Big Kahuna. This was something unimaginable to the narrow-minded Mustache Petes.

Luciano ingratiated himself to Maranzano while still working for Masseria. He agreed to hit Masseria in exchange for taking control of his rackets. Luciano arranged to meet Masseria at an Italian restaurant in the Coney Island section of Brooklyn. Masseria felt safe there. He knew the owner and he knew the turf. When Luciano went to the bathroom, four men entered and blasted Masseria into the next dimensional plane, where only he knows how he was received by his Higher Power.

Luciano was questioned by the cops but feigned innocence. One Mustache Pete down, one more to go.

FACT

Though called "the Morello Gang," the outfit was headed by Iganzio Saietta and Ciro Terranova, the men who ousted Morello. Rarely does a crime family change names when it gets a new boss. Even when celebrated hoodlum John Gotti, known for his ego, took over as head of the Gambino crime family, he did not change the name.

Lucky Luciano had made a secret deal with Maranzano to whack Masseria, but he also had plans to take care of the other Mustache Petes. The death of Masseria was only half of Luciano's business plan.

Maranzano was now *Capo di tutti Capi* (the Boss of all Bosses). He summoned mobsters from all over the country for a convention. They decked the halls with religious iconography to fool the feds and any other law enforcement officials who might want to crash the party. It was not a meeting of the Holy Rosary Society.

It was at this meeting that the Mafia flow chart that became "the five families" was hashed out. Maranzano was the CEO, and he appointed five VPs who would each head a "family." The heads of the criminal households would be Joseph Bonanno, Phil and Vincent Mangano, Charlie Luciano, Joseph Profaci, and Tom Gagliano.

Despite the Mafia's supercilious claims of honor, the old adage that there is no honor among thieves is a universal truth. Soon after this arrangement was made, Maranzano created a hit list that included most of his top lieutenants, including Lucky Luciano. He knew that one or more of these Young Turks would be already plotting to usurp him. The shooter was to be a particularly nasty killer aptly named Vincent "Mad Dog" Coll. Luciano was as lucky as ever. He got wind of the conspiracy and took preemptive measures.

When sides were chosen in the Castellemmarese War, so named because the two rival Mafia dons and many of their underlings were from the Sicilian town of Castellemmare, it shaped up as follows. The Maranzanos had among their ranks future bosses Joseph Bonanno, Joseph Profaci, Thomas Lucchese, Joseph Magliocco, and Gaetano "Tom" Gagliano. The Masseria team had Lucky Luciano, Frank Costello, Joe Adonis, Vito Genovese, Albert Anastasia, and Carlo Gambino.

Luciano learned that he and Vito Genovese were to be summoned to Maranzano's office, where Coll would be waiting to off them. He also learned that the long arm of the Internal Revenue Service had its sights on Maranzano. His organization was to be the subject of an IRS audit.

The Taxman Shooteth

Luciano sent four hit men to Maranzano's office posing as IRS account-ants, and they killed Maranzano and his bodyguards in a massacre. Mr. Lucky also arranged the elimination of forty or so rivals nationwide. The era of the Mustache Petes was over, and Luciano was now the Boss of all Bosses.

Luciano, perhaps having been influenced by American democracy and corporate structure, rejected the title. He resolved that the five families would remain intact and, along with Meyer Lansky, formed the National Crime Syndicate, also known as "The Commission." The Commission became the organizational structure of organized crime in America for the rest of the Mafia's glory days. It is still believed to exist in a somewhat emasculated form.

In the next chapter we will take a more comprehensive look at the life and bloody times of Lucky Luciano, the man who made the modern Mafia the powerful and profitable business it became. (E)

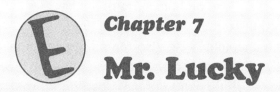

Chapter 7
Mr. Lucky

Lucky Luciano made the Mafia an even more formidable force to be reckoned with, expunging the Old World thinking and creating the modern Mafia. There is more to Luciano's story than this tumultuous period. He lived a long life and was one of the most ruthless and successful gangsters of the twentieth century.

Little Rascals

Mr. Lucky was born Charles Luciano in Sicily in 1897. Like so many other millions of Europeans in the nineteenth century, who heard tales of a promised land where the streets were paved with gold, his family set sail for America and learned that the hype did not match the reality. Nevertheless, it was a land of opportunity for those on both sides of the law.

Young Charlie entered the criminal milieu at the tender age of ten, when he was arrested for shoplifting. He also ran a juvenile "protection agency," offering to protect the weaker boys for a few pennies. It was a no-win scenario for the boys—if they did not pay Charlie for protection, they were promptly pummeled by him.

America is not really a "melting pot." It is more like beef stew. All the ingredients commingle in the pot but have their singular uniquenesses. The immigrant Mafiosi that came to America as boys and adolescents were raised in this atmosphere and were more willing to interact with other ethnic groups. This is how the Mafia became Americanized.

One of the kids refused to pay up. This feisty little fellow was another immigrant child, a Jewish kid from Poland named Meyer Lansky. Lansky stood up to Luciano, and they became fast friends and lifelong partners in crime. From this "Bowery Boys" youth sprang the most successful crime outfit in American history.

Drug Dealer

We sometimes think that drug use in America was something that exploded on the scene in the '60s, but drugs have been around for millennia. Lucky Luciano did time in a reform school for dealing heroin and morphine in 1915. A year later he was on the New York Police Department's short list as the suspect in several murders. And he was a member of the infamous Five Points Gang. All before the age of twenty.

Every gangster was in the bootleg business during the 1920s, including

Luciano. He mingled with other young hoodlums who formed a virtual *Who's Who* of gangland: Meyer Lansky, Bugsy Siegel, Joe Adonis, Vito Genovese, Frank Costello, Dutch Schultz, Arnold Rothstein, and even an Irishman called Big Bill Dwyer. Luciano had no prejudices about mingling with hoods of all stripes. His fraternization with Irish and Jewish gangsters was frowned upon by his boss, who was Joe "the Boss" Masseria. This conflict led to one of the first Mafia bloodbaths—the Castellemmarese War (detailed in Chapter 6).

Charles in Charge

After the Castellemmare War, Lucky Luciano was the top Mafia don. He did not get the nickname from surviving the near-fatal beating that left him with a fashionable scar on his cheek, an emblem befitting his status as a tough guy. He was called Lucky because of his handicapping acumen. He could pick winners at the racetrack with uncanny accuracy. And most of the time the races weren't even fixed.

FACT

Lucky Luciano had the posthumous distinction of being named by *Time* magazine as one of the 100 "Builders and Titans" of the twentieth century. He was placed in the same company as Walt Disney and Bill Gates.

Mafia men do not have a wide circle of friends, but the friends they have are held close. Luciano maintained business and personal relations with the tough little kid who steadfastly refused his shakedown intimidation. There would not have been a Lucky Luciano without a Meyer Lansky, and vice versa.

An FBI agent said that Meyer Lansky could have been a CEO if he had wanted; he was that skilled a businessman. Cynics may suggest there is little difference between a Mafia don and the CEO of a multinational corporation. In any event, the "Little Man," as he was affectionately called, was a business and criminal mastermind.

He was born in Poland, and his real name was Maier Suchowljansky. He paved the way into the Cuban gambling rackets in the years before

Fidel Castro's revolution and "wet his beak" (an old Sicilian expression for taking a cut of the action in a certain territory) in rackets in his hometown New York and across the river in New Jersey, as well as in Chicago, Detroit, and eventually in Las Vegas and on the West Coast. Together Luciano and Lansky, even as young men, dreamed of a gangland "syndicate" that would span the country and unite organized crime families across America.

The Commission

Luciano and Lansky maintained the basic structure of Maranzano's Commission. The other East Coast boys were Joseph Bonanno, Vincent Mangano, Joseph Profaci, Tom Gagliano, and Stefano Magaddino of Buffalo. Al Capone's successor in Chicago, Frank Nitti, was also a member. After Nitti, Frank Sinatra's crony Sam Giancana was affiliated with the Commission.

FACT

Film buffs take note: Frank Nitti was not thrown off a roof by Eliot Ness as depicted in the 1987 movie *The Untouchables*. It was a nice Hollywood ending for the hoodlum, but alas, it did not happen. Nitti committed suicide rather than face a prison term in the late 1930s.

The Commission was modeled after many a corporation, with the equivalents of a CEO and board of directors and middle management types. The local leg breaker could be equated to the mailroom guy. For years the Commission was made up of mostly Italian and Jewish gangsters. The "Big Six" included Frank Costello, Joe Adonis, Meyer Lansky, Tony Accardo, Jake Guzik, and Longy Zwillman. However, the Jewish influence faded over time and essentially died when Meyer Lansky died. The sons of the Jewish gangsters, for the most part, did not follow in the family business. The next generation went into legitimate careers. Lansky even saw that one of his sons went to West Point. The sociocultural phenomenon of Jewish gangsterism lasted just a single generation in America.

One of the reasons that the Commission was a long-lasting success was because it was structured as a board of directors, each with equal power and no one man in charge. There were men who came to be regarded as the "Boss of Bosses" from time to time, but all major decisions were voted on, and no one man had veto power.

Tough Guys in Time Out

Much of the role of the Commission was to mediate and settle disputes between rival families in the United States, and to keep things running smoothly with the Sicilian Mafia in the old country. Bad boys were put in the Mafia version of "time out," which usually meant being murdered. It has been estimated that the National Commission included 1,700 members in twenty-four families nationwide. The bigwigs were from New York's five families, but there were also representatives from Buffalo, Philadelphia, and Chicago. Families in smaller cities were controlled by the families in larger cities. For example, the Chicago boys controlled all the Midwest families in Kansas City, St. Louis, Milwaukee, and Detroit.

The Dream Is Over

The legacy Lucky Luciano and Meyer Lansky had left behind suffered an irrevocable blow in 1986 when the heads of the five families were successfully prosecuted and convicted for their crimes. This was long after Luciano and Lansky were gone, of course. It is believed that the Commission exists in a truncated and weakened form these days, mostly on the East Coast. This is the Mafia of the fictional Tony Soprano, with none of the panache of its flamboyant founders.

Check out a book called *The Last Testament of Lucky Luciano* by Martin A. Gosch and Richard Hammer for some interesting reading about this famous mobster. Be forewarned, however, that many experts on the Mafia doubt the truthfulness of many of the authors' claims.

Unsafe Sex

Lucky Luciano was a high-profile gangster. Unlike the low-key Meyer Lansky, Mr. Lucky was often seen at the trendiest nightclubs hobnobbing with the glitterati of the day. The high life took its toll. Prostitution was one of his many rackets, and his familiarity with the prostitutes gave him multiple bouts of gonorrhea and syphilis. When the Mafia ventured into the drug business, Lucky Luciano made sure that he got as many of the prostitutes hooked on heroin as he could, to better control them. This also made them turn their profits right back to him to feed their addiction. But the law was growing impatient with the mob run amok. The government went after Lucky Luciano in the form of Special Prosecutor Thomas Dewey.

Lucky Luciano

Courtesy of AP/Wide World Photos/Remo Nassi

▲ Reputed mobster Charles "Lucky" Luciano sips a drink during a news conference he called in the bar of Rome's Excelsior Hotel, June 11, 1948. Luciano said he wanted "to set the record straight." At extreme left is AP writer Johnny McKnight.

Lucky Luciano, at the end of life, had this to say about his legacy. "I learned too late that you need just as good a brain to make a crooked million as an honest million. These days you apply for a license to steal from the public."

Dewey Defeats Lucky

Thomas Dewey aggressively went after the prostitution racket in New York. Forty brothels were raided and 100 or so women were arrested. Many of them told sad tales of their lives and their many abuses at the hands of the syndicate. Soon Luciano had a large group of women spilling the beans to the law. Never mind the other rackets; Dewey compiled an airtight case against Luciano in the prostitution business alone. And this was enough to put him away.

Feeling the heat, Luciano decided to take in the waters at Hot Springs, Arkansas. This Southern "Sin City" was a vacation spot for the Capone mob. Luciano was caught in Hot Springs and taken back to New York City in a heavily guarded railroad car. The unthinkable had happened. Lucky Luciano had been arrested and was put on trial. Even more astoundingly, he was convicted and sentenced to thirty to fifty years in the Big House.

FACT

Many people thought Thomas Dewey was an overly ambitious prosecutor who was himself a crooked man, but many of those who made the claim were in the Mafia. It is true that Dewey used his crime buster reputation to propel him to the office of governor of New York before losing the presidential election to Truman in 1948.

On the Inside Looking Out

Luciano was sent to the Clinton State Prison in upstate New York. The prison is also referred to as Dannemora, and was not considered to be as "comfortable" as Ossining, known in the vernacular as "Sing-Sing," just a few miles north of Manhattan. Mr. Lucky, Boss of Bosses, became known as Number 92169 and put to work in the laundry room. In short order he went from laundering ill-gotten booty to washing other convict's undies.

Dannemora was not a model modern rehabilitation facility. It was positively medieval, with none of the amenities to which Mr. Big had grown accustomed. However, his influential pals on the outside saw to it that he had certain privileges.

Uncle Sam Wants Lucky

Lucky Luciano was locked up from 1936 to 1942. He was allowed as many visitors as he liked, and no record was made of his male callers. Thus he continued to pull the strings and run the syndicate from his claustrophobic prison cell. And when America entered World War II after the Japanese attack on Pearl Harbor, the godfather found a surprising ally in a distant uncle—Uncle Sam.

FACT

There are 548 pages on Lucky Luciano available through the Freedom of Information Act. Much of the government's information is no doubt classified, however. Evidence suggests that the links between the mob and the government sometimes ran deep. Luciano worked with military intelligence during World War II.

Before Italy switched sides and joined the Allies in 1943, it was allied with Nazi Germany. Benito Mussolini, Italy's fascist dictator, had made many enemies among the Sicilian Mafia. The old political adage "the enemy of my enemy is my friend" suddenly applied to relations between the United States government and the Mafia. Meyer Lansky let it be known that Luciano would be of valuable assistance in the war effort. It was suggested that he could help with espionage in Sicily and he could help keep the New York waterfront safe from the threat of Nazi saboteurs. Sabotage was a serious threat, and who better than the gangsters who ruled the docks to "police" them for the government?

Luciano was moved to Great Meadows Prison in Comstock, New York. This was a Club Med compared to the dank Dannemora. From this new base of operations he continued to run his underworld enterprises and help the Office of Naval Intelligence by providing information about German military activity on the island of Sicily. Military intelligence agents made numerous clandestine trips to Luciano's prison cell to secure his assistance.

The Mafia was happy to oblige. Mussolini's government had cramped the Mafia's style for over a decade, and they would be glad to see the dictator ousted. Ironically, when the American and British forces liberated Sicily, they also released hundreds of Mafiosi from Sicilian prisons, thinking they were political prisoners of the fascist government.

Room Service

Lucky Luciano was granted gourmet meals, plenty of booze, and even the pleasure of female companionship while incarcerated in Great Meadows. He also expected an early release from prison as a reward for his contribution to the war effort. It is ironic that the man who had him locked up, Thomas Dewey, was also the man who commuted Luciano's sentence. Dewey had used his success battling the mob as a political stepping-stone to the office of governor of New York. He probably did not feel too devastated in pardoning Lucky Luciano. Dewey pardoned Luciano at the request of the federal government. They wanted Luciano's cooperation in the war effort. He then used his contacts in Sicily to help the Allied forces. As part of Luciano's prison release deal, he was deported back to Italy, since he had never become an American citizen.

You Can Go Home Again

Luciano left America in 1946, never to return. He settled in Naples under the watchful eye of the Italian authorities. He could not travel more than a few miles out of town, and all foreign visitors had to be reported to authorities. Being a gangster and thus naughty by nature, he frequently broke the rules. Absence did not make the heart grow fonder between him and his old buddy Meyer Lansky. Luciano felt Lansky was not allowing him to sufficiently "wet his beak" in the lucrative American rackets. Luciano was still the de facto head of the Commission, but since he was deported, his influence naturally faded, and Lansky assumed more power.

Luciano's luck finally ran out when he died of a heart attack in 1962. Thus ended the violent life and times of a man who made a nice living through nasty means and helped create a modern criminal empire.

FACT

Lucky Luciano was not publicity-shy at the end of his life. In fact, he suffered a fatal heart attack while waiting at the Naples airport for a visitor—not one of his Mafia buddies but a Hollywood producer who was interested in making a movie about the famous gangster's violent life.

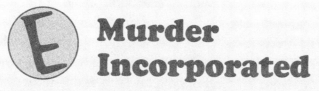

Chapter 8

Murder Incorporated

One of the most murderous elements of the Commission merits a closer look. These gangsters decided it would be beneficial to have an elite corps of killers permanently on the payroll, just as any business will routinely contract the services of an exterminator. These guns for hire were known collectively as Murder Incorporated.

The Killer Elite

Lucky Luciano and Meyer Lansky determined that a security force was needed for their business. More than a security force, it was a ruthless hit team that "rubbed out" the opposition, giving extreme meaning to the term "hostile takeover."

Murder Incorporated was an internal execution squad. It did not go after law enforcement officials, journalists, or politicians. As we shall see, a celebrated gangster was himself whacked when he became hell-bent on violating this code. The old saying that the Mafia "only kills its own" was attributed to Bugsy Siegel, a friend of both Luciano and Lansky.

Going Dutch

The man who proved that the Mafia expected the mandate of Murder Incorporated to be obeyed was Dutch Schultz. Dutch Schultz was born Arthur Simon Flegenheimer in the Bronx in 1902 to Jewish parents. He was something of a mama's boy and remained close to her until his untimely demise. In a perverse way, he remained true to his mother's deep faith.

Dutch Schultz

Courtesy of AP/Wide World Photos

◄ This is an undated photo of Arthur "Dutch Schultz" Flegenheimer.

Schultz was a man on a spiritual quest. Sometimes he would claim he was practicing Judaism, other times he considered himself Catholic. He was a gangster who gave a lot of thought to the afterlife. He considered himself a religious hood.

FACT

Similar to the plot of the movie *A Bronx Tale*, young Dutch Schultz grew up on the mean streets of the Bronx and became starstruck by local mob boss Marcel Poffo. He began to work for Poffo and never looked back to the straight and narrow road.

He began his criminal career in the Bronx. Sent to prison at the age of seventeen, he was a problem inmate and was transferred to a harsher prison from which he promptly escaped, only to be soon recaptured. Committing the crime was a badge of honor among his Bronx buddies, who gave him the snappy tough guy moniker "Dutch Schultz."

Like all Mafiosi, he was involved in the bootlegging racket during the '20s. His area of expertise was beer, and he and his cronies controlled the beer distribution in the Bronx and Upper Manhattan. His gang was comprised mostly of Jewish and Irish hooligans. Two of his associates went by the names "Fatty" Walsh and Edward "Fats" McCarthy. Obviously these lads were sampling the merchandise.

Dutch Schultz was known as the "Beer Baron of the Bronx." He made his name muscling in on the bootleg business of Irish saloonkeepers who did not shut down operations during Prohibition. They simply went underground and became involved with the underworld. Schultz moved on to bigger things, but like many a "gifted" man, he got his start in the Bronx.

Schultz was a maverick and a free agent during his career in crime. He was invited to join the notorious Commission by Lucky Luciano. During the Castellemmarese War he sided with Joe "the Boss" Masseria. When Maranzano won the war, Schultz found himself on the new Boss of Bosses' enemies list. Maranzano immediately felt threatened by the Young Turks nipping at his heels. Anyone who was anyone in underworld circles was on that list. Maranzano was the one who was killed, and Dutch Schultz survived, thrived, and continued running the restaurant business, the attendant food service unions, and bookie joints.

Along Came Dewey

Thomas Dewey was the United States Attorney for the Southern District of New York. He had decided to take on the powerful and deadly underworld forces that were menacing the good people of New York City and the surrounding area. The so-called harmless vices of drinking, gambling, and prostitution were not so harmless in the eyes of Dewey, and the accompanying bloodbaths by rival gangsters were giving the city a bad name. The free-flowing dough corrupted many a law enforcement official, judge, and politician. And civilians occasionally died in these mob wars, particularly in a nasty protracted feud between Dutch Schultz and "Mad Dog" Coll.

FACT

Like the cowboys who would "ride shotgun" on a stagecoach to protect the passengers from outlaws, Dutch Schultz performed the same function on trucks that hauled bootleg booze in and around New York City and its suburbs.

Dewey learned the lesson from the arrest and conviction of Chicago's Al Capone and sought to nail mobsters on income tax fraud. If it was good enough for Big Al, it might work with the New York Mafia. Schultz's bootlegging business came under scrutiny. While under indictment for tax fraud (it was estimated that he owed the IRS $92,000 and could face forty-three years in prison), Schultz went on the lam. He went "into hiding" for twenty-two months but never left New York City. He was seen in public often, confirming Dewey's concerns about local political and police corruption. Theoretically, Schultz could have been picked up rather easily, but he continued to take in the nightlife and other diversions that New

York City had to offer, all in plain sight of the press, paparazzi, and the police force. He was in hiding, but given the corruption in the police force and among politicians, he did not have to vary his routine very much.

The early 1930s saw the end of Prohibition, a new president in the White House, and a new mayor in New York. Fiorello LaGuardia, also known as the Little Flower (the English translation of his first name), had run as a reform candidate determined to use one of the planks of his political platform to whack the Mafia upside the head. It is possible that, as an Italian, he was particularly angry at the bad reputation the Mafia gave the rest of his people. Though most Italians had nothing to do with the Mafia, many non-Italians assumed that every new neighbor whose name ended in a vowel must be affiliated in some way with La Cosa Nostra.

QUESTION?

What is a "policy racket"?

This was a numbers game that was popular long before state governments made it legitimate and legal in the many lottery games of today. Policy rackets thrived in poor neighborhoods, where people dreamed of making a big score and improving their lot in life.

Dutch was feeling the heat. J. Edgar Hoover declared him Public Enemy No. 1. In 1934 Dutch turned himself in. He became a media darling during his two trials, the first ending in a hung jury and the second in an acquittal. Luciano may have been named Lucky, but Schultz was proving very fortunate as well.

But not for long. The government indicted Schultz again, and he had had enough. He wanted to whack Dewey, which would be a violation of the Commission's rules against killing politicians. Murdering a prosecutor who was so squarely in the public eye would do much more harm than good. Dewey's wife had received threatening phone calls, and there was a $25,000 reward for his murder. The Commission would not sanction the hit on Dewey, and maverick Dutch boldly announced that he was going to "make it so" anyway. The truth is that his cronies fully expected him to go to jail on income tax evasion charges. They were already spending the money from his interests that they planned to take over in their mercenary minds and were more than a little disappointed when he beat the rap.

When Luciano had his suspicions confirmed by Albert Anastasia, alias the "Mad Hatter," a.k.a. "Lord High Executioner of Murder Incorporated," that Schultz was fully intent on assassinating Dewey, he knew what he had to do. The Commission's decrees were final and not to be ignored. The price a Mafioso paid for so ignoring them was the ultimate price.

On October 23, 1935, in the Palace Chop House in Newark, New Jersey, Dutch Schultz and three of his associates found themselves in a pitched gunfight with Murder Incorporated. Schultz died in a nearby hospital days later. He converted to Catholicism on his deathbed, and his delirious dying ramblings are a legendary stream of consciousness mob-speak rant that inspired beatnik author William S. Burroughs to fashion a work called *The Last Words of Dutch Schultz: A Fiction in the Form of a Film Script.*

Dutch Schultz
lies wounded

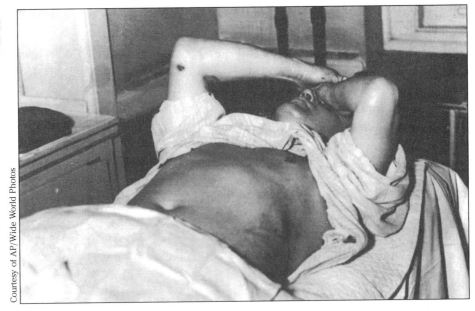

Courtesy of AP/Wide World Photos

▲ Mobster Dutch Schultz holds his head in agony as he lies in his hospital cot, his arm and chest wounds exposed, in Newark, New Jersey, on October 23, 1935. Schultz and his bodyguards were shot by rival gangsters in a massacre and he died the next day from his gunshot wounds. He was born Arthur Flegenheimer in the Bronx, New York, in 1902.

FACT

Albert Anastasia's nickname, the Lord High Executioner, comes from medieval England and the hooded and hatchet-wielding man who carried out death sentences in the Tower of London. The Mafia is known for its morbid sense of humor.

When Lepke Met Sparky

One of the two top members of Murder Incorporated was Louis Lepke, born Louis Buchalter. His first mob antics involved breaking strikes by the garment workers' unions through threats and intimidation (and worse) during the 1920s. He paired with Lucky Luciano in the bootlegging racket and later became the main hit man for Murder Incorporated, carrying out hundreds of hits. He was eventually convicted of a narcotics charge, but while in jail some informants ratted him out, and he ended up convicted on a murder rap. In 1944 he and two other Murder Incorporated alumni, Mendy Weiss and Louis Capone (no relation to Al), met their maker courtesy of Old Sparky (a slang expression for the electric chair) in Sing-Sing. Lepke was the only high-ranking member of the Commission to suffer such a fate. The No. 2 man of Murder Incorporated had been promoted long before then. His name was Albert Anastasia.

ESSENTIAL

For more information on the vicious gangster Louis Lepke, look for the 1975 movie *Lepke,* starring Tony Curtis. Hollywood loves gangster movies, so just about every hoodlum of note got a movie made about his life. Most were long gone by the time Hollywood got around to filming their stories.

Most of the members of Murder Incorporated were Jewish gangsters. They were methodical hit men. They operated out of a Brooklyn candy store. They did not operate without orders, and their hits were well thought out and for the most part dispassionate. Hits had to have the unanimous approval of the Commission. The operated nationally, so they got to see America as they plied their trade. A simple shooting was the common form of execution, but staged accidents, faked suicides, and the occasional garroting were also accepted practices. Often the law had to write the murders off as missing persons cases, when the bodies were never found. Most hits remain unsolved, except for those revealed by the rats that squealed, and until Anastasia took power, they remained insular in their targets. If you had no business dealings with the Mafia, you were in no danger of getting whacked. No one will ever know for sure, but conservative estimates place the number of hits somewhere between 500 and 700 in its ten-year reign of terror.

FACT

There were many Jewish gangsters in the early days of the Mafia, and many of the hit men in Murder Incorporated were Jewish. The tradition ended with that generation, however. Unlike the Italians, the sons of the Jewish mobsters went on to legitimate careers. Meyer Lansky even sent his son to the West Point Military Academy.

Murder Incorporated came to an end when several low-level members were arrested and began to "sing" to the authorities. The most famous was a man named Abe Reles, who was called the "Canary." He gave the police information on about 200 murders in which he was directly or indirectly involved. He was in police custody when he decided to "take a dive" out of a hotel window. It is unlikely that he took his own life out of guilt over turning traitor. It is generally assumed that he was given a gentle nudge.

The Mad Hatter

He was not a cute character from *Alice in Wonderland* despite the nickname given him. Albert Anastasia was one of the most vicious members of a vicious profession. Every man has his strengths and weaknesses. Anastasia was more into the bloodlust aspect of the Mafia than the bottom-line business side, and though he was a killing machine, his inability and lack of enthusiasm in other areas of Mafia operations led to his downfall.

Though the Mafia maintained that murder was just a business practice, the men who gravitated to Murder Incorporated were not content to simply shoot a man. They had many grisly techniques in their repertoire, including burying a mobster alive in the sand beneath a Brooklyn boardwalk.

Anastasia got his start on the Brooklyn docks, rising in the ranks of the mob-controlled longshoreman's union. He was a hot-tempered hood who killed another longshoreman early in his career. This faux pas landed him a reserved room on death row. He was granted a second trial when four of the witnesses who had testified in the first trial suddenly reversed their statements. When four key witnesses suddenly went missing before the second trial could be held, Anastasia walked. This happened time and time again in the history of the Mafia.

In other trials over the years, witnesses had a tendency to turn up dead, guaranteeing acquittals for Anastasia. One man and his wife vanished, never to be heard from again. The fact that blood stains splattered their home was a clear indication of foul play. Another man was found in the trunk of a car in the Bronx, and yet another was dumped in the Passaic River in New Jersey.

Needless to say, Anastasia's singular skill was put to good use during the Castellemmarese War. He served Lucky Luciano with gleeful enthusiasm during the violent power struggle. He was one of the four-man hit team that whacked Masseria. And given that publicity would have been bad for his particular line of work outside of Mafia circles, we will never really know how many people met their end at the Mad Hatter's hands.

Power Plays

Anastasia was a main player in the plan to get Lucky Luciano released from prison in order to help the war effort. One of the selling points to the government was that Luciano would help police the New York City docks. In order to make a valid case for Luciano's importance, Anastasia apparently began to create some havoc on the waterfront. It is believed that he ordered his boys to set fire to the French luxury liner *S.S. Normandie* and to place the blame on Nazi saboteurs. The vast amount of water used to extinguish the fire filled the ship and caused it to capsize. The manufactured crisis fooled the feds and helped Luciano get generous amenities in prison and ultimately a commuted sentence.

Coming Up

Luciano and fellow mobster Frank Costello could keep Anastasia on a reasonably short leash. Anastasia was a loose cannon, and cooler heads in the Mafia kept a watchful eye on him. He was loyal to these two bosses. Though loyal, he was unstable, they felt. In a Mafia version of the Peter Principle, Anastasia was promoted to the level of his incompetence. He was made boss of the Mangano crime family by his two benefactors, much to the indignation of Vince Mangano. This created an enmity that ended when Mangano's brother was murdered and Vince joined the ranks of the mysteriously missing folks who got in the way of Anastasia's ambition.

Louis Lepke was betrayed by a boyhood friend with the curious name of Moey Dimples. While Lepke waited to meet his maker on death row, Moey had a few more dimples impressed upon his person in the proverbial hail of bullets.

His benefactors backed up Anastasia's claim that he had uncovered a plot against him and his actions were in self-defense. As a result, the Commission deemed the hit justified and Anastasia was free from reprisals. For a little while at least.

Anastasia enjoyed his new position, but his handlers had their own reasons for promoting him. Frank Costello was in the midst of a rivalry with Vito Genovese as the two crime lords vied for control of the interests and rackets of the recently deported Lucky Luciano.

Anastasia was more interested in killing than making lucrative business deals. His lack of subtlety and finesse made him a liability rather than an asset in the long run. He ordered the hit of a man he saw on television. The man had testified as a witness against celebrated bank robber Willie Sutton. Sutton was the man who, when asked why he robbed banks, offered the now-famous reply, "That's where the money is." Anastasia was outraged at the witness's attitude and had him murdered. This of course violated the mob's unwritten rule not to mess with outsiders. It shines too much light on their shadow world and creates too many problems. The fact that a high-level Mafioso would so casually order a hit raised the red flag for the other members of the Commission. Anastasia's explanation was an offhanded, "I hate stoolies."

The mob was mortified by this brazen and reckless act. Costello needed Anastasia, so he could not cut him loose, but their enemies seized the moment. Genovese surreptitiously turned other mobsters against Anastasia, including the Mad Hatter's No. 2 man, Carlo Gambino.

Just a Little off the Top

Anastasia wanted a piece of Meyer Lansky's Cuban casino action, and Lansky refused. This increased the bad blood between the two. Lansky, who we will see in the next chapter did not shirk from rubbing out even his closest friends, had no compunction about taking a proactive stance against Albert Anastasia. Lansky decided to not wait for Anastasia and Genovese to solve his problem for him. He ordered a hit on the Mad Hatter.

FACT

The 1960 movie *Murder, Inc.* starring Peter Falk chronicles the history of the assassination wing of the Mafia and was released only three years after the celebrated hit on Albert Anastasia.

On October 25, 1957, Anastasia went to the barbershop of the Park Sheraton Hotel in New York City. Two masked men entered and the Lord High Executioner was himself offed in a hail of bullets. The fact that his bodyguard did not quickly join his boss in the barbershop after parking the car indicates that there was a conspiracy in his own family, no doubt led by the man who succeeded him, Carlo Gambino. And thus the Gambino crime family came into being. Ultimately, Gambino betrayed Genovese and switched to the side of Lansky and Frank Costello. They helped entrap Genovese in a drug rap that sent him away for life.

Albert
Anastasia's
murder

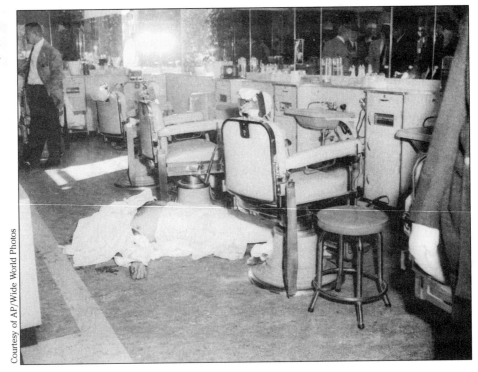

Courtesy of AP/Wide World Photos

▲ The body of Mafia boss Albert Anastasia lies on the floor of the barbershop at New York's Park Sheraton Hotel after his murder in October 1957. Anastasia's crime family was taken over by Carlo Gambino.

The end of Murder Incorporated did not mean the end of Mafia violence. However, the days of an organized and efficient "Praetorian Guard" were over (the Praetorian Guard was a unit of bodyguards in ancient Rome who protected the Roman emperor). Ⓔ

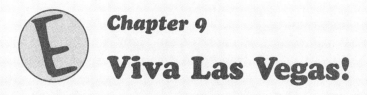

Chapter 9

Viva Las Vegas!

Las Vegas is also known as "Sin City," the place where you can indulge your deepest, darkest fantasies and maybe even make your fortune. The Mafia was a fixture in Vegas during its glitzy glory days and transformed it from a wild and woolly honky-tonk town to the entertainment capital of the world.

Here Come the Boys

Gambling casinos existed before the Mafia got to Las Vegas. Gambling was legalized in 1931 by the state of Nevada. The early casinos were more like rowdy honky-tonks and cowboy hangouts than the modern casinos that would soon spring up in the desolate wilderness. Who would have thought that a bunch of immigrant kids from New York's Lower East Side would become the power brokers and robber barons in the Wild West? When the Mafia decided to "Go West, Young Hoodlum," they sent an emissary to the Promised Land and, so the legend goes, he put Las Vegas on the map.

Don't Call Me Bugsy!

As we learned in the previous chapter, Bugsy Siegel was a member of the New York gang nicknamed Murder Incorporated. A Jewish kid from the mean streets of the neighborhood called Hell's Kitchen, he was also a charismatic and good-looking guy who had ambitions to be a movie star.

Meyer Lansky is the most famous of the Jewish Mafia men, and is considered one of the founding fathers of Las Vegas. Lesser-known but influential gangsters Moe Sedway and Dave Berman may not be household words, but they could also be on a Mount Rushmore of Vegas founders.

Siegel also had a crackpot plot to personally assassinate Italian dictator Mussolini. He hated him on two counts—as a Mafioso and a Jewish man. Mussolini had jailed many Sicilian Mafiosi and adversely impacted business, and he was an ally of Adolf Hitler. Even before the concentration camps were liberated at the end of the war, there were stories about what was happening to European Jews under Hitler's tyranny.

Siegel planned to ingratiate himself with members of the Italian aristocracy, get invited to Italy for an audience with Mussolini, and whack the dictator the good-old American Mafia way. It never happened, and the rational Meyer Lansky was deeply concerned whenever his friend would ramble on about this crazy scheme.

Bugsy Siegel

Courtesy of AP/Wide World Photos

◀ Benjamin "Bugsy" Siegel poses after apprehension in Los Angeles on April 17, 1941, in connection with an indictment returned in New York charging him with harboring Louis "Lepke" Buchalter.

When Dewey turned up the heat, the gang split up. Meyer Lansky went to Havana, Cuba, to open and operate casinos in conjunction with the government of the island's dictator, Batista. Bugsy Siegel went off to Las Vegas.

FACT

Nevada is the only state where prostitution is legal. Travel across state lines and you will get locked up, but in Nevada it is as acceptable as a trip to the convenience store. There is considerable debate over the legalization of prostitution.

While most hoods kept a low profile, Siegel was one of the first of the celebrity gangsters. Tall, dark, and handsome, he became a darling of the Hollywood set, many of whom got a vicarious thrill flirting with danger. Starlets who went for the "bad boy" type needed look no further than a psycho mobster murderer. Yes, "Bugsy" was not named after the wisecracking cartoon rabbit. His name came from his mercurial temperament and tendency to fly off into violent rages, which in the parlance of the underworld was called "going bugs." He did not like the name and would prove its validity by pummeling the poor soul who called him "Bugsy" to his face.

There were several thriving casinos in the downtown section of Las Vegas: the Apache, the Northern, the Boulder, the Las Vegas, the Golden Nugget, and the Horseshoe. Siegel looked toward the outskirts of town to an area called "the strip." He set about building his dream casino. It was to be a touch of urban sophistication in the middle of the desert. His vision became the Flamingo Hotel.

How's Your Bird?

The Flamingo was an opulent and expensive establishment, too costly for Bugsy's backers back East, including his boyhood friend Meyer Lansky. Theoretically, it should have been the best of both worlds. The Mafia could step out of the dark shadows and into the neon light of semi-respectability. They could indulge in familiar vices, but in this oasis in the desert it was all perfectly legal. Bugsy, however, spent far too much money building the Flamingo, and some suggested that he was skimming money off the construction costs and putting it in his own pocket. After all, he had expenses. He lived a lavish lifestyle, had an extravagant mistress, and was even taking acting lessons. He had the grandiose ambition to outdo Clark Gable and Cary Grant as Hollywood's latest leading man.

Mafiosi were not above mixing business with pleasure. Mob boss Sam Giancana, in addition to being a *compadre* of Frank Sinatra, also reportedly had a long-term relationship with Phyllis McGuire of the popular singing group the McGuire Sisters.

Others believe it was his girlfriend Virginia Hill who was skimming the money. She was a "bad girl" straight out of a B movie. Bugsy was smitten with this failed starlet and career gangster's moll.

An Eye for an Eye

Bugsy Siegel's mismanagement and possible outright thievery earned the wrath of the boys back East, including Meyer Lansky. Their $1 million investment had ballooned to $6 million, with no sign of a profit in the foreseeable future. Mob mythos has it that Lansky stayed the inevitable execution twice, but ultimately endorsed the execution of Bugsy Siegel.

The splashy opening of the Flamingo brought out Hollywood's brightest stars, but after a couple of days they returned to Tinseltown, and the Flamingo was an empty monument to a hubris-laden hoodlum whose time had run out.

For an entertaining film version of this tale, check out the 1991 Warren Beatty movie *Bugsy*. Beatty gives an excellent performance, as does Ben Kingsley as Meyer Lansky.

Bugsy was in the posh Hollywood home of his mistress Virginia Hill and he mentioned that he smelled flowers. Spiritualists have often said that those soon to be deceased often smell a fragrant whiff of flora just before the end. The air soon filled with the acrid scent of cordite as gunmen blasted Bugsy Siegel into "the big sleep." One of his baby blue eyes that had made many a starlet swoon was found at the other end of the room. Bugsy was gone, but Las Vegas was just getting started.

Mob Rule

With the vainglorious Bugsy Siegel out of the picture, less flamboyant but more efficient mobsters flooded Las Vegas. The less publicity hungry Lansky took over the Flamingo and had it running smoothly and profitably within a year. He also was the brains behind the Thunderbird casino. The Sands hotel was also controlled by Lansky, along with Frank Costello and others. Francis Albert Sinatra was brought in to attract the tourists. The famous Rat Pack antics, about which more later, took place at the Sands, and the 1960 Rat Pack movie *Ocean's Eleven* was filmed by day at the casino, while they performed nights at the Sands. Sinatra's name on the marquee filled the hotel and the coffers of the clandestine criminal element.

Other gangsters filled out the mob roster of hidden ownership of Las Vegas's biggest casinos. The Cleveland mob owned the Desert Inn. Sinatra's compatriot Sam Giancana had interests in the Sahara and the Riviera, along with the Fischetti brothers and others. The New England contingent hung their fedoras in the cloakroom of the Dunes.

The Teamsters Pension Fund, as administered by the notorious Jimmy Hoffa, loaned millions to the Mafia to build their casinos up and down the Las Vegas strip. The hardworking Teamsters shared in none of the booty, however.

Not satisfied with making money as hidden partners in the casino business, the mob had other methods of making money. The mob wouldn't be the mob if they didn't do something illegal in the world of legalized gambling. The most popular method was called skimming.

When the oodles of cash and coins were collected and taken to the "counting rooms" of the big casinos, a certain percentage was "skimmed" off the top and sent as tribute to the big crime families. This was cold cash free and clear, not subject to the grasping talons of the Internal Revenue Service. In a cash business where the moolah was flowing, the money made via skimming was astronomical.

The Rat Pack

Las Vegas has always been an almost surreal place, and as a source of pop culture entertainment it is unrivaled. Entertainers have always flocked to Vegas. There was plenty of money to be made, there were many ways to liberally indulge vices, and many got a vicarious thrill hobnobbing with the hoodlum element. Perhaps no entertainer was more enamored of the Mafia and its brethren than Frank Sinatra.

Sinatra had an association with the mob going back to his early days as a saloon singer. Almost every singer and comic had to contend with the Mafia, since the mob has a long history of involvement in the clubs and venues where they perform. Most performers of that generation accepted this fact and for the most part got along with their employers. Sinatra, by all reports, had a schoolboy romanticism of gangsters. And when he was down on his luck and his career was in a slump, it was his mob friends who still paid him to sing in their saloons. Sinatra was nothing if not loyal to his friends, and when the Vegas party was in full swing, he was there in spades. And he brought his Hollywood sidekicks along for the ride. Together they created a slice of pop culture lore that continues to fascinate people everywhere.

Ring-a-Ding-Ding

Sinatra, who was given the option to purchase 9 percent of the Sands Hotel by his goombahs, performed there often, always packing the house. And a sold-out crowd of Sinatra fans inevitably wandered over to the slot machines and gambling tables. Sinatra got it in his head to make a movie in Las Vegas. This became the 1960 film *Ocean's Eleven*, more memorable as a time capsule of an epoch than as a cinematic masterpiece.

Sinatra's pals included Dean Martin, Sammy Davis, Jr., Peter Lawford, and Joey Bishop. They filmed *Ocean's Eleven* by day, and performed at the Sands by night. The show was called "The Summit," named for the Cold War conferences between the United States and the former Soviet Union. Their endless stream of "ad-libs" was for the most part written by Bishop, and in the grainy black and white snippets that survive, the antics seem juvenile and not particularly funny. Sammy Davis stands for some ethnic humor that would make even the politically incorrect of today a little uncomfortable. The audience is loving it, however. And the performers seem to be having even more fun than the adoring throng. Smiling in the shadows was the Mafia. Every time Sinatra sang "Luck Be a Lady," the lack of lady luck for the hapless gamblers filled the pockets of the gangsters.

One positive thing Old Blue Eyes did was help break the race barrier in Las Vegas. Black performers were not allowed to stay in rooms at the hotels in which they performed to sold-out crowds and standing ovations. Velvet voiced crooner Nat King Cole was instructed not to make direct eye contact with the swooning fur-adorned and bejeweled ladies in the audience. Black performers had to withdraw to a shantytown on the wrong side of the tracks at the end of the show.

FACT

Do you think you overpaid for the last concert you attended? For $5.95 (in 1960 dollars), you could have seen the Rat Pack in concert— and that price included dinner! Sinatra and friends were fixtures in the Golden Age of Las Vegas.

One day Sinatra announced that he would not go on unless his chum Sammy could stay at the Sands and play blackjack at the tables and swim in the pool. Sinatra helped pave the way for integration in Las Vegas. The Mafia did not fret much either way. Green was the only color that truly inflamed their larcenous hearts.

One of the best friends the Mafia had in Las Vegas came from an unlikely source. In the ultimate example of "strange bedfellows," many of the workers, pit bosses, and managerial types in the casinos were Mormons. The faithful of the Latter-day Saints do not drink alcohol, coffee, or gamble. But they are not forbidden to work in casinos. They can be surrounded by vice as long as they do not succumb to its seductive allure. And they are also scrupulously honest and hard working. It was a strange alliance that served the Mafia well.

FACT

The Sands Hotel was the nexus of Rat Pack antics. New York mobster Doc Stracher was the front man and Old Blue Eyes owned a percentage. It was purchased by Howard Hughes in 1967.

Sinatra's organized crime connections

Courtesy of AP/Wide World Photos/HO

▲ From left, standing: Gregory DePalma, Frank Sinatra, Thomas Carson, Carlo Gambino, Jimmy "The Weasel" Fratianno, and seated in front, Richard "Nerves" Fusco, pose together in a dressing room at the Westchester Premier Theater in New York, September 26, 1976. The photo was used as evidence in a federal mob trial. (Note that someone unknown has been covered up to protect his identity.)

The Howard Hughes Era

The Mafia's end in Vegas began when the poster boy for eccentric millionaires, Howard Hughes, decided he wanted to make the town his life-size Monopoly board. The old hoods were ready for retirement. They had done more than "wet their beaks." They had gorged themselves on the sumptuous Las Vegas smorgasbord. It was a great run for the underworld.

Hughes was an enigmatic and megalomaniacal mega-millionaire who made his money in the aviation arena and also dabbled as a Hollywood mogul. Like Alexander the Great, he looked for more worlds to conquer, so he headed to Las Vegas. He bought seventeen casinos. The old hoods went back home with their loot and the young ones remained, but their power and influence were diminished. "Respectable" robber baron capitalists proved more than a match for the shady underworld and their shifty shenanigans.

Al Capone missed the boat vis-à-vis Las Vegas. In the 1930s he had interest in a gambling joint in Reno, Nevada, but did not have the foresight to see the potential millions to be made in the still wild and woolly western state.

It did not happen directly through Howard Hughes, however. He lost a bundle, sold out, and left town after a few years. Or rather his handlers did. It is generally accepted that Hughes was rapidly descending into madness during these years, and upon his death several years later his corpse looked more like that of a homeless man than one of the richest men in the world. Emaciated with long hair and nails and covered in sores, he had left his handlers to rule the empire while he died an ignominious death.

The Last Shout

The Mafia reasserted itself in the post-Howard Hughes days, but the 1970s and 1980s saw the mob under attack from both the feds and the Wall Street crowd. FBI probes and indictments sent many a mobster packing, and legitimate businessmen and corporations filled the void. The Tropicana, the Stardust, Desert Inn, Circus-Circus, Caesar's Palace, the Fremont, the Aladdin, the Sands, the Riviera, and the Sundance all fell out of mob hands, and the Dunes and the Marina were demolished in the inexorable juggernaut of respectability.

The Golden Age of Vegas had come to an end. Many mobsters were convicted and went to prison. Chieftains of the Kansas City, Cleveland, Milwaukee, and Chicago mobs felt the long arm of the law unceremoniously shove them into an eight-by-ten cell.

Today, Las Vegas resembles more of a giant theme park for adults than the naughty "Sin City" of its heyday. Millions of people still flock there every year and drop billions of their hard-earned bucks on the gaming tables and in the slot machines. In the sanitized big hotels and their environs you can see pirate ships battling in cement ponds, and re-creations of the Eiffel Tower and the Great Pyramids. Big corporations own the town now, and while it may be more family-oriented, the ineffable quality of charm is long ago and far away.

Just as the remake in 2001 of *Ocean's Eleven*, high-tech caper that it is, lacks the finger-snapping cool, and irreverent hijinks of Frank Sinatra and his Rat Pack, so Las Vegas is a pale shadow of its former self. Say what you want about the Mafia—they knew how to throw a party.

Chapter 10

Crime Kings in Camelot

The Mafia's tentacles extend into every area of the American experience. Hollywood and politics are not immune to the nefarious doings of underworld types. In this chapter we will look at a time when all these elements intersected and possibly helped to elect a president—and perhaps then conspired to assassinate that very same president.

Crooning Kingmakers

The infamous yet beloved Rat Pack did more than make the ladies swoon and crack each other up with less-than-spontaneous ad-libs. Their leader, Frank Sinatra, had aspirations to be a kingmaker. And he just might have succeeded. The Rat Pack reportedly helped John F. Kennedy win the presidency of the United States in 1960.

Frank Sinatra, Dean Martin, and Sammy Davis, Jr. all had obligatory associations with the Mafia. Mob influence permeated just about every nightclub and entertainment venue in the country. Sinatra for one was quite chummy with the mobsters; Dean Martin, who had Americanized his name but still was known as "Dino" to his friends (and some fans), was nonchalant and not particularly respectful toward "the boys."

Peter Lawford, a singularly "unhip" addition to this randy band of aging bad boys, was there in large part because of his direct connection to the Kennedys. He was married to Patricia Kennedy, JFK's sister. Together these men decided they would do what they could to aid the presidential ambitions of Senator John Fitzgerald Kennedy.

The Kennedy Tradition

The Kennedy Dynasty was founded in part on the bootleg whiskey trade during Prohibition. The family patriarch, Joseph Kennedy, was a rumrunner during the Golden Age of the mob. He was an associate of none other than Frank Costello and Meyer Lansky. He was part owner of a racetrack and a heavy gambler. Even after Prohibition his mob ties continued.

FACT

Joseph Kennedy lived to bury three of his sons, plus endure many other family tragedies, including a crippling stroke that left him paralyzed and speechless in his last years.

Like many men with mob ties, he craved respectability. His fortune was made in the underworld of violence and criminality, and he pushed his sons to succeed in the legitimate world. In 1938 he was appointed ambassador to the Court of St. James, a fancy phrase for England, by President Franklin Delano Roosevelt. This was an irony because Kennedy came to America as a poor Irish immigrant, and the relations between the English and the Irish had been, with typical British understatement, strained over the millennia. He had to resign after he advocated the policy of appeasement regarding Nazi Germany. This gave him the reputation as a Nazi sympathizer at a time when Roosevelt was inclined to enter the war as an ally to Great Britain against Hitler.

Sins of the Father

Joseph Kennedy's first-born son, his namesake and the first one on whom he had transferred his dreams, died during World War II. The burden then fell on his second son, John Kennedy. A hero in that same war, he was elected to the House of Representatives and the Senate after that. As a senator, he announced his intentions to seek the presidency in the election of 1960.

His opponent was Richard Nixon, who had served as vice president for eight years under the popular Republican president and war hero Dwight Eisenhower. In addition to his formidable wealth and good looks, Kennedy had an arsenal in the liberal glitterati of Hollywood. And foremost among the constellation of stars was Frank Sinatra and his pals.

Rumble in West Virginia

John Kennedy had one significant obstacle in his quest for the White House—he was a Catholic. There was a strong anti-Catholic sentiment among some, particular in the Bible Belt Protestant South. The ostensible fear was that JFK would be taking his orders from the Pope in Vatican City.

John Kennedy's main opponent in the Democratic primaries was Minnesota Senator Hubert Humphrey. Beating Humphrey in Southern states was key, and the primary in West Virginia (a state that was 95 percent Protestant) was seen as a make-or-break vote for Kennedy. It would take a miracle for the New England Catholic to score a win in this unfriendly land. Divine or diabolical intervention was required. God stayed out of the political fray, so the Mafia reportedly tipped the balance of power.

John Kennedy and Richard Nixon came to Congress together in 1946 and were friends for a time before becoming rivals. Both attained the highest office in the land, and left it in unusual circumstances (assassination and resignation, respectively).

Old Joe Kennedy asked Frank Sinatra to ask his "friends" to use their influence to help JFK win the primary. Sinatra approached his pal, Chicago mob boss Sam Giancana. Giancana exerted pressure on the rank and file of the Teamsters and other unions to vote for Kennedy. This may have made the difference. JFK won the primary, Humphrey bowed out of the race, and JFK was assured the nomination of the Democratic Party.

One Brief Shining Moment

Kennedy beat Nixon in what was the closest election in history until the 2000 Bush versus Gore contest. And he had help with it, too. Mobster Sam Giancana, Mayor Richard Daley, and other crooked politicians in the city of Chicago allegedly stuffed ballot boxes to ensure a Democratic victory. Similar deceit is said to have occurred in Texas. Even with their help, the difference was only about 100,000 votes. JFK became president, and because he was a handsome man with a beautiful wife, his administration was compared to King Arthur's Camelot, which was also a hit Broadway musical at the time. The Camelot mystique was as close to reality as the Lerner and Loewe musical was to real life in the British Isles of circa A.D. 500.

FACT

John Kennedy's decision to make his brother Robert the attorney general of the United States was a very controversial move. The Kennedys were despised by many Washington insiders, and in the eyes of their enemies this was just another example of the unrestrained arrogance of the patrician Kennedy clan.

Kennedy and Sinatra's star power merged politics and entertainment in an elaborate inaugural ball that Sinatra produced. He used his influence to have the cream of the Hollywood crop in attendance. Ironically, Sinatra performed the same function for the 1980 and 1984 inaugural galas of President Ronald Reagan.

JFK made his brother Robert Kennedy the attorney general of the United States. RFK made a crackdown on organized crime the primary focus of his activities. Needless to say, the Mafia was outraged. They had helped these guys get in office, and now they were under attack. Added to the "strange bedfellows" irony was the fact that JFK and Sam Giancana reportedly shared the same girlfriend, party girl Judith Campbell, who had been introduced to them both by none other than Sinatra.

The Big Chill

The Kennedys were not especially grateful to the men behind the scenes who helped them get elected or the entertainers who campaigned tirelessly for JFK. Sammy Davis, Jr. was reportedly asked to postpone his wedding to white actress Mai Britt until after the election and was not invited to the inaugural gala. And Sinatra also got a big kiss-off. JFK had agreed to stay with him at his Palm Springs, California, estate when he traveled to the West Coast. When RFK urged JFK to distance himself from Sinatra, the president decided to stay at Bing Crosby's house instead. Sinatra had been renovating his compound at great expense, including adding quarters for the Secret Service and a helicopter landing pad. With this rejection, Sinatra went ballistic and trashed the place in a rage. Thus ended the friendship between the Chairman of the Board and the Crowned Prince of Camelot.

November 22, 1963

President John F. Kennedy was assassinated while riding in a motorcade in Dallas, Texas. It was a national tragedy that, along with the Vietnam War and the Watergate scandal, ended America's innocence. Politicians and the military-industrial complex were now suspected of creating more harm than good. They were no longer assumed to have the best interests of the citizenry at heart. In the passing decades many people have questioned whether the putative assassin, Lee Harvey Oswald, acted alone, or even fired a shot on that fateful day. Conspiracy theories abound, and the Mafia figures in many of them. The mob certainly had a bone to pick with Kennedy, but could the gang shoot straight? Could this confederation of goombahs orchestrate such a hit? Or was the Mafia one cog in the malevolent machinery of a vast conspiracy? The theories are legion.

Cuba Libre!

The Mafia was entrenched in the island nation of Cuba prior to 1959. The island was ruled by the Batista government, a cruel dictatorship that was very friendly to United States business, both legitimate and illegitimate. Meyer Lansky was the hood who personally dealt with Batista in a mutually beneficial business arrangement. The Mafia flourished under Batista's regime, but the well suddenly went dry.

In 1959 Fidel Castro won a hard-fought revolution and ousted the Batista regime. A former major league baseball player and onetime seeming friend of the United States, Castro became allied with the Soviet Union after his victory, and the island became a communist enclave, only ninety miles from the coast of Florida.

Bay of Pigs

Before Kennedy became president, there were plans to invade Cuba and oust Castro. It would not be an attack by American armed forces; instead the assault would come from exiled Cubans who had planned and trained in the United States with the help of the CIA. Kennedy did not veto the plan when he took office, but when it was launched, he refused, at the last minute, to aid the assault with air cover from the United States Air Force. It was a total disaster, and thousands of exiled Cubans were killed or captured. Those taken alive probably came to wish that they had died on the beach.

Kennedy made many enemies in many circles by his refusal to provide air support in the Bay of Pigs invasion. He earned the hatred of the Cubans who wanted their nation back, those in the CIA who felt betrayed and humiliated, and American big business, which had enjoyed great profits in Cuba. And of course the Mafia, for whom Cuba was once a cash cow and pleasure palace. Rumors have always suggested that there was a strong Mafia-CIA connection where Cuba was concerned. Both organizations had a vested interest in removing Castro. And the rumors have been flying for decades that both groups may have joined forces to take revenge on JFK.

FACT

Frank Sinatra stuck his neck out for the Kennedys and literally put his life on the line. When RFK launched his crusade against organized crime, the mob considered "whacking" the Rat Pack. FBI wiretaps reveal that Sam Giancana vetoed the idea because he liked hearing Sinatra sing "Chicago," a jazzy anthem to his kind of town.

The Usual Suspects

Attorney General Robert Kennedy launched an aggressive prosecutorial campaign against the Mafia. Given all that they had done to help JFK get elected, they were indignant. In the Mafia code, when someone does you a favor you are indebted to them. Favors are expected to be appreciated and returned when the marker is called (a gambling expression meaning the repayment of a debt). The Kennedy brothers had showed no honor in the eyes of the mob. And these are a bunch of fellows whose bad side you most definitely do not want to be on.

The Mafia should have had some clues this was coming. Robert Kennedy aggressively took on Teamster boss Jimmy Hoffa during the 1950s congressional hearings on racketeering. JFK was also on the committee, called the McClellan Committee. The Mafia should have surmised that the Kennedys would not change their tune when one brother became president and appointed the other the "top cop" of the land.

President
Kennedy
signs gam-
bling bill

Courtesy of AP/Wide World Photos/Bill Achatz

◀ President Kennedy, September 13, 1961, as he signs three bills creating tough new laws to help combat gambling and racketeering. In the background from left: Senator Kenneth Keating, R-NY; FBI Director J. Edgar Hoover; Attorney General Robert Kennedy; Justice Department officials Harold Koffshy and Edward Joyce; Chief Counsel Jerome Alderman of the Senate Investigations Subcommittee; and Herbert Miller of the Justice Department.

Oswald and Ruby

Mere hours after JFK's murder, lone oddball Lee Harvey Oswald was picked up for the murder. With forty years of hindsight, many people feel it was all too convenient, a neat and tidy solution to the murder. Making things especially tidy was Oswald's murder in the Dallas Police headquarters by a local strip club owner and small time hoodlum, Jack Ruby.

Lee Harvey Oswald was no doubt a strange loner. At age seventeen he enlisted in the Marines, worked in top-secret facilities, learned the Russian language, and ultimately renounced his American citizenship and defected to the Soviet Union. The circumstances of his defection and his return are curious and full of the stuff that makes a conspiracy seem possible.

Ruby burst out of the crowd and shot Oswald, thus ending the possibility of a trial in which potentially explosive information might have come to light. Ruby claimed his reason was the desire to spare first widow

Jackie Kennedy the pain and suffering of a protracted trial, where she would have to relive the horrific event over and over. There appears to have been more to the story, however.

FACT

Dean Martin was not starstruck by the Kennedys and the Mafia like his pal Frank. He was a laid-back guy who did not take himself or those around him too seriously. In his way he was a martini-sipping Zen master.

As a nightclub owner, Ruby naturally had connections with the Mafia. He was also involved with an organization called the Fair Play for Cuba Committee. This group supported anti-Castro Cubans in exile in their efforts to reclaim their island nation. This Mafia-Cuban connection plus his seemingly easy access to Oswald feeds the conspiratorial fires.

Jack Ruby, born Rubenstein, was a long-time, low-level mob figure. Born in Chicago, he ended up moving to Dallas to help his sister run a nightclub. He also spent time in New Orleans and made trips to Cuba on mob business in the pre-Castro era. His strip club made him a popular, if sleazy bon vivant in town, and a shady pal of the corrupt element within the Dallas Police Department.

It was those connections that probably allowed him access to the police station that Sunday morning to plug Oswald in plain view of dozens of law enforcement officials and on national television. Ruby died of cancer in prison in 1967. He took his secrets with him.

Carlos Marcello and Oswald

Lee Harvey Oswald was born in New Orleans, and his uncle was a member of the local Mafia. The mob boss of the New Orleans family was Carlos Marcello. The Oswald-Marcello connection fuels speculation that the mob was using him as a patsy, the fall guy for their mob hit. But Oswald's military background, his defection, and welcome return to the United States (he should have been arrested for treason upon his return), also suggest links to the clandestine world of spies and counterspies.

Marcello is quoted by Mafia informants as saying, "You cut off the head, the tail dies." This has been interpreted as his intention to kill the president to get at his brother. He is also alleged to have said, "Get a nut to do the job." This is an obvious reference to the troubled young Lee Harvey Oswald.

Trafficante Violation

In 1978 there was a Congressional Committee investigating assassinations. The ultimate finding of the committee is that there was a "probable conspiracy" in the death of JFK. The "lone gunman" theory has been disavowed by the government, though members of the committee maintained that Oswald was indeed the triggerman. Among the voluminous testimony given to the Warren Commission (the Congressional investigation that produced thousands of pages and is today regarded as generally unsatisfactory), much involved the Mafia. Santo Trafficante, a mobster active in the Cuban casinos, told a Cuban associate that he need not worry about Kennedy's re-election in 1964. The veiled threat is obvious.

The House Assassination Committee took great pains to pin the conspiracy on the Mafia. Oswald's mob connection and his assassination by a known mobster closed the case. There was a conspiracy, they admitted, but it was the Mafia and nothing but the Mafia.

Will We Ever Know?

As Joe Pesci, playing the frenetic David Ferrie in the movie *JFK* says, "It's a mystery wrapped in a riddle inside an enigma." Perhaps the mob was behind the assassination. Perhaps it played a small role in a larger scheme. Or maybe the Mafia is ironically being used as a patsy by a deeper, darker more insidious conspiracy. The Mafia, as powerful as it is, was possibly used as the fall guy by a force that makes them seem like penny-ante grifters. Perhaps our descendents will one day know the whole truth, when classified government documents are opened to the public, a process that has been happening gradually, although the last of the documents still won't be available for two decades.

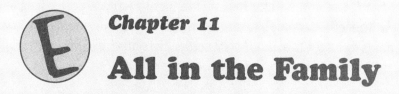

Chapter 11

All in the Family

The organized crime outfits that have become known as the "five families" of New York have had their share of family ties, family feuds, and very violent family affairs. In this chapter we look at the history and the cast of characters of these dysfunctional families.

The Bonannos

Joseph Bonanno, also known as Joe Bananas, died in 2002 at the ripe old age of 97 in the dry sunny climes of Arizona. He was the first Mafia don to violate the sacred code of Omerta. The way he did it was a little different than the low-level "rats" who sang for the feds. He was not only the first Mafia don to break the oath; he was the first to write a best-selling tell-all memoir. In fact his memoirs were used against him in a court of law. Sometimes "wiseguys" are not very smart. Ego has been the downfall of more than one Mafia don.

FACT

For most of his professional career, Joe Bonanno kept so low a profile that he might not have been recognized in a line-up. He was the antithesis of the flamboyant Mafiosi. That changed when he was forced into retirement. He became quite chatty in his old age.

Bonanno ascended to power when Salvatore Maranzano, one of the Mustache Petes, was killed in 1931. It was the culmination of years of the Castellemmarese War that rid the streets of the Mustache Petes and established a New Underworld Order. The twenty-six-year-old Bonanno, hand-picked by Lucky Luciano himself, was the youngest man ever to become head of a family.

Leading the Family

It was a small family, but Bonanno ran a tight ship. His was a presence that commanded respect. He was a natural leader of men, one of many Mafiosi who could probably have done much good in the world with their people skills had they been inclined toward the straight and narrow.

Bonanno made alliances with more powerful dons. He made his family's fortune through gambling, loan sharking, and eventually, as all Mafia families did, drugs. Uneasy is the head that wears the crown, as the fella said, and in the 1960s the aging Bonanno believed that there was a conspiracy among the other crime family leaders to kill him. He believed that among the conspirators was his own cousin. Bonanno planned to hit all of his enemies in one fell swoop and become the Boss of Bosses. This action probably inspired *Godfather* author Mario Puzo when he had Michael Corleone kill the dons of the five families in one afternoon.

ALERT!

For an inside history of the Bonanno family, check out Gay Talese's book *Honor Thy Father*. It is written in cooperation with the Bonannos themselves, so the other four family members might disagree with the spin within this book.

The fictional Michael Corleone was somewhat more successful. In Bonanno's version, one of the hit men assigned to the task, Joe Colombo, switched allegiances and spilled the beans to the opposition. The Commission summoned Bonanno to appear, but he refused and went into hiding.

Though the crime families are usually called by the name of the founder or the current don, they are not like royal families, where the heir assumes the throne. It has only happened occasionally. Joe Bonanno wanted his son to succeed him, and most within the family were not too impressed with this princeling. The Commission countermanded Bonanno's wishes and appointed a hood named Gaspar DiGregorio as new head of the family. Bonanno was kidnapped, and he vanished. It is believed to have been a staged kidnapping. He was poised to appear before a grand jury, so it is possible that it may have been a set-up to avoid the heat.

Going Bananas

Joe Bonanno emerged from his mysterious disappearance after nineteen months. He declined to say where he had been. Some believe he had been a prisoner of the Commission. It is thought likely that he was set free on the condition he would leave the crime scene quietly and permanently. He did no such thing. The Banana War, as the local news media liked to call it, was on. The Commission had replaced Gaspar DiGregorio with a hood named Paul Sciacca after DiGregorio botched a hit on young Bill Bonanno and his boys. Sciacca's team was no match for the Bonannos. Nevertheless the war went on for years during the 1960s. It was an extended trip "to the mattresses," as the Mafia calls a protracted gangland war. Bonanno, getting on in years, suffered a heart attack and headed for Arizona and retirement. The Banana War ground to a halt, and Sciacca took control of Bonanno's Brooklyn rackets.

Final resting place of Joseph Bonanno

Courtesy of AP/Wide World Photos/Jay Hayt, Pool

▲ A cemetery worker pushes the casket of the late Joseph Bonanno into the family crypt on May 20, 2002, at the Holy Hope Cemetery in Tucson, Arizona. Bonanno, the notorious gangster known as "Joe Bananas," ran one of the most powerful Mafia groups in the 1950s and 60s. He was remembered as a man of honor by his family.

The barbaric and extremely violent Carmine Galante took the reins of the Bonanno family. Galante was tough and fearless and more than a little sadistic. He was universally unpopular with the mobsters from all five families. The Commission had wanted Bonanno out of power so they could better control the unruly family, and in Carmine Galante they had a far worse and more reckless and violent loose cannon. The hit on Galante was a unanimous decision from all the members of the Commission both in New York and across the country. Galante was whacked to the relief of all in 1979. The psycho hood known as "The Cigar" lived and died with a stogie in his mug. When he was whacked in Joe and Mary's Italian Restaurant in Brooklyn, his cigar never even fell out of his mouth.

ALERT!

Under the don-ship of Rusty Rastelli, the events that formed the basis for the Mafia movie *Donnie Brasco* occurred. FBI agent Joseph D. Pistone infiltrated the family, lived the lifestyle, became friends with Dominick "Sonny Black" Napolitano and Benjamin "Lefty Guns" Ruggiero, and then betrayed them, sending several family members to jail and prompting the "disappearance" of Napolitano in the 1970s.

Galante was replaced by Rusty Rastelli, who returned to the role after an absence of many years. He brought the family into the video pornography business and an expanded role in drug trafficking. The long-gone Mustache Petes were probably turning in their graves.

These activities got the don into trouble. Rastelli went to prison, where he died in 1991. He was replaced by Joseph Massino. According to the feds and those in the know, as of 1998 the Bonanno crime family remains very powerful in an era when most Mafia families are in serious decline.

Meet the Colombos

Like Joe Bonanno, Joe Profaci took over a crime family when the Castellemmarese War ended. The crime family bore his name during his lifetime. He had a reputation as a cheapskate Mafioso. He charged members of his family the equivalent of union dues. Each soldier and capo (literally "captain" in Italian, meaning a Mafioso who supervises the soldiers) had to fork over $25 a month for the privilege of being in the family. And he always made sure he "wet his beak." He was also not thought highly of by his fellow dons, yet he remained in the job until his death from natural causes.

He was so unpopular that there was a mutiny in his ranks. Three brothers—Joey, Larry, and Albert Gallo—and others were dissatisfied with Profaci's reign and were making plans to oust him. This came to be known as the "Gallo Wars." Profaci used the old "divide and conquer" technique employed by the ancient Romans (with whom the Mafiosi liked to compare themselves). He pitted one against the other and thus thwarted a hostile takeover of the family.

New York's five families were forever fighting each other, but the Colombo family earns the distinction of fighting within its own ranks. No less than three uncivil "civil wars" were fought in its bloody history.

The Don Is Dead

Joe Profaci died in 1962 and was replaced by his underboss, Joe Magliocco. He faced a potential gang war with the Gambino and Lucchese families. They were muscling in on the Colombo family's interests. At the time, Joe Bonanno stood with the Colombos, and the boss of the Genovese family was doing time and had his own problems.

This was when Bonanno orchestrated the hits of Gambino and Lucchese. Magliocco backed him up. This caused the Banana War. We learned earlier what befell Bonanno. When hit man Joe Colombo betrayed the men who hired him by telling the intended targets, Magliocco threw himself on the mercy of the Commission. His life was spared, but he died of natural causes a few months later.

Ethnic Pride

Joe Colombo was rewarded by Carlo Gambino for the warning about Bonanno's planned hit, and was made the don of the family that henceforth bore his name. He was one of those gangsters who liked the limelight. Bonanno, Profaci, and others kept a very low profile. Men like John Gotti and others get swept up in their own celebrity and bring about their own downfalls. Colombo was such a man.

Joseph Anthony Colombo Sr.

Courtesy of AP/Wide World Photos

▲ Organized crime boss Joseph Anthony Colombo Sr. is shown in 1971.

Joe Colombo thought it would be a good idea to exploit the ethnic pride of Italian-Americans by staging a series of public rallies that would equate anti-Mafia sentiment with anti-Italian racism. He accused the feds of being anti-Italian in their prosecution of the Mafia. The first rallies got a lot of media attention, something a level-headed Mafioso does not want. Carlo Gambino was fed up with the man he recommended as don. Gambino told Colombo to stop—or else—and Colombo refused.

In 1971, Joe Colombo received a shot in the head at one of his rallies. The perpetrator was an African-American who was killed at the scene by a police officer. He was not a "lone gunman," as was believed at the time. He was working for Gambino, and did not expect to be the "patsy" and fall guy. Colombo did not die immediately, however. He lingered in a vegetative coma for seven years before finally dying.

Ciao DiBella

Thomas DiBella took over as don of the Colombo family after Joe Colombo's shooting. He was an old timer who had served in the lower levels of the Mafia since its glory days. He did not stay in power long. He transferred power to Carmine Persico. Persico went to prison, and DiBella acted as boss, with Persico pulling the strings from jail. Yet the Mafia goes on and on. These days the Colombo family is reportedly still in operation, but on a smaller scale. It is one of the two smallest Mafia families. They are small but ornery, and they allegedly still have interests in the usual rackets, including pornography, counterfeiting, and other unsavory enterprises.

FACT

Colombo family member "Crazy Joe" Gallo had many celebrity friends. He was married in the home of actor Jerry Orbach and was murdered in a restaurant after seeing pal Don Rickles perform at the Copacabana. At least he had a few laughs during his last night on earth.

The Genovese Family

The celebrated and infamous Lucky Luciano was the first head of this crime family. It did not get its better-known name of Genovese until many years later. When Luciano was sent to prison in 1936, his henchman Frank Costello took over.

Costello was a different breed of don. He was not a micromanager, nor was he into the sensational aspects of being a gangster. He was more like quiet Meyer Lansky, who pulled strings and made bundles of money and stayed out of the headlines. Costello was a "big picture" guy who looked beyond New York City to expand his family's interests as far west as Las Vegas and as far south as Cuba. Costello was affectionately called "the Prime Minister" because of his diplomatic skills, and his ability to delegate leadership made his family a lot of money.

Vito and Costello

Vito Genovese had served as Luciano's underboss, and by all rights he should have succeeded Mr. Lucky as boss. Genovese, however, left the country to avoid a murder charge and was languishing in Italy. After World War II, Genovese came back to America, where he was expected to stand trial for the murder. As often happens in Mafia murder trials, key witnesses were themselves mysteriously murdered. As a result, Genovese remained a free man.

Vito Genovese and Frank Costello vied for control of the crime family for many years. Genovese chipped away at Costello's power with a series of small but significant moves. A series of hits eliminated many of the top guns in Costello's corner. Costello countered by talking the hot-headed Albert Anastasia of Murder Incorporated into killing his bosses, the Mangano brothers. This kept the balance of power in Costello's favor for a few more years.

Frank Costello preferred negotiation to assassination and was a shrewd and skilled leader of men. And lucky, too. He survived a shot to the head, which only grazed him, by a hit man who could not shoot straight; Costello lived to tell the tale.

In 1957 Genovese orchestrated the barbershop murder of Albert Anastasia and staged an unsuccessful hit on Costello. Costello was shot and wounded in the lobby of his luxury apartment building on Manhattan's Central Park West. The hit man who missed was allegedly Vincent "the Chin" Gigante, who went on to be one of the Mafia's most colorful characters.

In the Anastasia hit, Genovese was helped by an Anastasia associate, Carlo Gambino, who then assumed control of Anastasia's outfit, now called the Gambino family. He quickly switched sides and joined an alliance with Costello and Meyer Lansky to take out the ambitious Genovese.

Frank Costello wanted to get out while the getting was good and enjoy his retirement. Rather than eliminate Vito Genovese through a violent coup, the Commission agreed to let Costello leave the underworld quietly and peacefully and in turn put Genovese in charge of the Luciano crime family. They were still conspiring against him, however. The other Mafia bosses set Genovese up in a bogus drug rap. He was sent up the river and never came back. He died in prison in 1969.

Eboli Virus

Genovese continued to control his empire from his jail cell. Mafiosi have often had special privileges while in prison. Gourmet meals, greater creature comforts, and even "dates" with women were arranged for the rich and powerful crime kingpins while behind bars. Genovese was monitoring gangland operations and even ordering hits. Nevertheless, he could not be a completely hands-on don from the little cell he shared with informant-to-be Joe Valachi. The men on the outside whom Genovese relied on were not the brightest bulbs lighting the underworld, and they could not compete with the machinations of the savvy Carlo Gambino.

FACT

Mob boss Frank Costello, when asked by a member of the Kefauver Committee investigating organized crime what he had done to serve his country, replied, "Paid my taxes."

Gambino was slowly taking over the Genovese family's rackets. Genovese's power was further diminished by the defection and damning congressional testimony of Joe Valachi, which is covered in detail in Chapter 15. The wily Gambino was becoming the new "Boss of Bosses," the most powerful don in the Mafia.

As mentioned, Vito Genovese died in prison in 1969, and his man on the outside, Tommy Eboli, was an incompetent don who ran things into the ground. He was not respected by his own men or the Mafia community at large. And if you're not a man of respect in the Mafia, your lifespan is often a short one. Gambino had Eboli killed in 1972 and appointed a hood named Frank "Funzi" Tieri to fill the slot. Though not a known name like a Gotti or a Capone, "Funzi" was an effective don who brought the Genovese family back to prominence while never forgetting that it was Gambino who put him there, and thus showed Gambino the proper deference.

When Tieri died in 1981, it is believed that "Fat Tony" Salerno took over, though other sources maintain that it was "Cockeyed Phil" Lombardo. The Genovese crime family became the second most powerful of the five families, second only to the Gambinos.

Taking It on the Chin

When Salerno was sent away for 100 years, the colorful and eccentric Vincent "the Chin" Gigante took over. The Chin had a unique way to keep the law off his case. And it almost worked. Gigante was often seen wandering around his Greenwich Village neighborhood in a bathrobe and talking to himself. This behavior caused wags to give him the moniker "The Oddfather." It was generally accepted that he was faking it in an effort to avoid prosecution for his many crimes via an insanity plea. The feds were not fooled. Secret wiretapped conversations revealed a sane and lucid criminal mind at work. In 1996 he was charged with murder and racketeering and was sentenced to twelve years in prison. Of course he has been obliged to delegate responsibilities to Dominick "Quiet Dom" Cirillo, but he is rumored to still be calling the shots from a jail cell in Texas.

Vincente
Gigante

Courtesy of AP/Wide World Photos

◄ Vincente L. Gigante, 29, looks out from behind bars at police headquarters in New York City on August 20, 1957. He was waiting to be arraigned on a charge of attempted murder in the shooting of Frank Costello. Standing behind Gigante is detective Nathan Ury.

The Gambino Crime Family

The Gambino family became the most influential and successful family in America under the leadership of Carlo Gambino and later the "Dapper Don," John Gotti. From 1957 until his death in 1976, Gambino made the family more powerful than the formidable empires of Lucky Luciano and Al Capone. It also suffered its greatest setbacks under the egotistical Gotti's flamboyant stewardship. (The rise and fall of John Gotti will be covered in detail in the next chapter.)

The Beginnings

The earliest incarnation of what was to become the Gambino family began in New York in the 1920s. These were the days when the Mustache Pete Joe Masseria was the Boss of Bosses of the Mafia. Alfred Mineo and Steve Ferrigno were bosses of the Brooklyn crime outfit until they were murdered in 1930 by, among others, Joe Profaci and Joe Valachi. The new bosses were the Mangano brothers, Vince and Phil. They ruled the roost until they were killed by their ambitious and psychotic henchman Albert Anastasia, who remained boss until his famous barbershop murder in 1957.

Under Anastasia's watch, which in turn was under the watchful eye of Frank Costello, the crime family grew in power and stature. But Anastasia was not nicknamed the "Mad Hatter" for nothing. The very skills that made him ideal in the role of "Lord High Executioner" of Murder Incorporated were a liability in the role of don. Being a don required more subtlety and diplomacy, things Anastasia did not have in abundance. He was a loose cannon who brought unwanted publicity to the Mafia.

Anastasia's henchman Carlo Gambino was a collaborator in Anastasia's murder, and Gambino assumed control of the family as a reward for a whack well done. And the crime outfit now took his name.

Changing Leadership

With Vito Genovese in jail and Frank Costello in retirement, Carlo Gambino became an intimate of the legendary Meyer Lansky and soon was the unofficial Boss of Bosses. It was unofficial because the structure of the Commission was just that, a committee with no top dog. This was designed to prevent conflicts and clashes of egos, which of course happened all the time despite the best efforts of the Commission.

Carlo Gambino

◀ Carlo Gambino, Cosa Nostra organized crime leader, is shown circa the 1930s.

Courtesy of AP/Wide World Photos

    Carlo Gambino became ill in the 1970s, and his underlings were jockeying for position as his heir apparent. Gambino did not choose his underboss Aniello Dellacroce, who would have been next in the chain of command. He chose his brother-in-law Paul Castellano. He gave Dellacroce the consolation prize of control of the family's Manhattan rackets. Carlo Gambino died in 1976.

    The Castellano-Dellacroce leadership was uninspired, and the Young Turk John Gotti was plotting and planning as he waited in the wings. Dellacroce was respected by the young soldiers and capos; Castellano was not. When they learned that Dellacroce was dying of cancer, they waited. Castellano was murdered two weeks after Dellacroce succumbed to cancer, and John Gotti became the new don.

The Lucchese Family

The Lucchese family is the smallest of the big five crime families. It does not have the name recognition factor that the Bonannos or Gambinos have. It has always had smaller membership and kept a low profile compared to the other families. It does, however, have the distinction of being the family whose activities are the source for one of the best Mafia movies, *Goodfellas*.

FACT

Lucchese family member Jimmy "the Gent" Burke got his nickname because, during his career as a hijacker, he regularly gave the drivers of the trucks he hijacked a $50 bill for their inconvenience.

The first don of the Lucchese family was Gaetano Reina. He controlled bootlegging in the Bronx under Joe Masseria. He switched sides and supported Masseria's rival Maranzano. When Masseria learned of his treachery, he was rewarded with a shotgun blast to the head administered by future crime family boss Vito Genovese. He was followed by a Mafioso with the same first name, Gaetano Gagliano. In a curious coincidence, the next don, who gave the family its name, was Gaetano Lucchese. But he Americanized his first name to "Thomas." Tommy Lucchese's area of expertise was corruption in the garment industry. The family was also heavily into loan sharking, hijacking, and drugs. The drug trade was done on the sly. This was the era when the Mafia was becoming increasingly involved in narcotics trafficking despite its outspoken "just say no" stance. The underlings dealt drugs but coyly declined to tell their bosses where the money came from when they handed over the bosses' take of the profits. The old Mafiosi turned a blind eye to the drug dealing because it was making them a lot of money.

Real Goodfellas

Paul Vario was a capo in the Lucchese family. In his circle was Jimmy "the Gent" Burke. Henry Hill was a punk kid who became enthralled by the neighborhood Mafiosi and fell under the influence of these older wiseguys who schooled him in the ways of gangsterism. Henry Hill's turn-coat testimony eventually sent both his mentors to prison, where they died.

Decline and Fall

Tommy Lucchese died in 1967. He was followed by Carmine Tramunti, who served as don until he was jailed for life. His replacement was a man with the nickname "Tony Ducks." Anthony Corallo was called that because of the many times he successfully beat the rap and ducked prison. He oversaw the Lucchese family's continued involvement in corrupt labor unions, the private garbage removal business, and construction projects.

Though a small family and not as well known as the others, its members and their hijinks inspired a Mafia classic, Martin Scorsese's *Goodfellas*. The Lucchese crime family also had more informants, snitches, and stoolies per capita than any other Mafia family.

Nothing lasts forever, however. In 1986, after twelve years as don, his ducking skills failed him, and he was finally imprisoned. He was sentenced to 100 years, and died in prison in 2000. His successor, Vittorio Amuso, was not amused when he himself was sentenced to life imprisonment in 1992.

A Rat Problem

Henry Hill is the most famous rat in the Lucchese family, but this family has had more of a vermin infestation than any other. Hill squealed in 1980 and went into the Witness Protection Program. "Little Al" D'Arco sang for the feds during the Amuso years. So did two badfellas named Anthony "Gaspipe" Casso and "Fat Pete" Chiodo. The family is barely a blip on the Mafia radar these days. Its glorious golden age is long past, and it has degenerated into, quite literally, a bloody mess.

The Apalachin Meeting

One of the most famous, infamous, and embarrassing moments in Mafia legend, involving all five major families and most of the smaller families, was the conference held in Apalachin, New York, in 1957. They revealed themselves as the gangs that couldn't think straight in this fiasco that put the Mafia squarely in the national spotlight, a place that most Mafiosi were prudent to avoid.

The Commission met regularly every five years. Needless to say they kept the locations private. Only the invitees and their close confidantes knew the locale. They would discuss business, amend grudges, settle debts, and make peace if necessary. In 1957 the meeting was held at the upstate New York estate of Pennsylvania mobster Joseph Barbara.

Law enforcement officials had been trying for years to identify the heads of the big Mafia families. They wanted to get a handle on the secret society's power structure and chain of command. The Mafia obliged them by gathering every major don under one roof. There is no existing agenda or itinerary of what was to be discussed at the meeting. Maybe it was the controversial drug-dealing dilemma. Perhaps the recent murder of Albert Anastasia and bungled hit on Frank Costello. None of the gentlemen in attendance deigned to discuss the affair. They probably did not have a chance to discuss much, since it ended rather abruptly.

Color Me Barbara

Joe Barbara did not know that he was under surveillance and had been for some time. He had received visits in the past from Joe Bonanno and others who the cops suspected were criminals. He also booked most of the hotel rooms in the small town of Apalachin. This raised a red flag for the state police.

Dons and assorted bodyguards and wiseguys descended upon the sleepy little community. Goombahs in pinstriped suits flooding the area must have looked a little conspicuous in a land of cows and cornfields. The local police sensed something was afoot, and they alerted higher authorities. On November 14, 1957, four law enforcement officers pulled up to the house in two cars. The dons assumed it was a raid and scampered into the woods in a less-than-dignified fashion. The wiseguys flew out of every available egress. Some ran off into the woods. Those who escaped by car were nabbed at roadblocks and were overnight guests of the New York State Police. All of them maintained that they were paying a call on their sick friend Joe Barbara. Barbara himself told the law that it was a convention of salesmen from the Canada Dry soft drink company.

FACT

Thirteen days after the raid at the conference, the FBI announced its new Top Hoodlum Program, officially beginning their crackdown on the Mafia.

The names of those detained is a *Who's Who* of hoodlums: Carlo Gambino, Paul Castellano, Tommy Lucchese, Joe Profaci, Joe Colombo, Vito Genovese, Frank Costello, Tony Accardo, Santo Trafficante, Carlos Marcello, and Sam Giancana.

Believe it or not, none of the approximately sixty dons were arrested, only detained for questioning. So little was known about the shadowy Mafia in 1957 that the cops had no idea that they had in one fell swoop nabbed the most vicious and successful criminal kingpins in the country. The shadow life of the Mafia was over.

Apalachin Agenda

Several sources offer different reasons for why the meeting was called in the first place. Joe Valachi said it was a coming-out party for the new dons, including Carlo Gambino. They were also there to grant clemency to Vito Genovese for his role in the Anastasia murder. The Mad Hatter was so despised and feared that no one was particularly sorry to see him go.

The brother of the late and not especially lamented Anastasia, who went by the name Anastasio, said that the objective of the meeting was to decide which misbehaving mobsters and which intrusive federal agents were to be whacked. Still another theory is that the whole thing was designed to set up and embarrass Vito Genovese, and the police were made aware of the meeting. Genovese was sent to prison on drug charges less than a year later.

Apalachin Aftermath

The Mafia was no longer a badly kept secret or a word that was only uttered in a hushed fearful whisper. Dons were on the covers of *Life* and *Look* magazines. The media was abuzz with all things Mafia, and even J. Edgar Hoover had to admit that it existed.

The FBI under the directorship of Hoover did very little to combat organized crime. Hoover steadfastly denied that there was a structured society of criminals who acted in unison to further their villainous goals. Hoover knew many reputed gangsters and was a big time horse player. He was either in denial or in collusion with the Mafia.

Hoover and his beloved bureau took a lot of heat in the court of public opinion and from the politicians in Washington, D.C. They wanted to know "what he knew and when he knew it," as they say in Washington. And if Hoover did not know anything about the Mafia, Congress wanted to know why. Hoover engaged in some aggressive damage control with a program he called the "Top Hoodlum Program."

The Top Hoodlum Program included wiretapping that was not the slightest bit legal, but that garnered reels and reels of Mafia chatter. These tapes were inadmissible in a court of law but provided valuable information and insight into the underworld.

After the Apalachin blunder, the Mafia entered American popular culture as a subject of fascination, outrage, and revulsion. Never again would the activities of these ruthless and brutal men remain completely in the shadows. They were now as famous as they were infamous, and their world was no longer an inner sanctum of clandestine criminality. The law turned up the heat, and the public loved to read about their exploits and see movies about them. Mafiosi would do the unthinkable and break their sacred vow of Omerta. Even some Mafiosi themselves would be swept away in their celebrity status. A prime example of this is our next subject, the infamous "Dapper Don," John Gotti. He was ultimately his own worst enemy and did more damage to himself and the Mafia than any informant or crusading crime fighter. Ⓔ

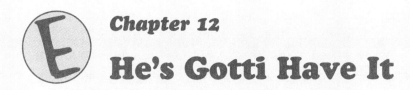

Chapter 12

He's Gotti Have It

The last of the flashy and flamboyant Mafia dons was John Gotti. In the 1980s and 1990s, he became the boss of the Gambino crime family. He was the first hoodlum since Al Capone to become a media darling. Like Capone, he contributed undeserved positive publicity and bogus charm to a nasty and brutish lifestyle.

Coming Up in the World

The glory days of the Mafia were long gone by the 1980s. Capone was ancient history. So were Lucky Luciano, Meyer Lansky, Bugsy Siegel, and the pantheon of hoodlums from the "good old days" of organized crime. The men who came up behind them were empty pinstripe suits by comparison. When Gotti came to power, all that changed. He was the last hurrah for the celebrity hoodlum.

Gotti was born in the Bronx in 1940. He came from a poor family. His family moved to Brooklyn, and the angry young kid found himself in the land of the wiseguys. They became his heroes. Like Al Capone a few decades earlier, he began his life in crime running errands for the local mobsters.

He became the member of a criminal street gang. Gotti was no "Fonzie," however. The gang was involved in car theft, robbery, and other criminal activity. He was arrested five times while still a teenager, but avoided any jail time, a bit of luck that would follow him through most of his career. His luck did run out eventually.

Married to the Mob

John Gotti married in 1962. His marriage was volatile, full of separations both by mutual consent and imposed by trips "up the river." After a brief flirtation with the legitimate world he quickly returned to a life of crime. The couple had five children. One would follow in his father's footsteps (less successfully), one would die tragically young, and another would write potboiler romance yarns, becoming the Jackie Collins of Mafia princesses.

It is not always easy when you are "married to the mob." The Gotti marriage was a tumultuous one. The hundreds of hours of FBI wiretaps reveal John Gotti complaining, "That woman is driving me crazy," referring to his wife.

The Ozone Layer

Gotti hooked up with the Gambino crime family when he joined a group of low-level hoods that reported to Aniello Dellacroce, who hung out at the Bergin Hunt and Fish Club, a storefront in a neighborhood in Queens, New York, called Ozone Park. Gotti's beat was nearby John F. Kennedy International Airport. The pack of thieves hijacked stuff that landed at the airport and had yet to make it to its final destination. If you have ever been told that the electronics or cigarettes you purchased "fell off the back of a truck," this means it was intercepted before it reached the merchant who bought and paid for it and was sold by the Mafia at a discount to the consumer and a big profit to the mob. Gotti and his crew would steal anything, and one of their favorite things to steal was women's designer clothing. In 1968 Gotti was nabbed in the back of one of his heist trucks by the FBI and went to jail for three years.

ALERT!

Got any John Gotti memorabilia? It might be worth more than you think. A ghoul who attended Gotti's wake and grabbed a memorial card from the funeral home sold it on eBay for over $300.

Gambino underboss Dellacroce took a liking to Gotti and promoted him to capo. When Dellacroce went to prison, Gotti had a direct pipeline to the Mr. Big of the outfit, Carlo Gambino. Gambino fancied himself a philosophical hood and introduced Gotti to Niccolo Machiavelli's book *The Prince*, a Renaissance masterpiece of amoral scheming. Who says leg breakers can't appreciate the classics?

Irish Need Not Apply

Kidnapping was a common means of intimidation among Mafia families in the 1970s. Members of one family would snatch someone from a rival family and demand ransom in the form of loot or other conditions. Often the kidnapped hood was released intact, on other occasions he was sent home on an installment plan, one piece at a time. Carlo Gambino's nephew was kidnapped and killed, and the old don wanted to put an end to the practice. An Irish gangster with the pugnacious sounding name of Jimmy McBratney was believed to be the killer. Gotti curried favor with his boss Gambino by sending the errant Irishman to meet St. Patrick. It turned out that McBratney was less of a brat than that. He was not the killer. Gotti got the wrong guy and did two more years in the slammer, but he got in good with his boss. That is an example of upward mobility, Mafia-style.

Room at the Top

Carlo Gambino died in 1976, surprisingly of natural causes. He had named Paul Castellano to succeed him. Gotti's first mentor Aniello Dellacroce's feelings were hurt. And when a sensitive mobster's feathers are ruffled, the fur usually flies.

Paul Castellano

Courtesy of AP/Wide World Photos/Mario Suriani

◀ Paul Castellano, 69, know as "Big Paulie," arrives at federal court n Manhattan for his arraignment on February 28, 1985. Castellano was the reputed head of the Gambino crime family and was described by law enforcement officials as the most powerful man in organized crime.

Gotti had been consolidating his power base and rising within the ranks. The McBratney murder had granted him the exalted position of "made" man. The heists crew that operated out of the Bergin Hunt and Fish Club were his guys now, loyal to the up-and-coming capo. The boss, Paul Castellano, did not have as high an opinion of Gotti. That in itself thwarted Gotti's ambitions. Gotti in turn did not like or respect Castellano.

A week before John Gotti's death, his brother, Peter, acting head of the Gambino crime family, and several others were indicted on sixty-eight counts of racketeering, including another brother and a nephew, both named Richard.

Much of Gotti's success occurred because he violated an old Mafia rule: no involvement in drugs. For many years it had been respected, but over the years the Mafia's insistence on this edict began to crumble. There was a lot of money to be made in the drug trade. Other criminal organizations were deeply involved in drug trafficking, and the Mafia was notorious for wanting a cut of someone else's profits.

The rules were bending in that it eventually came down from on high that anyone caught dealing in drugs would be killed, emphasis on the "if they were caught" loophole. Eventually the old dons turned a blind eye to drug dealing when they saw the vast wealth that filled the family coffers.

Bye Bye Paulie

Paul Castellano, also known as Big Paulie, was in hot water. In the early 1980s the government was aggressively going after the heads of the five New York families. They were being prosecuted under charges that came to be called RICO (Racketeer Influenced and Corrupt Organizations). Castellano learned that he was going to be indicted in at least two RICO cases. Gotti seized upon the old don's vulnerability and began planning his demise.

Big Paulie got a big surprise as he got out of his car to walk the few paces into Sparks Steak House in Manhattan. It was December 1985, and Christmas shoppers crowded the busy city sidewalks, dressed in holiday style. Four gunmen administered six bullets to Castellano's head just to be on the safe side. John Gotti cruised by in a passing car and surveyed the carnage. Another Mafia transfer of power had been successfully staged. Gotti was the Big Boy now.

Paul Castellano is assassinated

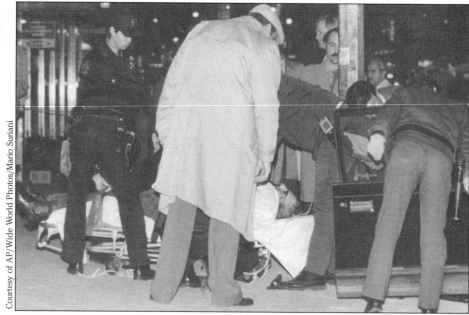

Courtesy of AP/Wide World Photos/Mario Suriani

▲ The body of mafia crime boss Paul Castellano lies on a stretcher outside the Sparks Steak House in New York after he and his bodyguards were gunned down December 16, 1985. Mobster John Gotti claimed the top spot in the Gambino family following the gangland shooting.

The New York media covered John Gotti's death and funeral for days, focusing on everything from the dapper suit he donned in death to man-and-woman-on-the-street interviews where naïve New Yorkers came to praise the murderer, not to bury him.

Castellano had not been respected as a don, and Mafia experts believe that the fact that he did not see this hit coming and take precautions was an indication of his lack of competence.

Little Boy Lost

The tragic story of the death of Gotti's son is worth telling because of what it says about Mafia justice. John Gotti's twelve-year-old son, Frank, was puttering around their Howard Beach, Queens, neighborhood when he was struck and killed by a car. The driver, John Favara, was a neighbor of the Gottis. Favara's son and little Frank Gotti were friends. They even had overnights in each other's homes. It was a terrible tragedy and clearly an accident.

Shortly thereafter, Favara began receiving death threats. The local police suggested that he move. He did not take these threats seriously at first. After all, it had been an accident.

FACT

John Gotti was a rebel and a hero to many a misguided citizen. He thumbed his nose at the New York City ban on fireworks with a lavish pyrotechnic display every July 4. So what if he killed people? some people thought. He threw a great party.

The word *MURDERER* was spray-painted on his car, and one of his friends, the son of an old mobster, urged him "to take a powder," slang for hastily leaving the scene. After Gotti's wife, Victoria, attacked him with a baseball bat, he changed his mind. He put his house up for sale and decided to get out of town.

He did not get very far. He simply disappeared one morning, never to be heard from again. The story was pieced together by veteran crime reporter Jerry Capeci many years after the fact. Witnesses saw Favara get clubbed and thrown into a van. The witnesses were intimidated and remained silent. It is believed that his body was dumped in a barrel that was filled with cement and ended up at the bottom of the Atlantic. The offending automobile was turned into scrap metal.

Another slightly different version had Favara getting a grisly death by chainsaw. His remains were then put in his car, which was compressed to the size of a one-square-foot slab of metal.

Mr. and Mrs. Gotti were in Florida when these events transpired. They were questioned upon their return, but as usual, there was no evidence to link them to Favara's disappearance. John Gotti did volunteer the unsolicited opinion that if something bad did befall Favara, it was no skin off his Cosa Nostra.

There is no doubt that little Frank Gotti's deaths broke the hearts of his grieving parents. There is also no doubt that it was a terrible tragedy, not murder or even manslaughter. Most parents would not take the law into their own hands. But the rules that the rest of us live by do not apply to the Mafia. They do what they please, usually in the shadows, and to get on their bad side, intentionally or inadvertently, is invariably bad news.

The Dapper Don

Gotti was a Mafia superstar in the 1980s, always nattily dressed and not the least bit camera-shy (he was even seen wearing makeup in public, just in case *Entertainment Tonight* showed up). No murderous thug since Al Capone enjoyed the adulation of a perverse press and public. The government continued to go after Gotti, with no success.

John Gotti

Courtesy of AP/Wide World Photos/Richard Drew

◀ Reputed mob boss John Gotti sits in New York Supreme Court in Manhattan, New York, on January 20, 1990. He was accused of ordering the shooting of a union official, but was acquitted.

From Teflon to Velcro

Gotti was a target from the moment he assumed control of the Gambino crime family in 1985. Even before that, he had been caught on FBI wiretaps over the years discussing all sorts of things, from criminal activities to complaining about his wife. Big Brother was monitoring Gotti.

Gotti beat his first rap as don in 1987. The government thought it had an airtight case and was stunned by the verdict. Gotti was acquitted again on another RICO charge. As is often the case with bureaucracies, in organized crime and the legitimate world, there were rivalries and in-fighting among the prosecution attorneys and the FBI agents who brought them the evidence. Gotti was acquitted again, and as a result he earned another nickname, the "Teflon Don." No matter what the feds threw at him, nothing stuck.

Gotti's daughter, romance novelist Victoria Gotti, eulogized him in the *New York Post* as the man who "taught her to dream."

Gotti was also acquitted on an assault charge in 1990. He had been accused of hiring a gang of "Westies" to shoot carpentry union boss John O'Connor. It was alleged that O'Connor demolished a restaurant of a man who had dared employ nonunion workers. The restaurant happened to belong to a soldier in the Gambino family. The Westies are an organization of Irish gangsters who operate out of a neighborhood once known as "Hell's Kitchen" on Manhattan's West Side. Gotti sent the Westies after him. They shot O'Connor, giving him, to be polite, a royal pain in the butt. If they were aiming for his head, they truly were the gang that couldn't shoot straight. O'Connor told police that he had no idea who would want to take a shot at him. He knew that next time the marksman might take better aim if he squealed on Gotti.

Witnesses always tend to lose their memories when questioned about their relationship with John Gotti. The *New York Post*, always good for a clever headline, once ran "I FORGOTTI" on their front page about one such witness who neglected to take his ginkgo biloba.

FACT

John Gotti's son John, known as Junior Gotti, made a mistake following in the family business. He lacked both the acumen and the dubious charm of his father. He eventually plead guilty to, among other things, lying on a mortgage application.

Bull in a China Shop

The next time around, the prosecutors were more successful. In fact, they were luckier than they could ever have imagined. They found the biggest "rat" ever to scurry into their midst, with enough information to turn the "Teflon Don" into the "Velcro Don," as Gotti later came to be called when his world began to fall apart.

Sammy "The Bull" Gravano was John Gotti's underboss in the Gambino crime family. He confessed to murdering nineteen people over a twenty-year period, an average of about one whack per year. The state knew he would be an invaluable asset in nailing the Teflon Don, so despite his many crimes he was granted immunity. His testimony not only brought down several members of the Gambino family, but also members of the Colombo and Genovese crime families. The Bull was granted immunity and entered the Witness Protection Program.

QUESTION?

What do John Gotti and Grandpa Munster have in common?
Believe it or not, John Gotti's defense team trotted out celebrities as character witnesses to tell the press what a great guy he was. Among them was the ancient Al Lewis, most famous for playing Grandpa on the beloved television classic, *The Munsters*. Talk about strange bedfellows—the Dapper Don and the Doddering Dracula.

Many mobsters believed that, while the Bull's testimony was certainly damning, the Dapper Don's rampaging ego was in large part to blame. Most mobsters prefer the shadows, and those who strutted and swaggered in the limelight invariably had their comeuppance.

Membership in the Gambino family dropped considerably. Many modest low-level capos and underlings were ordered to meet with Gotti at his social club, despite the fact that everyone knew that it was under constant FBI surveillance. Camera-shy hoods were obliged to have their picture taken lest they earn the wrath of Don John. It was common knowledge that the FBI was watching and listening to everything that was said in the club, but Gotti would make his minions line up and pay homage. He would also speak with self-destructive candor. The Bull and the others were alarmed and angered by the Dapper Don's egotism and big mouth. He had begun, as many celebrities do, to believe his own publicity and consider himself as "untouchable" as Eliot Ness.

When Gotti got wind of another indictment, probably charging him with the murder of Paul Castellano, he ordered Gravano to go into hiding. Gotti knew Gravano would be subpoenaed to testify. Sammy the Bull stayed in various resort areas: the Poconos, Florida, and Atlantic City. When he retuned to New York City, Gotti demanded he meet him at the same social club that everyone on both sides knew was wired better than a home entertainment center. They were not there fifteen minutes before the feds raided the joint.

FACT

John Gotti, if he was to be believed, was perfectly at peace with himself. He was quoted as saying, "All I wanted was to be what I became."

The two men and others were arrested and denied bail. At a hearing, excerpts from the hours and hours of tapes were played. Gravano learned what Gotti had been saying about him when he was not around. He was putting the blame for the Castellano hit on Gravano's shoulders. Locked up together for months before their trial, the two men developed an even deeper dislike for one another. Gravano is the one who is called the rat, but Gotti and the Bull were both rats trying to escape the sinking ship at the other's expense. The feds wanted Gotti more than Gravano, so they offered the Bull a deal.

John Gotti's
funeral
procession

Courtesy of AP/Wide World Photos/Robert Spencer

▲ Cars with floral arrangements lead the funeral procession of reputed mob boss John Gotti as it winds through the Queens borough of New York, Saturday, June 15, 2002. Gotti died in prison of cancer at the age of 61.

Circus, Circus!

The final John Gotti trial was, to no one's surprise, a media circus. Sammy the Bull was now Sammy the Rat in the local papers. Gotti's people initiated a smear campaign, calling him everything from a homosexual to a compulsive womanizer. The defense team called as "character witnesses" the venerable late actor Anthony Quinn, the decidedly un-venerable actor Mickey Rourke, and Al "Grandpa Munster" Lewis. The three celebs told the press and TV reporters what a great guy Gotti was.

When Gravano, who had been sequestered at a Marine Corps base in Virginia, took the stand, that was, as they say, all she wrote. He placed Gotti at the scene of the Paul Castellano murder and fingered him as the man who orchestrated the hit.

In 1992 Gotti was convicted and given a life sentence without the possibility of parole. For many years it is believed he ran things from behind bars. But eventually health problems took over. He was diagnosed with cancer and lingered gravely ill for many years in a prison infirmary.

Death of a Don

John Gotti succumbed to cancer on June 10, 2002, at the age of 61. The Associated Press eulogized him as follows: "John Gotti, who swaggered, schemed and murdered his way to the pinnacle of organized crime in America only to be toppled by secret FBI tapes and a turncoat mobster's testimony, died at a prison hospital Monday while serving a life sentence."

FACT

Sammy the Bull has made it back into the news in recent years. Living in Arizona as "Jimmy Moran," he became involved in trafficking the popular drug known as Ecstasy. He was arrested along with his wife, son, daughter, and son-in-law. A real family affair.

John Gotti delivered his own obituary right before he was sent to jail. It is naturally more colorful and more hubris-laden than the press reports that covered his death. The Dapper Don was nothing if not full of himself. "I'll always be one of kind. You'll never see another guy like me if you live to be 5,000."

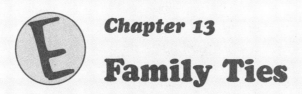

Chapter 13

Family Ties

Al Capone's Chicago mob is the stuff of legend, and New York's five crime families are the most powerful, but organized crime is a national institution. The Mafia's grasping tentacles reach all across the fruited plain from sea to shining sea. This chapter looks at some of the smaller Mafia crime families across the land.

East Coast Mafia Families

The Buffalo, New York, mob was founded by Stefano Magaddino. He was a member of the Commission from its inception and one of the elder statesmen of the Mafia. Buffalo's location near the Canadian border made it ideal for the bootleg business. The Buffalo mob was integral in the pipeline of transporting whiskey from Canada into the United States. Magaddino also had another business that catered to those who ran afoul of him—a mob-run funeral home. The Buffalo mob extended its influence west into Ohio and up into Canada.

Buffalo Mafioso Stefano Magaddino was the older cousin of New York City gangster Joe Bonanno. They were not kissing cousins, however, unless you count the "kiss of death." The Buffalo resident was intensely jealous of his more successful younger cousin, and neither would have been displeased to see the other whacked.

In the 1960s old man Magaddino accepted the inevitability of the drug trade and let two Young Turks operate in his territory, but when they were arrested, he did not help them out. After one of the brash young mobsters vowed to get even, his body was found in rural upstate New York carved like a Thanksgiving turkey, strangled, and incinerated. Old man Magaddino died of natural causes at the ripe old age of eighty-two.

Boston/Providence Crime Family

The Boston Mafia family was started by Gaspare Messina. He was succeeded by Phil Buccola, who was in turn replaced by Raymond Patriarca, Sr. He moved the headquarters of the family to Providence. Patriarca remained the don until he died in 1985. His son, Raymond Patriarca, Jr., took over. His claim to fame is being caught on tape during an initiation ceremony. Made men were admitted into the inner sanctum and took the vow of Omerta. The tapes allowed outsiders, for the first time, to hear the actual ceremony. All involved went to jail.

Northeast Pennsylvania Crime Family

This Mafia family operates out of Pittstown, Pennsylvania, and the surrounding environs. It was founded by Santo Volpe, who was followed by John Sciandra as head of the family. Joseph Barbara had Sciandra whacked in 1940 and was the don until 1959. It was in Barbara's summer home in Apalachin, New York, that the famous 1957 raid of the Commission took place.

Pittsburgh, Pennsylvania

Stefano Montasero was the boss of Pittsburgh during Prohibition. He was whacked, as was his successor Guiseppe Siragusa, who was one of the forty Mustache Petes wiped out in the wars of the late 1920s that culminated in 1931. Like many Mafia families in smaller American cities, its glory days are behind it, and it is a shadow of its former self. This can be said of the Mafia in general. It is believed that its remnants are clustered in the Northeast.

Newark, New Jersey

When most people think of the New Jersey Mafia, *The Sopranos* comes to mind. There was a New Jersey crime family for more than a hundred years before Tony Soprano and his cronies hit the small screen. The first don was Big Phil Amari who reigned for over twenty years. He was replaced by Nick Delmore. Sam the Plumber DeCavalcante took over after that, and the crime family became known by his name. Given its close proximity to New York City, the family was always second to Joe Bananas and the other heads of New York's mighty five families.

The New Jersey crime family is believed to be the basis for the hit HBO series *The Sopranos*. This critically acclaimed television show is said to be a favorite of today's Mafia. Famous informant and now Internet entrepreneur Henry Hill says he is a devoted fan, and that it is a very realistic portrayal of the modern Mafia.

Rochester, New York

Rochester, a small city in upstate New York, was under the thumb of the Buffalo crime family for over forty years. It broke away in the 1960s courtesy of the ambitious Valenti brothers. As in all Mafia breakups, the parting of ways was not an amicable one. The bloody battles and the federal prosecutions that went on over the next couple of decades diminished this crime family to one of negligible significance and zero influence in the big Mafia picture.

Tampa, Florida

New York and Chicago got all the media attention and became part of Mafia folklore, but the Tampa mob was very active and profitable. It had a great ride during Prohibition. Florida is geographically ideal for smuggling, given that the Bahamas and Cuba are a short cruise away. The family also, like most Mafia families, made its fortune in gambling, assorted heists, and infiltration of the unions.

The Tampa family also had no compunction about getting into the narcotics business. They were one of the first families to aggressively get into the game. The Tampa mob also had connections in Cuba. The island nation was a paradise and a playground for the mob and wealthy Americans who went there to gamble and indulge in other vices. This all changed when Castro seized power in 1959.

FACT

Members of Newark's crime family, the DeCavalcantes, were actually overheard on wiretaps watching *The Sopranos* and discussing whether the on-screen antics were based on their lives. There are no bigger mob movie and TV fans than Mafiosi.

The most famous Tampa Mafioso was Santos Trafficante, Jr. He succeeded his father in the family business and had a very long and successful career without ever going to jail or getting whacked. His claim to fame among conspiracy buffs is that his name comes up in the many theories about the assassination of President John F. Kennedy.

He and New Orleans boss Carlos Marcello, were named in a congressional investigation into the Kennedy assassination in the 1970s.

Midwest

Gaspare Milazzo established the Detroit family in 1921. He was retired in a shower of bullets in a hostile takeover by a rival named Gaetano Gianolla in 1930. He remained in charge until 1944. Joe Vitale took over and had a twenty-year run as boss. He was followed by Joseph Zerilli and later by Jack Tocco. Tocco often picketed city hall with the audacious charge that the persecution of the Mafia was based on anti-Italian prejudice. The Detroit Mafia was ravaged by a series of indictments and convictions in the late 1990s.

FACT

The Detroit crime family's specialty was labor racketeering, since Motor City was a big union town. Its most infamous son, Jimmy Hoffa, was president of the Teamsters Union and had known mob connections. Rumor has it Hoffa now resides under a goal post in Giants Stadium in New Jersey.

Kansas City

Kansas City was a town that was raucous in its own right before the Mafia arrived. Scarface DiGiovanni arrived from Sicily in 1912. Like many Sicilian gangsters he left the old country with a price on his head. DiGiovanni and his gang made a bundle of money and terrorized the town during Prohibition. They preyed on their own, as was often the case. It was the law-abiding Italians and Sicilians who suffered before the gangs grew powerful enough to menace the general population. Though there were many other gangsters and many violent gang wars, it is believed that Scarface DiGiovanni remained in power until his death in 1967 after enjoying a jail-free life of crime and a comfortable retirement.

Madison, Wisconsin

This may seem an improbable locale for a Mafia family, but the FBI says one existed there, and its don was a man named Carlo Caputo. Caputo and the alleged Mafia family are like Bigfoot sightings. People swore it was out there, but it was not an "in your face" family like the boys in New York and Chicago.

Most of the Midwest Mafia families were mere satellites of the big time outfit in Chicago. They did not have the manpower or the firepower to challenge the gang in the Windy City and thus remained small-time operations whose members are largely anonymous.

The shadowy Caputo is alleged to have had ties to the Chicago and Milwaukee mobs, but less is known about him than his more famous associates. Caputo came to Madison in 1940. He was successful in real estate and opened two restaurants. All seemingly legitimate enterprises. Caputo did thirty days in prison for income tax evasion and continued to expand his seemingly above-board businesses. When an associate of Caputo's named Joseph Aiello died a natural death, the FBI probed into his affairs and determined that the men were a two-man operation, the smallest Mafia family in history. Caputo died at the age of ninety and went to his grave denying the government's charges. If he was in the Mafia, one wishes that all crime families could be so low key and nonviolent.

Milwaukee, Wisconsin

The Milwaukee Mafia family began as a subsidiary of the Chicago organization. The first don was Vito Guardalabene. Guardalabene was followed by his son Peter. When the Commission was formed, they determined that Milwaukee would remain an extension of Chicago. The Milwaukee and Kansas City mobs, with the help of the corrupt Teamsters Union, got in on the Las Vegas casino boom in the 1970s. Unbeknownst to the hard-working rank and file of the Teamsters, their pension fund funded the Stardust Hotel and other casinos. And the mob made plenty of money "skimming" off the top in the casino counting rooms before it was reported to the IRS.

After the debacle of infighting and law enforcement crackdowns that plagued the entire Mafia in the second half of the twentieth century, the influence of this crime family is now nil.

St. Louis, Missouri

The St. Louis crime family thrived during Prohibition and had more than its share of gang violence. Vito Giannola was the first St. Louis don. The most famous was Anthony Giordano. The St. Louis mob appears to have had an independent streak. Its leadership did not attend the Apalachin conference that ended in disaster. Giordano was a skilled leader, and as a result he projected an image of power and influence that the family did not really have. It was a second-tier family. This was evident after Giordano's death—the family went into its death throes after the don's demise.

FACT

The gangsters of St. Louis had colorful names for their families in the days of Prohibition. The most powerful organizations called themselves the Green Ones, the Pillow Gang, the Egan's Rats, the Hogan Gang, and the Cuckoos. Eventually one familiar name, the Mafia, reigned supreme.

Wild West

The Dallas mob is most famous for one of its low-level members, Jack Ruby, who gunned down Lee Harvey Oswald after he was arrested and charged with the assassination of President John Kennedy. Ruby was an intimate of the local don, Joe Civello. It is alleged that corrupt members of the Dallas Police Department let Ruby into police headquarters to shoot Oswald on national television. The Dallas family was under the control of the larger New Orleans Mafia. It was never a particularly powerful and influential crime family, and it is believed to be no longer in existence.

The Denver Crime Family

This underworld outfit began in the 1880s and was more like a Western movie than a gangster melodrama. The first boss was a French-Canadian named Lou Blonger. He ran saloons that also featured prostitution as an attraction. This was common in the Old West. Blonger's career lasted from the wild and woolly 1880s until the 1920s, when he was finally imprisoned.

To counter the mob violence, the citizenry turned to an equally unsavory organization, the Ku Klux Klan, to restore order. The mayor, chief of police, and many cops were Klansmen. The KKK did not vanquish vice in Denver, they controlled and profited from it. The American Legion took on the Klan and won, eliminating the KKK's influence in the police force.

The Italians finally arrived in the 1930s in the persons of Pete and Sam Carlino. They brought their brand of bootlegging into the Wild West. Gang wars that rivaled those in Chicago followed. The Mafia tamed the Western town and has run its underworld their way ever since.

Los Angeles, California

Though founded by Joseph Ardizzone, the most influential Los Angeles Mafioso was Jack Dragna. He made inroads into Hollywood but was bullied and browbeaten by Bugsy Siegel when the Commission sent him out to California to muscle in on the L.A. territory. Bugsy Siegel took the time to make a screen test. The vainglorious gangster had dreams of becoming a movie star.

Dragna was replaced by Frank DiSimone, followed by Nick Licata and then Aladena Frattiano. He was nicknamed "Jimmy the Weasel" because he was one of the many rats who broke the vaunted vow of Omerta and informed on his *paisan*.

San Francisco, California

The Bay Area crime family never reached the exalted heights of the East Coast families. The first don was named Frank Lanza, and he was the boss during the good old days of Prohibition. Many a Mafioso left his heart, and other body parts, in San Francisco. Two other dons followed before Lanza's son James took over in the 1960s. He was not a grandiose hood who loved the limelight. As a result, the San Francisco family has always been low key, despite some unwelcome publicity courtesy of *Life* magazine. It is now the ultimate in low profile—it is history.

San Jose, California

Onofrio Sciotino was the lyrically named founder of this low-key California family. He was replaced by Joseph Cerrito, who like San Francisco's boss, did not appreciate the free publicity he got after the infamous 1957 Apalachin conference, when all the world suddenly became aware of the dirty little secret that was the Mafia. Today this branch of the Mafia family tree has withered and died.

QUESTION?

Did a mobster ever sue the press for libel?
Joseph Cerrito of San Jose, California, sued *Life* magazine when the periodical identified him as the head of the San Jose crime family. The case was eventually dismissed.

The New Orleans Mafia

The New Orleans crime family was the first in America. As discussed in Chapter 3, Sicilian immigrants came to New Orleans in the 1860s. Along with the hard-working, decent folk, there was an insidious criminal element that quickly took root and began a reign of terror that culminated in the murder of the New Orleans chief of police, and a subsequent lynch mob attack that made the term *La Mafia* a household world in the United States. In the twentieth century, the name of Carlos Marcello was synonymous with the New Orleans Mafia.

Carlos Marcello was a teenage bank robber who was ratted out by his own brother. Carlos returned the money and was not prosecuted. This brush with the law did not deter him from a life of crime. He planned to rob the same bank again but was ratted out yet again, this time by two of his would-be heist men. He served four years in the brutal Louisiana state prison in Angola. His father had bribed local officials to get his son a pardon. This was a technique that Marcello took to heart in his long criminal career.

Though its tentacles once spanned the land with branches in every major city from sea to shining sea, it is believed that the Mafia has been severely diminished, and its territory is now limited to the Northeast.

Marcello became the owner of a saloon called the Brown Boxer, after the popular boxer of the day, Joe Louis, in an African-American part of town named Gretna. The bar became a source for drugs and gambling as well as alcohol. The diminutive Marcello also served as bouncer. Though only five-feet-four-inches tall, he was a feisty little guy. He was a "made" man in the New Orleans Mafia by the age of twenty-five.

Independent Mafiosi

The New Orleans mob was always very independent. It went its own way and did not answer to the Commission up North, which regulated just about every other Mafia family large and small. Just as the American South is regarded as laid back, with people and events that move along at a leisurely pace, so too the New Orleans Mafia's structure was a looser confederation of individuals and groups of criminals. There was more autonomy than in other Mafia families. Greedy overlords eager to "wet their beaks" were not always trying to insert themselves into the minutia of day-to-day operations.

Carlos Marcello continued to thrive and feign influence and prestige in the New Orleans rackets. He had his sticky fingers in drugs (including marijuana), gambling, and also in less harmful enterprises that the Mafia has always had an interest in—pinball machines, jukeboxes, and vending machines. The Mafia is still involved to these enterprises to this day.

Marcello and Costello

The New York Mafia was keenly aware of the goings-on in the Deep South. They had no influence over and only minimal interaction with their brethren south of the Mason-Dixon line. Lucky Luciano's right hand man Frank Costello made inroads into the New Orleans Mafia with the help of a corrupt Louisiana politician.

Frank Costello was in charge of the lucrative and very illegal slot machine business in New York City. Crusading Mayor Fiorello LaGuardia was elected in 1933 and began to make like difficult for the Mafia. LaGuardia was an Italian-American who wanted to eradicate the stain that the Mafia had given his people, the majority of whom had no connection to organized crime. Slot machines were seized and destroyed. LaGuardia had many a photo opportunity personally smashing slot machines for newsreel cameras.

Huey Long, the former governor of Louisiana, approached Costello and agreed to act as broker in a deal to ship the surviving slot machines from New York down to New Orleans, where they could be used for fun and profit. Carlos Marcello made sure the machines were prominently displayed for public consumption in gambling joints, bars, and brothels in New Orleans and the surrounding communities.

QUESTION?

What is the longest reign of a Mafia don?
Stefano Maggadino ruled the Buffalo crime family for fifty years until his death in 1974. No other don approaches this tenure. They were ousted by either natural or unnatural causes long before they could celebrate this milestone anniversary.

The Northern Mafia also opened a nightclub in New Orleans called the Beverly Club. The men behind the scenes were Frank Costello and Meyer Lansky. They made Marcello a partner.

Don Carlos

Carlos Marcello became the don of the New Orleans crime family in 1947. He did so through nonviolent means. A conference was held, and he was appointed by the other members of the New Orleans crime family. It created bad blood but no bloodshed. It was an unusual example of Mafia power transference. Most involved someone getting whacked.

Marcello shared the philosophy of most of his fellow gangsters. In a sense they were akin to the political Libertarian Party, which endorses the legalization of drugs and prostitution. Marcello believed he was giving the people what they wanted. He wasn't concerned with whether or not people's lives were destroyed by drug abuse or alcohol addiction—that was the individual's responsibility.

When the Kefauver Committee came to town in 1951, Marcello was called in for questioning. The full name of the committee was the Special Committee to Investigate Organized Crime in Interstate Commerce. Senator Estes Kefauver was the ambitious politician who earned the enmity of many a Mafioso.

Carlos Marcello "pleaded the fifth" 152 times during his questioning. He was essentially claiming he was guilty of something but unwilling to incriminate himself by answering. His smug demeanor also earned the ire of the committee, and he was cited for contempt, but the six-month jail sentence was later overturned on appeal. Kefauver was outraged and publicly announced his desire to see Marcello deported back to Italy. This had happened to Lucky Luciano earlier and was doable, since Marcello had never become a United States citizen. Carlos Marcello became a reluctant celebrity and received the derogatory nickname "Midget of the Mafia." He was five-foot-four in lifts.

Bayou Boss

Marcello is not as well known a name as Al Capone or John Gotti, but he surpasses them in longevity and in the success of his career. His sphere of influences included most of the Southern and Western states, including California, plus pre-Castro Cuba, the Caribbean, and Mexico. His illegal income funded numerous and diverse legitimate businesses. He operated without hassles and interference from the Commission up North.

He continued to have dealings with a government determined to shut him down. Years after the Kefauver Committee, the McClellan Commission was after him. Two prominent members of this congressional committee were the Kennedy brothers, John and Robert, who would continue to harass the Mafia into the older brother's presidency. And perhaps they paid an awful price for their meddling.

ESSENTIAL

> Carlos Marcello had an ominous credo: "Three can keep a secret if two are dead."

The Kennedy brothers questioned Marcello, who was as disdainful of them as he had been of the Kefauver Committee. Maybe more so. No doubt Marcello was well aware that their father, Joe Kennedy, made his fortune in the bootlegging business during Prohibition. He didn't think that these preppie pipsqueaks could do him much harm. He had not anticipated one of them becoming president and making the other the attorney general. Marcello pled the fifth over and over again and made no attempt to hide his contempt of the Kennedy brothers.

Guatemala or Bust

Marcello had never bothered to become an American citizen. As a result he was subject to deportation. To combat this, he had a bogus birth certificate created that said he was born in Guatemala. He did not want to be returned to Italy or to his actual birthplace, Tunisia, in North Africa. When Robert Kennedy became attorney general he deported Marcello to Guatemala. Marcello was humiliated. He had a terrible ordeal trying to get back into the United States, including being stranded in the Central American jungles by the local military and wandering lost in the rain forests for three days. He was not without influence and eventually made it back to the United States. He sued Robert Kennedy for illegally deporting him. Mafia informants maintain that he spoke openly of killing not the pesky RFK, but his brother President John Kennedy.

Lee Harvey Oswald

There are myriad conspiracy theories about the assassination of JFK. Some place the blame squarely at the Mafia's doorstep. Many mention the Mafia as a player in a vast, dark scheme worthy of *The X-Files*. There are also some who think Lee Harvey Oswald was a lone gunman.

There facts are disturbing. Lee Harvey Oswald's uncle, a man named Dutz Murret, was a bookie for the New Orleans Mafia. Oswald's mother was linked to several soldiers in the mob. The man who killed Oswald, Jack Ruby, had ties to the Dallas crime family, which was more or less a subsidiary of the Marcello organization. Is it possible that the Mafia used this outcast and oddball Oswald for their hit and then had him whacked to avoid discovery? Future generations will know when the classified files are revealed. Carlos Marcello was in a New Orleans courtroom being found not guilty of his false birth certificate charges on the afternoon of President Kennedy's murder.

FACT

His name notwithstanding, Russell Bufalino was not head of the Buffalo crime family. He led the western Pennsylvania family and was considered a suspect in the disappearance (and probably murder) of former Teamster boss Jimmy Hoffa.

In an interesting coincidence, Marcello was also in court being acquitted of another charge on the afternoon that Robert F. Kennedy was assassinated in 1968. There are some conspiracy buffs that try to link Marcello not only to RFK's murder, but also the killing of Martin Luther King, Jr. in the same year. Though the "lone gunman" explanation is also questionable in both these murders, the strongest circumstantial evidence links the mob boss with the JFK assassination.

End of the Line

Carlos Marcello and the New Orleans mob continued to prosper and avoid the long arm of the law for many years. But nothing lasts forever, and eventually the FBI caught up with him. In a yearlong surveillance operation, the feds accumulated hundreds of hours of damning recordings of Marcello mouthing off on a variety of topics, including his criminal activities. His office had been tapped, and many turncoats had worn wires in his presence. In 1981, after decades of seeming invulnerable, the don of the New Orleans Mafia was found guilty of violating the RICO law. He was also convicted on other charges in other states, and when all the prosecutors compared notes, he faced seventeen years in prison; he was seventy-two years old.

He bounced around several federal prisons in the six years he was incarcerated, most of them minimum-security "country club" institutions. He developed Alzheimer's disease in prison and was released. The mighty little man who ruled a massive criminal empire, killed many men, and ordered the killings of many more (possibly even a United States president) degenerated into dementia and infantilism and died in 1993.

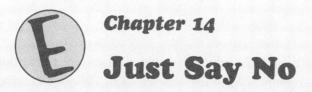

Chapter 14

Just Say No

For years the Mafia had a love/hate relationship with the world of illegal drugs. The Mafia protested much about its unwillingness to get involved with drugs, but to some extent they always were, and finally the allure of the big money became too great. In this chapter we will look at the Mafia's involvement in the drug trade.

Drug Abuse in America

Contrary to what many people believe, drug use in America did not begin with the hippies in the 1960s. Drugs have been popular since humans first discovered the natural kick in certain chemicals and plants and then learned to refine and fine tune them for greater potency.

In the late nineteenth century, "opium dens" were easy to find. Patrons could go into these dimly lit and seedy establishments, usually run by Chinese immigrants, smoke opium, and be provided a cot to recline on to enjoy their drug-induced reverie. There were numerous opium-based drugs openly sold in the marketplace. Children's medication was often laced with opium.

When opium was outlawed, addicts turned to a legal substitute— heroin. Yes, heroin was legal in the United States. In 1898 the Bayer pharmaceutical company touted heroin as a nonaddictive substitute for the highly addictive painkiller morphine. Astoundingly, even Coca-Cola was laced with cocaine for a time in the nineteenth century. Drugs have always been around, and there has always been a subculture of addicts.

FACT

Many drugs that are now illegal were readily available and enthusiastically consumed by the general public. Vin Mariani was a popular drink in the nineteenth century. Made of cocaine-laced wine, it was served in saloons and bistros in Europe and America.

Some people were aware of the gravity of the drug problem. And they were not simply Bible-toting temperance types. Sir Arthur Conan Doyle, author of the Sherlock Holmes stories, was also a medical doctor like his fictional character Dr. Watson. Doyle's fictional mouthpiece regularly warns Sherlock Holmes about the dangers associated with Holmes's cocaine use. Dr. Doyle, through the voice of Dr. Watson, was in the minority in his belief about the insidious nature of cocaine, but he and other medical men were ahead of their time in their belief that it was much more than a harmless recreational drug.

Lawmakers Crack Down

The first attempt by the government to control the use of narcotics by Americans was the Harrison Narcotics Act of 1914. It did not do much good. It required businesses that dealt in opium and cocaine products to register with the federal government and, of course, taxed them a penny per ounce on items they shipped through the United States postal service. Doctors were allowed to dispense heroin, opium, and morphine to patients "for medicinal purposes." This resulted in the first versions of "rehab centers." Like the methadone clinics of later decades, these facilities tried to break people's morphine addiction by giving them heroin. Morphine addiction became a serious problem for many American soldiers during World War I. In 1923 the Supreme Court decided to make it illegal for doctors to prescribe heroin and morphine for any reason. Did government interference end the scourge of drug addiction in America? Of course not. All it did was make the trafficking of drugs go underground. And there was an organization in place ready, willing, and able to take up the slack and make billions over the remainder of the twentieth century. Enter the Mafia.

The Chinese Connection

Prior to the Mafia's entrance into the drug business, most of the heroin consumed by America's addicts came from China. A smaller supply came from the Middle East and the Corsican gangs in Marseilles, who would ultimately team up with the Mafia. During World War II this whole network was nearly broken by the fortunes of war. The fighting on land and sea in and around Europe and North Africa and Japan's invasion of China effectively dismantled the source of the heroin's manufacture and the trade routes over which the drug was shipped. Since the supply was not there, the demand diminished in the United States. Then the United States intelligence community made it possible for the Mafia to become extremely wealthy drug kingpins and flood the land with the addictive poison.

Just as the Sicilian Mafia had problems when the fascist government of Mussolini came to power, so too did Chinese organized crime fail after the Chinese communist revolution of 1949. The peasant class suffered either way, whether it was from the menace of the criminals or the cruelty of the totalitarian regime.

Just Say Yes

Even before the Supreme Court decision made these drugs illegal, the Mafia had dabbled in drugs. Mafiosi acted as if it were beneath them, but they greedily salivated at the money to be made. The New Orleans Mafia was dealing drugs, including marijuana, in the nineteenth century. Marijuana was popular in the local African-American community in turn-of-the-century New Orleans. The Mafia talked a lot about keeping it away from children and from Italian and Sicilian neighborhoods. There was always racism within the Mafia in addition to its deep insularity, so it did not much care what drugs did to destroy other ethnic groups.

The Mafia crime families in the North were slower to jump on the narcotics bandwagon. The old guard from the Old World wanted nothing to do with it. There was plenty of money to be made in the bootlegging, gambling, and prostitution rackets. These were regarded as "harmless" vices by many people, even law enforcement officials, who often turned a blind eye when these activities were going on right under their noses.

Drug trafficking was another matter altogether. When the Young Turks wiped out the old guard in the Castellemmarese War, the new and Americanized leaders of the Mafia reconsidered staying out of the drug trade. They had a peripheral role in the business anyway. Their Jewish pals such as Meyer Lansky, Dutch Schultz, and Legs Diamond were already involved in the heroin business in the 1920s. The new Boss of Bosses, Lucky Luciano, decided that the Italians should get a piece of the action.

When Prohibition was repealed in 1933 after the election of Franklin Delano Roosevelt, the Mafia turned its sights on the heroin racket. The decision made good business sense. Though there were fewer drug addicts than drinkers in the country, the profit margin would be much higher, and drugs would be easier to smuggle. Packets of powder do not noisily clink-clank in crates when being unloaded off ships in the dead of night.

FACT

As the Mafia's power and influence has dwindled, other forces have moved in to take up the slack. Russian and South American organized crime groups are reportedly keeping the illegal drug trade a brisk and profitable enterprise.

Part of Luciano's plan was to turn the approximately 1,200 prostitutes (who earned him $10 million a year) under his control into heroin addicts. They would not create problems, and they could be easily manipulated that way. The prostitutes would work to support their habit and buy the product from the Mafia. They would be immediately returning the pittance they earned back into the pockets of their Mafia masters. During his exile in Italy, Lucky Luciano masterminded the modern heroin trade. They should have left him in the slammer.

The Italian Connection

The United States government thought they were getting rid of a rotten apple when they deported Lucky Luciano back to Italy. What they really did was send him off to the old homestead so he could organize a very efficient and effective drug trafficking empire. They kicked him out, and he sent back tons of heroin that filled the Mafia's coffers and made life miserable for the addicts and those in their intersecting circles for years to come. Luciano immediately renewed old acquaintances in the Sicilian Mafia when he returned to the Mediterranean region.

It was a labyrinthine trail that took the heroin from its source to its destination as nickel bags in American cities and towns. And Lucky Luciano oversaw the whole sordid affair until his death in 1962. It is estimated that the number of heroin addicts in the United States increased from 20,000 to 150,000 in the twenty years after World War II.

The trek began in the Middle East, where it was in its morphine base form. Luciano's main source for the morphine base was a shady character in Beirut, Lebanon. Sami El-Khoury secured the raw opium from Turkey, oversaw its transformation into morphine base in Lebanon, and sent it along to the laboratories in Sicily and Marseilles, France, for its final metamorphosis into heroin. It seems that just about everyone in Lebanon was on the take. Members of the police force and airport and customs officials were generously bribed, which enabled the trafficking to run smoothly with no interference from pesky law enforcement officials.

On to Sicily

In Sicily, Lucky Luciano had several secret laboratories where morphine was processed into heroin. Luciano had minimal interference from the law from 1949 to 1954 until some investigative journalists ran some pictures and a story in a Rome newspaper. One lab was shut down, but the impact to the business as a whole was negligible.

The Mafia's involvement with drugs and the increasing number of snitches are directly connected. Since drug trafficking carried very serious jail time and law enforcement officials were less likely to look the other way, low-level hoods were more likely to cut deals.

Luciano was not the only Mafioso who was deported after World War II. More than a hundred big and little fish were kicked out of the United States, but their penchant for larceny did not diminish. Nor did they all return to Italy when deported. Luciano had his men placed in big cities throughout Europe. Therefore he had many agents and operations in places across the European continent. If one tentacle of his hydra-like empire was cut off, it would not have jeopardized the enterprise as a whole.

Back in the USA

Meanwhile, Luciano had stayed in close contact with his old pals back in America. Meyer Lansky was controlling Luciano's interests in America, and Lansky organized the American end of the drug empire. Lansky worked with the Trafficante crime family of Florida to oversee drug smuggling from the Caribbean and Cuba. Smugglers also delivered through Canada, and some audaciously unloaded their product right off the shores of New York City, much as they had done in the bootlegging days.

Luciano was not allowed back into the United States, but nothing prevented him from visiting Cuba, a mere ninety miles off the coast of Florida. Cuba was a haven for the Mafia until 1959. Luciano went to Cuba in 1947 for a meeting with the American crime bosses to discuss their plans. The Mafia bribed the entire corrupt government of Cuba and secured their services in making Cuba the last stop before drug distribution in the United States. The United States government was well aware of Luciano's presence in Cuba, and it put pressure on the Cuban government to revoke Luciano's visa and force him to return to Italy. He did return there, but not before he had accomplished his goals. The distribution network in America was established.

Meyer Lansky
is arrested

Courtesy of AP/Wide World Photos/Zimmerman

◀ Meyer Lansky, with hat, New York City underworld figure, escorted by detectives, February 11, 1958, on his way to booking at West 54th Street Police Station.

The pleasure paradise of Cuba was not the only cooperative island in the Caribbean for the Mafia's drug trade. Many other island nations were not as wealthy as Cuba; in fact most were quite poor. They welcomed the infusion of cash that the Mafia paid for its assistance.

The French Connection

Marseilles, France, was another city where clandestine laboratories refined morphine base into heroin. The Sicilian Mafia was getting sloppy, and there was a series of arrests. In the 1950s the Mafia began to shut down the Sicilian labs and contract the work out to the Corsican crime families. Corsica is an island in the Mediterranean Ocean, and Marseilles is a port city in the south of France. It is the port from which the French imperialists left to seek their fortunes in North Africa and Southeast Asia. The city has an international flavor, like most great metropolises with active sea commerce and busy docks. It was a fertile breeding ground for a criminal element, just as New York City and New Orleans were and are for the American Mafia. In the case of Marseilles, the local villains were the Corsican gangsters. French pulp fiction portrays Marseilles the way American writers of hardboiled crime fiction treat Chicago of the 1920s.

ALERT!

Lest you think that drugs are a harmless vice and strictly the purview of the Mafia, consider that recent evidence suggests that terrorist organizations are funding their activities through drug dealing in the United States.

The Corsican mob lacked the elaborate organization of the rest of the Mafia. It was comprised of close knit and insular clans who worked together for the greater evil. They have always had a track record of working for the highest bidder, and have occasionally been employed by the Americans. It is generally accepted that the CIA paid the Corsican mob to break the striking communist labor unions. The Corsican mob's association with the CIA made them an extremely powerful crime family and in effect made Marseilles the largest heroin producer in the Western world.

Meyer Lansky made a personal trip to Europe to, among other things, secure the services of the Corsican mob. Lansky established the clandestine financial network for organized crime activities that involved Swiss bank accounts to avoid scrutiny by the IRS. Swiss banks prided themselves on protecting the anonymity of their depositors by issuing numbered, not named, accounts and jealously guarding the identity of their clients. This enabled the Mafia's finances to remain secret from inquisitive American authorities who were eager to freeze or seize their assets. Eventually Meyer Lansky bought his very own bank in Geneva, Switzerland, to eliminate the middlemen.

Meyer Lansky's European jaunt also took him to Rome to see his old friend Luciano and then on to France to negotiate with the Corsicans. A deal was struck, and in short order Marseilles became the heroin-producing capital of Europe and the major supplier of heroin to the United States.

Check out the movie *The French Connection* to get a glimpse of how the drug trade affected the lives of working-class cops on a heroic crusade to end the scourge in New York City. It is not a mob movie per se, but it gives you a flavor for what the Marseilles drug connection was like and the damage it caused our country.

Dumbed Down Dons

Back on the United States home front, the Mafia adapted to the times, and the drug trade became more and more a part of Mafia business and more and more in the open. The Mafia's pretense of civility and its vaunted code of honor gave way to the inherent greed of its members. The Mafia went from avoiding involvement in narcotics to involvement with reservations to outright and enthusiastic drug trafficking. As the old dons died and the Young Turks took over, they were less concerned about the nasty nature of the drug trade and more interested in the profits they made.

Chapter 15

The Rats

Despite the code of Omerta, the vow of silence every "made" Mafioso makes, there have been many "rats" in the mob's violent history. Breaking Omerta was punished by death, so the rats sought refuge with their former enemies, the G-Men. This chapter introduces you to some of the more famous, or infamous, depending on your sympathies, Mafia informants.

The Valachi Papers

Joseph Valachi was the first informant to get national attention. His testimony was covered on national television. The events that transpired to land Valachi on the witness stand were a soap opera that could rival *The Sopranos*.

Joe Valachi became a member of the Mustache Pete Salvatore Maranzano's organized crime family in the 1920s. He was officially "made" in 1930 and served at the pleasure of Maranzano until the don's murder in 1931. After that Valachi was a soldier in the Luciano family, reporting to Vito Genovese.

Valachi was an unrepentant hoodlum. He was a numbers runner, leg breaker, ruthless murderer, and in later years a drug trafficker before he was finally locked up. He was in prison on a fifteen- to twenty-year sentence for a drug charge when he decided to re-evaluate the oath he took when he was made.

Two's Company

Joe Valachi was in a federal prison in Atlanta, and he found himself sharing a cell with none other than his old boss Vito Genovese. Genovese became head of the Luciano crime family after Lucky Luciano was deported back to Italy. The family eventually assumed his name. Things grew tense for the cellmates when Genovese began to suspect Valachi of turning traitor. Valachi had not done this yet or even considered it. Genovese in essence gave Valachi the push into the pantheon of notorious rats.

FACT

Attorney General Robert F. Kennedy's war on organized crime turned up the heat and made turncoats of many Mafiosi. He called the Mafia "the enemy within," a hostile force within our borders out to undermine the American way.

Kiss Me, Guido

Vito Genovese publicly gave Joe Valachi the "kiss of death," meaning that he was now a marked man. His days were numbered. There were three attempts on his life while behind bars. Even in prison, the Mafia could conduct business and have men killed. Valachi knew he would soon be whacked.

He got wind of who the hit man might be and killed him. Valachi, however, was a wiseguy who would never be nicknamed "The Brain," as was Meyer Lansky. Valachi had killed the wrong man. The stone killer who had seen so much violence in his life felt perhaps his first pangs of conscience when he learned that the man he clubbed to death with an iron pipe was not the man he thought he was. His sentence was amended from fifteen to twenty years to life imprisonment. It was then that Valachi fulfilled Vito Genovese's prophecy and become an informant.

Sing, Sing a Song

Valachi was placed under witness protection and guarded by 200 United States marshals. They were not going to let the Mafia get their hands on their prize songbird. The mob offered a $100,000 reward for Valachi's head on a platter. Valachi appeared before the McClellan Committee in 1963. His testimony received national and international attention. He fingered 317 organized crime members and brought the name *La Cosa Nostra* into the vernacular. The testimony was enlightening but produced no quantifiable results. No one Mafioso was jailed based solely on Valachi's testimony.

ALERT!

There is much braggadocio and one-upmanship among low-level Mafiosi. It is therefore necessary to take much of Joe Valachi's testimony with the proverbial grain of salt. A man in his position would not be told much about his superior's plans, and his fellow soldiers tended to lie about their exploits to feed their egos and enhance their reputations.

Valachi had no entrée into the inner workings of the Commission. He could only speak of his own experiences. The lawmakers in Washington and the public were treated to a worm's eye view of the workings of the

Mafia. There was probably much braggadocio in his testimony, and plenty of unreliable hearsay. Nevertheless, his pronouncements painted the picture of a brutal, nasty, and ruthless world: speaking of honor and codes while double-crossing and backstabbing, going to church on Sunday and beating a man to death on Monday, sexually distancing themselves from their wives when they became the mothers of their children while keeping girlfriends on the side.

Spin City

The Mafia orchestrated something akin to a publicity campaign against Valachi's testimony. Not everyone on the side of the law bought a lot of Valachi's claims either.

Although the rats began to desert the sinking ship in the 1960s, there were some notable informants in the Mafia's Golden Age. A man named Louis Shumway was one of Al Capone's bookkeepers who turned on his boss. Fearing for his safety, he was spirited out of the country until it was his turn on the witness stand.

Vito Genovese was not considered the Boss of Bosses by most in the know. Even in far-off Italy, Lucky Luciano remained the boss until his death in 1962. And Luciano's mouthpiece in America was his old friend Meyer Lansky. Valachi, not the brightest bulb in the underworld, and more than a little xenophobic, did not give Lansky his due simply because he was Jewish.

Other Mafia informants claimed Valachi talked out of both sides of his mouth long before he turned rat. And claims surfaced that he might have been an informant long before he officially went to the feds.

Another attack on his character was in his Mafia nickname. He had been called Joe Cargo as a young man but over time other Mafiosi began calling him "Joe Cago." According to mob sources, they were not simply mispronouncing his moniker. It was a sign of how they felt about him. *Cago* is an Italian word for feces.

Joe Valachi was released from prison and died of cancer in 1971. It is a surprise and a mystery why none of his former associates found him and whacked him. Before his death, Valachi cooperated with best-selling author Peter Maas on the book *The Valachi Papers*. At least Valachi exacted revenge on his old boss. Vito Genovese lost much of his power as a result of Valachi's testimony, and the crime family he controlled lost its pre-eminence as the largest and most powerful of the five families.

King of the Hill

Another infamous rat in the history of Mafia informants is Henry Hill. Henry Hill was played by Ray Liotta in one of the best and most realistic gangster movies, Martin Scorsese's *Goodfellas*. And in a very appropriate twist for these very twisted times, he is the first Mafia informant to have his very own Web site.

A Brooklyn Tale

When Hill was a small boy on the mean streets of Brooklyn, he was enthralled watching the local wiseguys. Like many a hoodlum before him, including Big Al Capone, he got his start running errands for the neighborhood gangsters, much to the chagrin of his parents.

FACT

A Mafioso must be fully Italian in order to be initiated into the family, take the vow of Omerta, and become a made man. Jimmy "the Gent" Burke and Henry Hill could never be made men because they were not full-blooded Italian. Burke was given the affectionate and honorary title of "the Irish Guinea."

He became entrenched in the seductive criminal underworld. One of his best friends was Jimmy "the Gent" Burke, another local gangster who, alas, would never be "made." Hill and Burke were half Irish, and because of that, no matter how many people they killed, they would never be admitted into the inner sanctum of the Mafia. For the record, Hill says he never killed anyone, though he was present at a few murders.

Hill was a member of the Lucchese Mafia family, one of New York

City's big five. His biggest score was an airport heist for which his cut was a mere $50,000 out of a cool $5.8 million. He felt he was entitled to a lot more. His life was also spiraling out of control. Drug and alcohol addiction and its attendant paranoia, plus the increasing stress of living in the dangerous underworld were bringing him to the breaking point. In 1980 he turned on his fellow goodfellas and became, in their eyes, a very bad boy.

Witness for the Prosecution

Most of the men that Henry Hill fingered, including Jimmy the Gent, were sent to prison. Burke died there. Dozens more were murdered as they squabbled over the distribution of the Lufthansa airport heist money. Hill went into the Witness Protection Program and was given a new identity. He remained in the program for seven years.

ALERT!

The movie *Goodfellas* tells the bizarre and violent story of Henry Hill and his descent into the maelstrom. From cocky wiseguy to drug-addicted loser seeking refuge in the Witness Protection Program, it is one of the best Mafia movies ever made. It is the flip side to the Shakespearean quality of the Corleone family.

Under his new identity, he continued to engage in criminal activity and even did sixty days in jail. He was arrested for drug dealing, assault, burglary, driving while intoxicated, and parole violation. The protection program, run by the United States Department of Justice, kicked him out, so he turned to the FBI, which has helped him remain in hiding since then.

Cyberfella

Henry Hill calls himself a "cyberfella" these days. He is also the author of a cookbook called *Cookin' on the Run*. Although his life will always be in danger, it would seem that his ego has compelled him to make potentially hazardous forays into the light. He has a Web site called ✐*www.goodfellahenry.com*. It is a strange mix of gallows humor, showmanship, and salesmanship.

Those who log on can buy copies of Mafia-related books and chuckle over his version of David Letterman's Top Ten List. Hill's parody is a list of Mafia slang expressions for murder. You can take an interactive tour of his old neighborhood and the mob hangout called Robert's Lounge. You can even buy an autographed poster of the movie *Goodfellas* that he suggests you purchase before he gets whacked. You can send him an e-mail and he might even answer.

These days Henry Hill is clean and sober and wants to forge a new career as a substance abuse counselor. He is also trying to sell some movie scripts to Hollywood and a half-hour mob comedy television pilot. Needless to say, his favorite show is *The Sopranos*.

Singing to the Feds

One of the most accommodating Mafia rats since Joe Valachi, and much more of an informed informant, was Angelo Lonardo, former boss of the Cleveland, Ohio, crime family. It is fascinating to hear the inner workings of the Mafia from the horse's mouth. He testified before the Permanent Subcommittee on Investigations of the Senate Committee on Government Affairs on April 4, 1988. He was being questioned by Senator Sam Nunn.

SENATOR NUNN: Thank you, Senator Roth. Mr. Lonardo, why don't you proceed.

MR. LONARDO: My name is Angelo Lonardo. I am seventy-seven years old, and I am a member of the La Cosa Nostra. I am the former underboss of the Cleveland organized crime family. I became a member of La Cosa Nostra in the late 1940s, but have been associated with the organization since the late 1920s. When I was "made" or became a member of La Cosa Nostra, I went through an initiation ceremony. I later learned that to be proposed for membership in La Cosa Nostra, you would have to have killed someone and stood up to the pressure of police scrutiny. Today, you do not have to kill to be a member, but just prove yourself worthy by keeping your mouth shut or by being a "stand-up" guy. However, if you are called upon to kill someone, you have to be prepared to do it. In my case, my father was murdered by Salvatore Todaro in 1927. In revenge, my cousin, Dominic Sospirato, and I killed Todaro. This is one of the reasons that I was proposed for membership in La Cosa Nostra.

MR. LONARDO CONTINUES: In the 1930s, my cousin John Demarco and I murdered Dr. Romano, the former boss of Cleveland, because Romano had a role in the death of my father, and we believed that he killed our cousin on the operating table. At the time, I was not a member of the LCN, but Demarco was. As a result of the Romano murder, Demarco was condemned to death by the Commission for killing a boss without okaying it with the Commission. I was excused for my part in the murder, since I was not an LCN member and did not know the rules. Later, I attended a meeting with Al Polizzi, the boss of Cleveland, in Miami, Florida. It turned out that this was a Commission meeting and that Polizzi was defending Demarco's murder of Romano. I did not sit in on the meeting, but afterwards Polizzi told me that he had "straightened out" Demarco's problem with the Commission.

The FBI was taken to task in 1999 for being a tad overzealous in its mob-busting efforts. The bureau was criticized for its protection of valued informants even while these snitches continued their illegal activities, which sometimes included murder.

MR. LONARDO CONTINUES: During the '30s, the Commission put a "freeze" on the making of new members. The Commission put the freeze on since families, especially in New York, were not making the "right" kind of people. Some individuals were even buying their way into the LCN. I have heard that one businessman paid $50,000 to join the LCN. Because of the decree, I was not made into the Cleveland family until the 1940s.

MR. LONARDO CONTINUES: John Scalish became boss of the Cleveland family around 1949. He took over for Al Polizzi, who tired of Cleveland and retired in Florida. In 1949, the Cleveland family had between fifty and sixty members. Scalish did not "make" any new members, so the strength of the Cleveland family diminished as its members aged or died. Scalish just did not want to make any new members. Even though a small organization, the Cleveland family became involved in Las Vegas casinos through their association with the "Jewish Boys," Maurice Kleinman, Moe Dalitz, Sammy Tucker, Tommy McGinney, who is dead, and Lou Rothkopf, also dead. In the late 1940s, Wilbur Clark began building the Desert Inn casino in Las Vegas, Nevada. Clark was in need of additional capital and eventually went into a partnership with "the Jewish Boys" in order to obtain the necessary funding to complete the construction of the casino. Kleinman, Dalitz, Tucker, McGinney, and Rothkopf were gamblers who owned the Beverly Hills Supper Club, a casino-type gambling operation in Covington, Kentucky.

MR. LONARDO CONTINUES: A few years after the Desert Inn was licensed and operating, "the Jewish Boys" gave Al Polizzi, John King, and Frank Milano a piece of the Desert Inn in exchange for the Cleveland family's protection. During the 1970s, the Cleveland family received money from two sources. The first source was the "skim" money from the Las Vegas casinos, and the second was our piece of the Pittsburgh family's Youngstown, Ohio, rackets. Our family received about $40,000 a month from Vegas and 25 percent of the Youngstown rackets, which would average about $5,000 per month. I did not learn about this arrangement until I became the underboss in 1976. The skim of the Las Vegas casinos started in the early 1970s. Starting in 1974, I began receiving about $1,000 to $1,500 a month from the family, through Maishe Rockman. I did not know where the money was coming from, but I suspected that it was from the Las Vegas casinos. I learned this from various conversations that I had with Rockman.

MR. LONARDO CONTINUES: In 1976, John Scalish died, and at a meeting at Scalish's house, Rockman told me and Jack Licavoli, who is also known as Jack White, that Scalish's wishes were that Licavoli become "boss" of our family. At first, Licavoli did not want the job, but I told him to take it, as those were Scalish's wishes. Later, Licavoli made Leo Moceri his underboss and Tony DelSanter his consigliere. One day, I asked Licavoli if he had gone to New York and introduced himself to Tony Salerno as boss of the family. Licavoli said no, and that he did not know that he had to do this. I told him that it was only right, out of respect, since the Genovese family represents us, Cleveland, on the Commission. After this conversation, Licavoli went to New York to introduce himself as boss of our family.

MR. LONARDO CONTINUES: Later in 1976, Leo Moceri was murdered. Moceri had been murdered on the orders of John Nardi. I became underboss after Moceri's death. After Licavoli named me underboss, he and I traveled to New York to introduce me to Salerno as underboss of the Cleveland family. I had known Tony Salerno since the 1940s, and out of respect for him and the Genovese family, it was proper to let them know of my appointment.

Not all mob informers are sleazy hoodlums out to save their own skins. In the Oscar-winning movie *On the Waterfront*, Marlon Brando's character Terry Malloy blows the whistle on the mob influence of the docks and suffers as a result. The movie was inspired by real events.

MR. LONARDO CONTINUES: When I became underboss, Rockman told me the details of the Las Vegas casino skim operation. Rockman told me that the skim started when Allen Glick approached Frank Balistrieri about Glick's obtaining a Teamsters pension fund loan so that Glick could purchase a Las Vegas casino. Balistrieri was the boss of the Milwaukee family. Balistrieri talked to Nick Civella, boss of the Kansas City family, since he controlled Roy Williams, who was a high official with the Teamsters. Civella told Balistrieri that he would find someone in Cleveland that could talk to Bill Presser. Civella got a hold of Rockman and asked him to talk to Bill Presser about getting a pension loan for Glick. Glick told Balistrieri that in return for the pension loan, he, Glick, would give the Milwaukee, Kansas City, and Cleveland families a piece of the casinos. Rockman also told me that Glick received the Teamsters pension loan and purchased the Stardust, Fremont, and Desert Inn casinos. I do not remember about him purchasing the Desert Inn, though. "Lefty" Rosenthal ran the skim operation in Las Vegas. Kansas City would get the money from Las Vegas and cut it up between themselves, Cleveland, and Milwaukee. Rockman would travel to Kansas City or Chicago to obtain Cleveland's share. Rockman controlled the money and would cut it up with Scalish's and later Licavoli's approval. Bill Presser and Roy Williams received about $1,500 a month for their role in the skim. The Cleveland family received a total of about $40,000 a month from the skim. Later, when a dispute arose in regard to the distribution of the skim between Milwaukee and Kansas City, Chicago settled the dispute and began receiving 25 percent of the skim. Chicago settled the dispute since Milwaukee and Kansas City answer to Chicago, the same way Cleveland answers to New York. To the best of my knowledge, the skim continued until at least 1984.

Joseph Valachi's Senate hearing

Courtesy of AP/Wide World Photos

▲ New York gangster Joseph M. Valachi sits at the witness table, facing members of the Senate Investigation subcommittee as he reveals more of the inner workings of a major crime syndicate in Washington, D.C., on October 8, 1963. In the background are four charts of crime families with names and pictures of mobsters identified by Valachi. From left are, Giuseppe Magliocco family, top; Joseph Bonanno family, bottom; Carlo Gambino family; Gaetano Lucchese family; and the Vito Genovese family.

FACT

The line sometimes blurs between cop and criminal. Such was the case with stoolie Robert Cooley. He worked both sides of the fence for many years before entering the Witness Protection Program to save his hide.

MR. LONARDO CONTINUES: Since the 1920s, my family has reported to the Genovese family in New York City. We always had a very good relationship with the Genovese family, and that is why they represent us on the Commission. The Genovese family also represents the Magaddino and Pittsburgh families. There is a separate Commission in Chicago. Chicago has control of all of the Western families, including Detroit. The Chicago Commission makes and enforces the rules for those families and settles inter-family "beefs." If there was a beef or problem that included New York families with Chicago on Chicago-controlled families, that dispute would be settled by members of both commissions having a sit-down and working out the dispute.

SENATOR NUNN: Mr. Lonardo, let me interrupt you right there and ask you just one or two short questions. Is there still a Commission, to the best of your knowledge, in Chicago?

MR. LONARDO: Up to the time I was out, yes.

SENATOR NUNN: What date was that?

MR. LONARDO: Well, I knew at the time I was in Lewisburg, and that was in 1984 or 1985.

SENATOR NUNN: Up until 1984, to your knowledge there still was a Commission of organized crime operating in Chicago?

MR. LONARDO: Yes, there was.

SENATOR NUNN: I would ask you the same question about New York. Was there still a New York organized crime Commission that basically controlled activities of La Cosa Nostra as of 1984–85?

MR. LONARDO: Yes. Mr. Chairman, I have been in the Mafia most of my adult life. I have been aware of it ever since I was a child in Cleveland. It has changed since I first joined in the 1940s, especially in the last few years with the growth of narcotics. Greed is causing younger members to go into narcotics without the knowledge of the families. These younger members lack the discipline and respect that made "This Thing" as strong as it once was.

At the same time, the government has successfully convicted many members, including most of the Cleveland family. However, this does not mean that La Cosa Nostra is finished in Cleveland or elsewhere. Many of the made "members," such as Anthony Liberatore, Tommy Sinito, and others, will be released in the next few years. In addition, there are many young men who are still in Cleveland who would have been "made" if we had had the time to do so before we were incarcerated.

SENATOR NUNN: Mr. Lonardo, you have broken with La Cosa Nostra's code of silence.

MR. LONARDO: Yes.

SENATOR NUNN: You have cooperated with the federal government.

MR. LONARDO: Yes, I did.

SENATOR NUNN: Tell us why, why did you break the code of silence?

MR. LONARDO: I was convicted and got life with no parole, plus 103 years. I know I will never get out of there alive and I miss my family very, very much.

Joe Dogs

Joseph "Joe Dogs" Iannuzzi was a member of the Gambino family. He was an inveterate dog-racing enthusiast. He worked for the Florida branch of the Gambino family but was promoted to the New York headquarters in 1971. The family came to regret this decision to promote him. He functioned as muscle for Paul Castellano. He made sure all monies owed were paid in a prompt and timely manner. And he broke the legs (or worse) of those who were tardy.

He eventually became guilty of the crime for which he was a punisher. He got in over his head with gambling debts.

FACT

Mob informant Vincent Teresa dismissed much of what fellow snitch Joe Valachi said as bogus and designed to inflate Valachi's own importance. Teresa went on to write a memoir, *My Life in the Mafia*.

He went on the FBI payroll as an informant in part to square his gambling debts. He started making payments but not enough to stave off a severe beating at the hands of three goons. By the time he was released from the hospital a week later, he had vengeance on his mind.

He tapped the phones of the loan shark Tommy Argo, to whom he owed the money. He got Argo to admit to the bookie action and the beating and turned the tape over to the feds. Argo was arrested and charged with attempted murder. Given his success with this operation, the FBI used Joe Dogs to help them with a project they called Operation Home Run.

Grand Slam

Joe Dogs opened and managed a gambling parlor in Florida called the Beach Side Nightclub at the behest of his Gambino bosses in New York. His partner in the operation was John Marino, a Chicago hood. Marino was really undercover FBI agent John Bonino.

Operation Home Run was a winner. The nightclub was wired for sound and video. Bonino was so convincing he was even made a capo in the Gambino crime family. A dozen mobsters were jailed, and the case against Paul Castellano was stronger. Eventually the rats were ratted out.

Needless to say, Joe Dogs was in the doghouse. The last refuge of many a rat is the Witness Protection Program. He remained in the program until he was kicked out after agreeing to appear on the David Letterman show. They say all dogs go to heaven, but one wonders if Joe Dogs was the exception. He died in 1987.

Brotherly Hate

There was little brotherly love for Philadelphia mobster Ralph Natale. He was the first Mafia boss to turn rat while still on the job. Usually the rats were small-time operators. This violation of Omerta stunned the Mafia and precipitated the downfall of the Philadelphia crime family.

Prior to Natale turning traitor, the big boss of Philadelphia was a man named Angelo Bruno. He was nicknamed "the Docile Don," because he was more loath to use violence than any of his predecessors or contemporaries. Under his stewardship, his family made a lot of money in the revitalization of nearby Atlantic City, New Jersey.

There is more money to be made through illegal gambling than legal gambling, and the Gambino and Genovese family bosses were not satisfied with the cut they were getting from Philly. Low-level punks in the Philadelphia family were either jumping ship or getting a piece of the lucrative drug trade. Bruno was losing power and influence, and the boys in New York finally ordered his assassination. He was murdered in 1980.

Power Grab

Underlings scrambled to be the top banana in the days after the Docile Don's demise. Twenty-nine New Jersey and Philadelphia mobsters were murdered in the bloody battles, including one of Bruno's killers, Antonio "Tony Bananas" Caponigro, and the man who replaced Bruno, Phil "Chicken Man" Testa. A few more murders eventually put Ralph Natale and Joseph "Skinny Joey" Merlino in power.

Everyone knows what a snitch, a rat, and a stool pigeon are. But have you ever heard of a "beefer"? That is yet another word for informant in the Mafia's colorful and creative "slanguage."

From Cop to Capo

The Natale/Merlino reign was a shaky one. One of the flies in the olive oil was a hoodlum named Ron Previte, who had been, interestingly enough, a Philadelphia police officer for ten years before going over to the Dark Side. He was the capo of a New Jersey crew.

Previte was unhappy with the leadership of Natale and Merlino, and their dynasty was built on sand. Previte turned back from the Dark Side to the Force. In this case, the Force was the FBI. He "wore a wire," meaning a recording device on his person. Hours of damning evidence was handed over to the feds. Natale and Merlino were indicted on drug charges.

Sammy the Bull's Senate hearing

Courtesy of AP/Wide World Photos/John Duricka

▲ Former Gambino crime family underboss Salvatore "Sammy the Bull" Gravano arrives April 2, 1993, for a hearing of the Senate Permanent Investigations subcommittee on Capitol Hill. Gravano was to testify before the subcommittee, which was holding hearings on corruption in professional boxing.

Boss Rat

Feeling the heat, Ralph Natale became a federal informant and witness for the government. His former partner in crime, Merlino, and ten others were indicted, and the charges were expanded to include attempted murder and murder in the first degree. The defection of a don sent the Philadelphia Mafia into anarchy and chaos from which it will probably never recover.

The Biggest Rat of Them All

Sammy "the Bull" Gravano, the man who brought down the regime of the "Dapper Don" John Gotti was covered in detail in Chapter 12, which follows Gotti's rise and fall. Gravano's songs to the feds were the most destructive to any organized crime family. And, like Henry Hill, the life he led under his new identity was as criminal as his behavior as John Gotti's underboss. You can lead a rat into the Witness Protection Program, but you can't make him go straight. Ⓔ

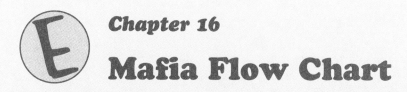

Chapter 16

Mafia Flow Chart

The Mafia has a structure and chain of command like any other corporation. There are CEOs who run things, boards to answer to, mid-level managers climbing their way up, and even accountants. In this chapter we look at the organizational structure of a typical family.

The Commission

The Commission was established by the Mustache Petes, the conservative Old World dons who were wiped out in the Castellemmarese War, which ended in 1931. The new breed of Mafioso, led by Lucky Luciano and Meyer Lansky, kept the basic structure of the Commission, also called the National Syndicate. The Commission is made up of the dons of the five big New York families and the lesser families in cities across the country.

Lucky Luciano

Courtesy of AP/Wide World Photos

◀ This is a 1946 photo of Mob Boss Charles "Lucky" Luciano taken in Naples, Italy.

The Commission was one of the most successful and long-running "corporate" entities in the history of American "business." For the most part it ran smoothly. Decisions were made and disputes were settled with a minimum of hard feelings. And when it came time to whack someone, a vote was taken. Hotheads who took it upon themselves to kill someone were often killed, especially if their target was someone outside the Mafia.

It is believed by law enforcement that the Commission is now a shadow of its former self, just as the golden age of the Mafia is long past. It lasted longer and accomplished much more than many American companies that have risen and fallen over the decades. It went into decline not because its structure was unsound but because the successive generations of Mafiosi became more ruthless and less artful in doing business. Despite the regular bursts of violence in the Mafia's bloody history, the founding fathers of the Commission were men of subtle finesse compared to those who followed.

Organization of a Mafia Family

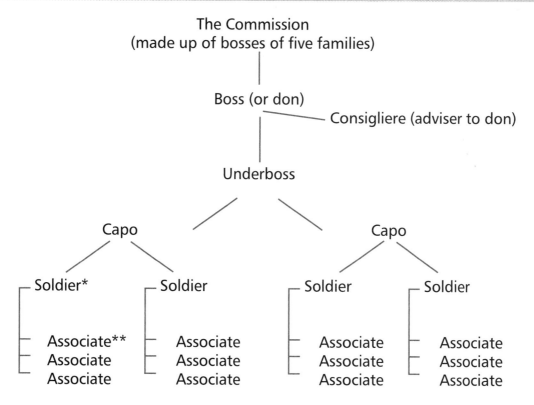

*There may be as many as ten soldiers under one capo.
**There can be any number of associates under a soldier.

The Administration

At the head of every Mafia family, there is one man who calls the shots. He is called the *boss*, the *don*, or sometimes the *godfather*. He confers with the heads of the other families in meetings of the Commission. He has usually achieved his exalted state through violent means, often through the murder of the previous occupant of the position. Directly below the boss is the aptly named *underboss*. He is the second most powerful member of the crime family. He deals with the day-to-day operations of the family and has a more hands-on approach than the don. He is also called by the Italian word *sottocapo*.

Third in this triumvirate is the *consigliere* or counselor. This person is the chief adviser to the don in all matters of policy. He is often but not always a lawyer. These three heads of the family are also called *the Administration*. Like the top officers in any legitimate corporation, these are the men who make the decisions, though in the underworld, termination has more finality than a pink slip.

Middle Management

At the lower levels of the Mafia, there is the *caporegime*. He is the equivalent of a lieutenant in the crime family. Usually called *capo* for short, he controls a crew of about ten or so underlings. Capo is also sometimes the diminutive of *capodecina*, which literally means "captain of ten." These crews commit the crimes and report the results and surrender the lion's share of the loot to the capo. He sees that it flows upward to their masters.

Below the capos are the soldiers. They are also known as *sgarrista*. These are the grunts who get their hands dirty. The crews carry out the heists, hijackings, and hits that make up the day-to-day workings of a typical Mafia family. The soldiers are all "made" men, meaning they have been indoctrinated into the family, taken the vow of Omerta, and have committed at least one murder. Lower ranking soldiers are called *piciotto*. Lower soldiers are made men, but they have to continue to work hard and prove themselves in order to get promoted to the rank of *sgarrista*.

Next down on the Mafia food chain are the *associates*. They are not made guys. They work with the crews in their various nefarious acts and are eager beavers who dream of being made. If they are not full-blooded Italians or Italian-Americans they can forget about it. As Henry Hill and Jimmy Burke of the Lucchese family were well aware, half-Irish need not apply.

As in any corporate structure, the talented rise in the ranks and the less-inspired men get stuck in middle management. Al Capone, John Gotti, and almost every other don worked his way up, usually over the bodies of his rivals.

Another name for associates who warrant special respect is *Giovane D'Honore*. These are not made men and usually non-Italians, but their contribution to the family business is appreciated. That person is also called "connected," meaning that he is tight with the family without being a member of the family.

Another key "white collar" gangster is the *contabile*, or financial consultant. This fellow does not get his hands bloody. He is the equivalent of a high-powered accountant. One thing is certain—this bean counter is sure to dot every "i" and cross every "t" and keep an accurate accounting. His masters would not tolerate accounting errors. The *chief corrupter* is the member of a crime family whose job it is to corrupt police, judges, elected officials, and others. The chief corrupter is not always in the hierarchal flow chart. The position need not be held by a made man. The requirement is someone with the means to influence the "legitimate" world.

Other Players

Other denizens of a Mafia crime family include the many "crews" that engage in all manner of mischief, including heists and hijacking. They report directly to the capo. Many of these junior league gangsters are called *cugines*. They are ambitious young hoods who desperately want to be made. Though valuable (they are more than willing to hit, whack, ice, or burn any target, since this is a prerequisite to being made), they are also regarded with a wary eye by the elder gangsters, since they may be a threat sometime down the line. They are also known as *Young Turks*.

For a look at the lowest rungs of the Mafia flow chart, check out the Al Pacino movie *Donnie Brasco*. While the *Godfather* saga concerns the CEOs, this movie shows you the blue-collar equivalent of the criminal world.

A *chairman* is consultant or adviser to the Commission, or National Syndicate. A *district man* is a crime family officer whose turf covers a small section of a city or suburban area. He is also sometimes known as an *area man*. A *field man* is a mobster-manager who supervises a group of numbers runners. A numbers runner would be an errand boy for the Mafia. He would visit regular customers, take the bets and collect the money and return it to the "office."

An *enforcer* is a tough guy who uses violence to send a message from his Mafia superiors. He is also known as a *leg breaker, head crusher, muscle*, and a *goon*. An independent is a bookie who is not a Mafioso, but pays a tribute to be allowed to stay in business. He is kind of like a franchise operation. Lowest of the low is the *empty suit*. He is a Mafioso wannabe, a hanger on who is regarded with contempt by the members of the family.

Climbing the Corporate Ladder

Unlike in legitimate businesses, men often rise in the Mafia through murderous means. Albert Anastasia killed his don to become the boss.

So did John Gotti. This is why a don can never truly be at peace. The vice president of sales may be concerned about an aggressive young salesman who is out to get his job, but it is unlikely that he will be whacked by the junior man. In the Mafia the higher you rise in the ranks the bigger the bull's-eye on your forehead.

People often run into difficulty when they hire friends and relatives. While Mafia "families" are not literal families, the don usually surrounds himself with his brothers and cousins. And when ambitious underlings resent the nepotism, the remedy is a little harsher than complaining to human resources.

On the lower rungs of the Mafia ladder, promotions can come more peacefully. A soldier can make capo without necessarily having to whack his superior; though, this being the Mafia, it does happen. Transfers of power naturally happen based on merit, but just like any other business, it is not always what you know, but who you know. A favored underling can rise within the ranks and surpass more deserving mobsters. You may have seen this in your workplace. It is a common occurrence. But at your job, giving someone a knife in the back is hopefully nothing more than a turn of phrase. In the Mafia it can be quite literal. The Mafia is "dog eat dog" taken to the extreme.

Chapter 17

Leadership Lessons of Don Corleone

Believe it or not, there are things that legitimate businesses and individuals can learn from the Mafia. No, it is not recommended to whack the CEO of a rival company as he sips cappuccino in an outdoor café. There are, however, some things we can learn from Don Corleone and his ilk.

Free Trade

In the opening scene of *The Godfather*, Bonasera the undertaker asks Don Corleone to kill the men who brutally raped his daughter. Corleone has had minimal contact with Bonasera, though Mrs. Corleone is the godmother to the victimized girl. The undertaker has avoided contact with the Mafia and tried to live in the legitimate world. When the judicial system does not give him the justice he is due, he looks to the underworld for vengeance.

Don Corleone bluntly reminds him of his hypocrisy and his brazen lack of respect. When the undertaker is sufficiently chagrined and anxious, Don Corleone agrees to have the men beaten up but not murdered, for that would be beyond justice. He also makes the potentially ominous remark, "Someday, and that day may never come, I'll call upon you to do a service for me." He eventually does call upon Bonasera to attend to the bullet-riddled remains of his oldest son, Santino.

FACT

Breaking the "glass ceiling" is a step into modern times that will likely never happen in the Mafia. There has never been a female Boss of Bosses. Of course, women play a role behind the scenes.

What can we learn from this? In business, never do something for nothing. Even pro bono work, which literally means "for the good" and is always done without compensation, is a valuable and positive public relations tool. Free trade and the barter system are some of the values that make America great. And just as Don Corleone makes the nervous Bonasera squirm a little, it is a common and not unreasonable business and personal tactic to make the other guy squirm a little, especially when he comes to you with an outrageous proposition.

Tit for Tat

Also, it is not prudent to overextend yourself. Do not do more than is necessary or put your business or reputation on the line. Bonasera asks Don Corleone to commit murder as a response to a beating. This is not "tit for tat," and could rebound against Corleone if ever discovered. "That is not justice. Your daughter is still alive," he tells Bonasera. When doing business or bartering, do not offer more than the other person is offering. You will lose out on the deal and may be regarded as a soft touch as well. Harsh as it sounds, an affable person who is always eager to accommodate will invariably come to be disrespected and ill-used. This applies to business dealings only. In matters of friendship, family, and affairs of the heart, generosity is to be encouraged. What you put forth in the way of positive emotions is returned many-fold.

Due Diligence

It is extremely important in business to check out possible leads, potential business mergers, and other dealings when your finances and reputation are at risk. The process for vetting such matters is called "due diligence." Learn all you can about your "opponent." Check the company out in Standard & Poor's. Make a few phone calls. Ask around. Rely on the network of contacts you have built over the years. Take nothing on faith. President Ronald Reagan turned the Russians' words against them when he used their phrase, "Trust, but verify," vis-à-vis the arms race. In business, it is a wise course to initially distrust and always verify.

Even in personal affairs, it is good to learn as much as you can. This is not to say you should hire a private detective to follow your significant other. But the more information you have at your disposal, the better.

The Mafia is big on rituals, but the rituals vary. The Sicilian Mafia and its American offshoot prefer medieval-like trappings and ceremony. The Mafiosi whose traditions originated in Naples, Italy, are informal by comparison.

Don Corleone does this when he sends the hulking Luca Brasi to visit Bruno Tattaglia. The Tattaglia family, with the help of Virgil Sollozzo, is going to start a drug dealing empire in America. Don Corleone declined to participate because he objected to the unsavory practice of drug pushing. Ever the pragmatist, he also knew that his friends in high places, the politicians, judges, and policemen on his payroll, might not remain in his corner if they knew he was dealing in drugs. He also suspects that the rival family is planning his murder.

Ancient Chinese Secrets

Don Corleone sends Brasi into the lion's den of the rival family as a pretend turncoat. This is a shrewd strategy straight out of Sun Tzu's ancient text *The Art of War*. This seminal work of military tactics is employed by businesspeople in today's cutthroat corporate milieu. Don Corleone has the right idea, but not every plan works out perfectly.

The enemy is on to Corleone and the unfortunate Luca Brasi ends up garroted and "sleeping with the fishes." Michael Corleone has his illegitimate nephew Vincent Mancini do the same thing in *Godfather III* with more successful results.

It is wise to understand one's enemy or rival and learn all about them in any way you can. In this information age, there are many resources to gather data.

Mum's the Word

A small-time pet shop owner with more ego than common sense announced to all the salesmen who came into his store that he was out to destroy the competitor who opened shop down the block. The competing store was part of a large superstore chain. The superstore manager got wind of the small time operator's claim and used the muscle of the corporate giant behind him to run more advertising and temporarily reduce prices to below cost until the little shop was run out of business.

This is what happens when you shoot your mouth off with not much to back it up. The old phrase used repeatedly during World War II, "Loose lips sink ships," is a universal truth. It is something the Mafia knows all too well.

During a conference with the menacing Virgil Sollozzo, Santino "Sonny" Corleone blurts something out and is shot an angry glance by his father. Don Corleone later admonishes him to "never let anyone outside the family know what you're thinking." Michael Corleone plays out the same scene with nephew Vincent Mancini in the third and final installment of the trilogy.

Your boss may welcome a free and open exchange of ideas and opinions in the boardroom. At a Mafia meeting, there is no "running it up the flagpole to see if anyone salutes." You follow orders—or else.

In the business world, this Mafia philosophy is the best policy. Corporate America is a kind of Mafia-lite. There is very little murder and mayhem, luckily, but as far as ruthlessness goes, today's corporate milieu is not a pretty place.

We no longer live in a world where people stay in the same company for a lifetime. And age and time in the firm have become almost meaningless. In fact they are a liability. You have to look out for yourself and protect yourself. And the best way to do that is to follow Don Corleone's advice.

Do not tell anyone what you are thinking regarding your personal feelings about the office goings-on. Never tip your hand. Water cooler gossips are noticed. Blowhards by the vending machines are heard. The walls have ears, and Big Brother CEO is watching you. Speak your mind in a reasoned and calm manner in your supervisor's office with the door closed, by all means. But be fully prepared to back up your case. Remain calm and try not to be bitter. Michael Corleone tells his nephew Vincent, "Never hate your enemy. It clouds your judgment." The same can be applied in manager-worker relations.

And always remember one of the most famous lines from *The Godfather*, a Mafia rationalization in fiction and in reality. When the man you thought was your pal because you are on the company bowling team together calls you into his office to terminate you, he might say, to ease his conscience, "It's not personal. It's business." Corporate America has its version of the "kiss of death."

1-800-MATTRESS

When competing Mafia families go to war for a long and protracted battle, they call it "going to the mattresses." This means that the battle will be a lengthy one. The mobsters assemble in a secret location and live like infantrymen in a barracks. This is where most of them will stay until the gunsmoke clears. In this makeshift barracks, mattresses are thrown on the floor. They crash on these after a hard day of gunplay.

FACT

There is no "pillow talk" about family business between couples in the Mafia. Wives are kept in the dark about the nature of their husband's business activities, and they probably would rather not know what hubby is doing at the office.

"Going to the mattresses" has entered the vernacular. Tom Hanks types it to Meg Ryan during an Instant Message pep talk in the movie *You've Got Mail*. It is a phrase meaning to persevere, to hang in there, and not to give up and quit. When the going gets tough, the tough get going.

The Business of America Is Business

The Mafia is the dark side of the American Dream. It is the distasteful underbelly of the capitalist, free market economy. Crime families have not fared well under dictatorships. Fascist dictator Benito Mussolini waged war against the Sicilian Mafia, and a dastardly Russian Mafia emerged after the fall of the Soviet Union. This is not to say that the dictatorships are on the right track. Everyone suffers under a totalitarian regime. Freedom is a memory, and dissenters are dispatched with cruel finality.

The Mafia knows quite well that it is a mirror image of its more legitimate counterparts with offices in the steel and glass high rises of America's urban centers. Meyer Lansky once said that the Mafia was bigger than U.S. Steel. They ironically called themselves the "captains of industry" during the mob's halcyon heyday.

When Don Corleone calls a meeting of the fictionalized version of the Commission in *The Godfather*, he is taken to task by the other dons for not sharing the numerous judges and politicians and corrupt police officials on his payroll. Another Mafia chieftain, Don Barzini, says Corleone is not being a pal by sharing, adding that, "Certainly he can present a bill for such services. After all, we are not communists." This gets a big laugh from the Commission.

In this respect, the Mafia is on the right track. The great Winston Churchill said it best when he remarked, "The inherent vice of capitalism is the unequal sharing of blessings; the inherent vice of socialism is the equal sharing of miseries." Yes, it is a flawed and imperfect system, and there are the haves and have-nots, but that is true of the socialist and communist regimes that have risen and fallen and remain in place in the world.

The Mafia was kicked out of Cuba after Fidel Castro's revolution in 1959. The reign of the dictator Batista and his henchmen was corrupt and the people suffered. But the peasant's lot did not improve under Fidel Castro. It remains an oppressive dictatorship, not a proletariat's paradise.

Always Have an Escape Route

Before you enter any business dealings, it is wise to always have a plan to back out of the situation gracefully and with minimal fallout should the plans go awry. The Mafia is adept at slithering away from a situation when the heat is on.

When young Michael Corleone decides to assassinate Virgil Sollozzo and corrupt New York City Police Captain McCluskey, the Mafia plans the hit down to the last detail, including the escape route. In all the successful mob hits in real life, the perpetrators get away scot-free. Some were fingered later by informants, but if not for the squealing rats, the careful planning and attention to detail were the decisive factors in a successful hit.

There is something we can learn about the Mafia's thoroughness in such matters. Michael Corleone always had a back door exit, or he relied on the people around him to have the initiative and wherewithal to provide one on the spot. When he found himself in Batista's Cuba as Castro's revolutionaries stormed Havana, Corleone escaped. When Joe

Zaza attempted to wipe out the entire Commission via a helicopter strike on their Atlantic City meeting place, it was his nephew Vincent who improvised a solution by blasting open a locked door and hot-wiring a limousine.

Personal Code

The real-life Mafia goes on and on about honor and codes of ethics but exhibits precious little of it in their daily affairs. It has been suggested by many, including Mafia experts and veteran crime reporters, that the *Godfather* movies are a romantic and unrealistic portrayal of the Mafia. There is something likable about the Corleones that is not very prevalent in the genuine article.

Even though that is most certainly the case, there is something to be learned from the fictional Corleones. If you eliminate the fact that they do occasionally kill people, there are codes of conduct lived by Don Vito Corleone and his son Michael that we can adapt to our lives.

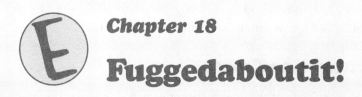

Chapter 18

Fuggedaboutit!

The Mafia has its own unique "slan-guage." Some words might be easy to catch on to, like using *whack* to mean killing someone. There's a whole host of terms that the mobsters use to talk about their illegal activities that won't appear in any dictionary.

Linguistic Legerdemain

Why would a close-knit and insular organization also develop a language all its own, full of unique and colorful turns of phrase to describe brutal and barbaric actions? There are several reasons. Since what they do for a living is almost always illegal, the Mafia began to employ euphemisms to describe their ruthless activities. If they were in mixed company the outside would not know what they were talking about.

Warm and Fuzzy Hoodlums?

Perhaps members of the Mafia sometimes feel guilt or pangs of conscience about their unsavory lifestyle. They are known to be the masters of rationalizations and have the ability to put "spins" on their doings and dealings that rival any elected official. Maybe the clever language can psychologically blunt the harsh reality of their misdeeds.

Funny Fellas

Another reason may be that the Mafiosi are a lot funnier than we give them credit. It is a sociocultural fact that cultures that have known oppression and hardship over the millennia, e.g. the Irish and the Jewish people, have a keenly developed and unique sense of humor. Certainly their American progeny do not suffer the atrocities that the Irish endured at the hands of the English for a thousand years and the Jews endured from just about everyone since before the Old Testament was chiseled in stone, but the residual sense of humor remains. It is full of irony and "gallows humor." Humor in the face of tragedy is the centerpiece of their wit.

The Mafia has a similar sense of humor but from the opposite perspective. They are the ones committing the crimes and inflicting the pain. They are the ones breaking the bones, corrupting the souls, and putting the bodies in "cement shoes." And they describe their evil antics with whimsical and even witty mordant irony, like smiling demons. People are often drawn to a flamboyant and unrepentant villain if he has a certain charm and finesse. Anthony Hopkins's Hannibal Lecter and Jack Nicholson's Joker in *Batman* and the Devil in *The Witches of Eastwick* are good examples.

FACT

The Italian and Italian-American Mafia are not the only organized crime outfits that have a vernacular all their own. The language of the underworld is used to keep outsiders ignorant of the clandestine and devious doings.

Thus the Mafia is often romanticized because of its portrayal in the movies and television. It is undeserved. The screenwriters who write about the Mafia have more wit than the street thug. And the quipping gangsters who helped develop "Mobspeak" as it is sometimes called are the minority. For the most part Mafiosi are as inarticulate as they are murderous.

How Can I Kill Thee . . .

There are many ways to kill a person in the Mafia handbook. And even more ways to describe it. Nowadays, with the numerous Mafia movies and the television hit *The Sopranos*, the secret is out. The general populace and the FBI wiretappers are not fooled by these once-cryptic code words and phrases.

As we know, the Mafia uses murder as the ultimate hostile takeover. It is a part of their business plan. It is part of the unwritten mission statement. But the Mafia does not kill with random bloodlust. The men in the Mafia who have done that have themselves been killed because of the problems their chaotic behavior caused. The Mafia practices due diligence before the headmasters give the order to kill an enemy. And when a person is killed it is usually done dispassionately, unless the target has done something particularly annoying to the dons.

A victim can be whacked, hit, iced, clipped, offed, burned, rubbed out, or popped. The hit man can *break an egg* or give his quarry a *serious headache*. They could be fitted with *cement shoes*, a *cement jacket*, or put in a *cement coffin*. This type of murder is specifically for burials at sea, when the body, sometimes alive and sometimes not, is weighted for deposit in the deep blue, where the incriminating evidence will never be found. Such a victim is said to be *sleeping with the fishes*.

A contract is put out on the target of a hit. This makes them *marked* for death. Another way to say it is to *put the X on* someone, as in *X marks the spot.* A more intimate way to order a hit is to publicly give the person the *kiss of death.* This means that his days are numbered. That person is now a *goner.* He is soon to be *put to sleep.*

ALERT!

If a Russian Mafioso goes into a politician's office and offers him *silver or lead*, the bureaucrat is likely to opt for the silver. This is a slang expression that offers the man the choice of a bribe or a bullet in the head.

The hit man may have already been told to *get a place ready*, meaning to find a good location to dispose of the body. That means he is *going*, as in "going, going, gone." The victim will then be *taken for a ride.* Or perhaps go out for an *airing.*

Maybe he will get *five times .38*, which is five bullets in the head with a .38 caliber revolver, or maybe be on the receiving end of a *Little Joe* if he failed to pay a gambling debt. A Little Joe is four shots in the head in two rows of two bullet holes. Neatness counts. He could also receive the *Italian rope trick.* That is strangulation. Or maybe a *Sicilian necktie*, which means being garroted with piano wire. On very rare occasions, the person may be given *a pass*, meaning his life has been spared on the mercurial whim of the don.

An *ice pick kill* means what it sounds like—an ice pick though the ear and into the brain. One thing you never want to hear a Mafioso say is the word *buckwheats.* He is not referring to the beloved tyke from the *Little Rascals* and *Our Gang* comedies. It is a slang expression for an especially grisly murder when the victim is mutilated and tortured for an extended period of time before being put out of his misery.

Native Tongue

One of the common ways that an ethnic group keeps outsiders from hearing their secret plans is to speak in its native language. Most of the new immigrants to America in the late nineteenth and early twentieth centuries spoke a language other than English. Most learned English with a desire to assimilate, but the native language was still spoken at home. The children of the immigrants were often bilingual, but their native tongues often faded from use in favor of the English language.

The native language could and was often spoken as a code to prevent others from understanding what they were saying. The Mafia employed this course of action, and many of the Italian expressions continued to be used by subsequent generations. There is something more musical about a "romance language" (Italian, French, and Spanish) than the "Anglo Saxon" English language.

Insults, Italian Style

If you do not like the looks of someone, you can say *Che bruta*, which means "How ugly you are." A similar slur is *Facia bruta*, which can literally mean "an ugly face" or simply be used as a generic insult. However, it would be unwise to say this to anyone in the Mafia. If someone is a motor mouth they could be called a *chiacchierone* or chatterbox. *Gira diment* means "going crazy," and *pazzo* or *oobatz: u'pazzu* means that you believe the person you are addressing is already crazy.

Mafiocracy is a slang word to describe the current state of affairs in Russia. When communism collapsed, the criminal element filled the void before true democracy could get a foothold.

A *Mortadella* is a loser. So is a *cafone*, also spelled and pronounced *gavone*. *Va fa napole* literally means "Go to Naples" but it is meant to say "Go to hell."

More Turns of Phrase

Most Mafiosi have a mistress on the side, even though they consider themselves to be fine husbands and fathers. A girlfriend is called a *comare*, while a male buddy is called his *compare* or *goombah*. Italian phrases that are substituted for the Mafia include *La Cosa Nostra*, which is translated as "our thing" or "this thing of ours," and *fratellanza* which means "brotherhood."

Capo di tutti Capi is much more lyrical than "Boss of Bosses," but they mean the same thing. An *amico* is a friend of the family who is not a member of the crime family, and an *amico nostro* is a way to introduce a stranger who is also a member of a Mafia family.

Omerta is the Mafia's vow of silence. Once a mobster is "made," meaning he is inducted into a family, he takes this vow. Violating Omerta is a death sentence. Another prerequisite for being made is that the inductee is a full-blooded Italian or Italian-American.

Pleasantries

On a lighter note, other expressions used by the Mafia do not imply malice or menace. *Piacere* is a greeting that means it is a pleasure to meet you. *Che peccato* is an expression of sympathy meaning "What a pity," and *Buon' anima* is a condolence and meditation on mortality that translates as "Rest his soul." And the Mediterranean mouthful *Col tempo la foglia di gelso diventa seta*, is an old Italian proverb that is rendered in English as "Time and patience change the mulberry leaf to satin," meaning that patience pays off in the long run with great rewards.

FACT

The Russian Mafia calls a front company that launders money and serves as a front for illegal activities a *panama*. This is probably derived from the common practice of using offshore, often Latin American, front companies by both legitimate and illegitimate organizations.

Business Language

The Mafia does business in a similar fashion to any multinational corporation, murder and mayhem notwithstanding. It has executive officers, middle management types, and drone-like workers. It also has a singular slang for its practices.

You may not think of the Mafia as a staunch proponent of "the American way." But the Mafia would not have thrived in anything other than a free market capitalist system.

In Mafia lingo, the *American Way* is not a patriotic slogan or part of Superman's super-mandate of fighting for "truth, justice, and the American way." It is the Mafia's phrase for the peaceful coexistence of rival crime families. A *big earner* is the Mafia's equivalent of Salesman of the Year. He is a member of a crime family whose activities made a lot of money for the team. It is not known whether he gets a gold watch on his twenty-fifth anniversary with the family.

ALERT!

In an example of linguistic détente, the Russian Mafia slang expression for a hired killer is the same as one of the many used by the American Mafia. They call a hit man a *torpedo*.

The Mafia's accounting practices are a little different than those of a legitimate corporation. Rarely if ever has the Mafia been successfully prosecuted by a paper trail. Yet the Mafia has a term called *the books*. It is an example of Mafia irony.

An early name for the Commission was *Captains of Industry*. Perhaps this is an ironic term, comparing themselves with the Carnegies, Vanderbilts, and other legitimate businessmen whom the Mafia believed to be, in their own way, as ruthless and corrupt as themselves.

Drugs and Alcohol

Of course much of the Mafia's business in its earlier days involved bootleg whiskey. In later years the Mafia dealt in drug trafficking. *Alkali* was a word for alcohol. *Alky racket* was slang for Prohibition, and an *alky cooker* was what they called a still, a device used for distilling alcohol. The *B-and-A racket* stood for beer and alcohol, another expression for Prohibition. When Prohibition became law, all distilleries and breweries became illegal, but gangsters as well as the thirsty private citizens decided that the party was not going to end because of some lawmakers in Washington, D.C.

Bootlegging seems innocent in comparison to the drug trade. *Babania* is a word for the drug traffic, especially heroin. It was forbidden for many years, but eventually the old dons looked the other way because of the big profits made in the narcotics business.

The *Bangkok Connection* refers to the drugs that wind their way from Southeast Asia to American shores for distribution at great profit by the Mafia.

Gambling

The Mafia also made a lot of money in the world of illegal gambling. *Action* covers the illegal gambling business. A *bookmaker* or *bookie* is the guy who takes illegal bets on horse racing and other sporting events. The *numbers racket* was the illegal precursor to state lotteries. A number was chosen at random and itinerant gamblers tried to divine the result. You had to be in it to win it. The gangster in charge is called a *numbers operator*. His assistant who takes the bets for the citizenry is called a *numbers runner*. And below the numbers runner is a low-level hood called a *drop man*. The percentage that the numbers operator and other Mafiosi have to pay to their bosses is called *giveup* or *tribute*.

Money Talk

The Mafia also has a unique language to describe money. A *nickel* is $500. Logically it follows that a *dime* is $1,000. Sometimes a *dollar* is also $1,000. So is the word *large*, as in "five large" being $5,000.

Frankenslang

A subset of "Mobspeak" is "Frankenslang." This is the phraseology developed by Frank Sinatra's "Rat Pack," a group of entertainers who were not Mafiosi per se, but who certainly moved on the fringes of that world. Any performer who worked in Las Vegas had to rub elbows with the mob. It was inevitable. The Mafia owned the place. The "Rat Pack" worked for the Mafia and were friends with many Mafiosi. They attended the same parties and shared the same girlfriends. There was plenty of crossover between Mafia lingo and the hipster patois of the Rat Pack. While not politically correct, there is a charm in the Rat Pack's idiom. In the 1950s and early 1960s the Rat Pack patter was the epitome of cool. By the end of the 1960s it was considered totally square. What once was hip now seems quaint.

FACT

Unlike the American Mafia, each Yakuza clan of the Japanese mafia has its own unique slang. A capo in the Bonanno family can understand a member of the Gambino crime family, but in Japan the clans often have a deeply secret slang that no one else can comprehend.

Here's to the Ladies

The Rat Pack made many slang expressions for members of the opposite sex. They are interesting as curiosities from a bygone era, but male readers of this book should proceed with caution before referring to your significant other by any of these antiquated terms of endearment.

Some of the complimentary terms for a woman that a Rat Pack hipster would like to get to know better are *barn burner*, meaning a very attractive woman. A petite woman was called a *mouse*, and a *beetle* referred to a well-dressed woman. *Broad* and *chick* were not insults but expressions of affection. So was *gasser*. *Dame* was not affectionate; in Rat Pack slang *dame* was not a compliment. A woman who liked to dance was called a *twist* or a *twirl* and a girl who appeared to be ready and willing for a little *hey-hey* (romance) was called a *tomato* in that she was ripe for the picking.

Likes and Dislikes

The Rat Pack was an opinionated clan. They considered themselves *big leaguers* and did not suffer *clydes* gladly. They were not good on names, so they would be likely to call you *Charlie* or *Sam*. They might greet you with *How's your bird?* This was an inquiry into the health and well being of your pelvic region. They had no time for *creeps, crumbs, bums, bunters, finks, punks,* or *Harveys*. If they said, *Let's lose Charlie*, it meant that they found your company not particularly stimulating. Similarly, if Frank told Dean that they were in *Dullsville, Ohio*, it meant that he was bored and wanted to *Scramsville*. Also if Sammy told Peter Lawford that it was raining and it was not, that was another code for wanting to split the scene. *Cash me out* also meant a desire to leave that particular *clam bake*. And if another of them blurted out *Hello!* to no one in particular, it meant he had just noticed an attractive woman.

Much of the Yakuza's elaborate slanguage contains naughty words and scatological phrases that are not fit to print here. And just as the Yakuza adopted a dress code straight out of Hollywood gangster movies, they borrowed some English words in a linguistic hybrid called "Japlish."

Certain Rat Pack expressions entered the vernacular and mean the same things today as they did in the swinging '60s. *Cool*, to *dig* something, a *gofer*, a *loser*, a *square*, and a *player* all are used today.

Chapter 19

The Mafia on Television

The two most famous mob shows on television are classic TV's *The Untouchables* and HBO's current hit *The Sopranos*. Both shows were and are controversial and also ratings blockbusters. They have been accused of defaming the reputation of Italian-Americans, yet are enormously popular with Americans of all ethnicities.

A 1950s Hit

Eliot Ness was the stalwart young federal agent when he was assigned to the Chicago office and began his campaign against Al Capone. He and his elite corps were called "untouchable" because they were unable to be bribed. This set them apart from many of their brother officers at the federal level and on the Chicago police force.

Ness got Capone on tax evasion charges, despite his many more malevolent transgressions. J. Edgar Hoover was intensely jealous of Ness's successes and did his best to thwart his upward mobility. Ness wrote his memoirs in the 1950s and died shortly thereafter, bitter and in obscurity. He did not live to see his autobiography become the source material for one of the most successful television shows in the new medium's history.

Robert Stack played Eliot Ness in *The Untouchables* TV series, which first aired in October 1959. The show ran until September 1963. After the 1987 movie was a big hit, Stack starred in the TV movie *The Return of Eliot Ness*. This was a purely fictional outing, and Stack was a little long in the tooth to play Ness, who died in his middle fifties.

Achieving Infamy!

The Untouchables was a violent program, a Tommy gun shoot-'em-up on the mean streets of 1930s Chicago. By today's standards it is rather tame, but it shocked many viewers in its initial network run. CBS received many protests from parents who were concerned about the impact the show would have on their children.

Most of the protests, however, came from Italian-American groups. The old Cagney and Bogart films rarely used Italian surnames for their characters, but *The Untouchables* made no secret of the ethnicity of its villains. Capone and his cronies were mentioned by name, and many felt this was an ethnic slur. In fact, the producers were sued by, among other people, Al Capone's widow!

You Got Some "Splainin" to Do

Desilu Productions, a company run by two classic TV icons, Lucille

Ball and Desi Arnaz, produced *The Untouchables*. At one point Desi received death threats and was obliged to travel with bodyguards. The ever-volatile Francis Albert Sinatra even accosted Arnaz in a Hollywood restaurant and chided him for his involvement in such a scandalous show. Desi, who often told Lucy she had some "splaining" to do, was now on the receiving end from Old Blue Eyes.

Eventually, some compromises were made. Once the series had exhausted the many historical figures in the Chicago mob, they decided to give the fictional villains non-Italian sounding surnames. And the actor who played "Nick Rossi," one of Ness's team, got more lines as a result. This was to highlight an Italian-American good guy on the show.

Eliot Ness's memorial service

Courtesy of AP/Wide World Photos/Tony Dejak

▲ Rebecca McFarland, vice president of the Cleveland Police Historical Society, second from left, watches as Cleveland Policeman Michael Doyle carries the ashes of former Cleveland Safety Director Eliot Ness, his wife Elisabeth, and their adopted son, Robert, at a memorial service on September 10, 1997 at Lake View Cemetery in Cleveland. The cremated ashes were later dispersed in a cemetery lagoon 40 years after the crimefighter, immortalized in the fictionalized *Untouchables* series, died at age 54.

FACT

Robert Stack, now so associated with the role of Eliot Ness, was actually a last-minute replacement for actor Van Johnson, who bowed out at the eleventh hour. Stack went on to make television history, imbuing Ness with a stoic manner and clipped speech patterns that were affectionately parodied by everyone from Leslie Nielsen to Dan Aykroyd.

Money Talks

The mob was not pleased with their depiction in *The Untouchables*. Rather than resort to the old horse's head in the bed trick, they hit the producers where it really hurts—in the wallet. (In the book and movie *The Godfather*, Don Corleone kills a movie producer's prize racehorse and leaves the head in his bed in order to intimidate him into giving someone a part in a movie.)

One of the sponsors of the show was L&M cigarettes, back in the days when tobacco advertising was allowed on TV. Many stars of the day puffed away as paid spokespeople. Mobster "Tough Tony" Anastasia threatened to use his clout with the unions to see that millions of cartons of L&M cigarettes would sit on the loading docks, unpacked by the longshoremen and undelivered by the truckers. L&M dropped its sponsorship of the show in short order, costing the network and all those concerned a lot of money.

Not every hood was indignant about *The Untouchables*, however. As in any other corporate hierarchy, the CEOs resented the bad publicity, but many of the rank and file were delighted. Many a low-level enforcer became wannabe screenwriters and actors. They contacted the producers with story ideas and suggestions that they would be "naturals" to play Ness's latest nemesis.

Staccato Delivery

The machine guns were not the only things with a rat-a-tat-tat delivery on *The Untouchables*. The show was narrated by the notorious newspaper and radio personality Walter Winchell, whose delivery was as rapid-fire as the Tommy guns in the garage on St. Valentine's Day. A slower yet nevertheless measured staccato was intoned by TV's Eliot Ness, Robert Stack. The two-part pilot revolved around Ness's pursuit of Al Capone. The earlier episodes were done in documentary style, and the gangsters Ness battled were based on real people, hence the controversy and the lawsuits. When real-life crime figures were exhausted, Ness took on fictionalized hoods and some real hoods the real Ness never encountered, such as the malevolent matriarch Ma Barker. Though the real Untouchables were long gone by World War II, the fictional Ness was still operating in Chicago in the 1940s and matching wits with Nazi saboteurs. *The Untouchables* ran for four seasons and has been in reruns ever since. It even inspired a movie version in 1987 (see Chapter 20).

A 1993 television version of *The Untouchables* that emulated the look and feel of the 1987 movie lasted only one season. Capone's bribes and bullets could not touch Ness and company, but they were done in by bad ratings.

Hitting the High Notes

The Untouchables of today is undoubtedly the HBO mega-hit *The Sopranos*. It is equally popular and as controversial as its 1950s predecessor. It takes the mob mythos into the modern era and adds new riffs and spins to old themes.

The Sopranos chronicles the life of Tony Soprano, a Mafia don beset by modern problems Al Capone and Lucky Luciano did not have to deal with. The story provides a sly counterpoint between the ordinary and the violent. Soprano, who lives in the dangerous underworld, goes home to the pedestrian problems that beset any American family.

He has marital problems. He has strained relationships with his kids. And he sees a psychiatrist. Yet when he goes to the office, his daily workload most often involves criminal conduct and occasionally murder.

This is what separates him from the other family men living in suburban New Jersey.

Its lead actors, James Gandolfini and Edie Falco, have won multiple Emmy Awards, and it is a favorite with the critics. Many people have subscribed to cable television specifically to see the antics of this dysfunctional Mafia family. The seasons are gradually being released on video and DVD as well.

They say a person cannot serve two masters and be faithful to both, but a man can apparently have two bosses. Steven Van Zandt, who plays Silvio Dante, works for mob boss Tony Soprano and plays guitar with "The Boss" Bruce Springsteen in the E Street Band.

One typical *Sopranos* episode that conveys all the elements that are designed to make it hip and edgy involve Tony Soprano's weekend in New England escorting his teenage daughter to exclusive and ritzy colleges for their open houses. While casing out the groves of academe he chances to spy a man he recognizes as an informant who squealed on the Mafia and entered the Witness Protection Program. He vanished without a trace into a new identity, and it is only by coincidence that Tony Soprano sees him. While keeping an eye on his daughter, conferring with a low-level hood back home, and talking to his wife, he stalks the rat and eventually murders him.

Meanwhile, back in New Jersey, his frustrated wife invites a cute young Catholic priest over for dinner and they watch a movie and experience some unconsummated sexual tension. The family man with everyday family problems and business problems is a common figure in television drama. Mob shows usually emphasize the criminal lives of their characters. This juxtaposition of the two worlds appeals to the millions of Sopranos fans.

Mafia for the New Millennium

The Sopranos is a new Mafia for the New Age. The old Warner Brothers gangster movies presented an image of hoodlums that suited the allegedly simpler times. Perhaps the times were not so simple in real life, but the movies portrayed them as such, and a conversation with your grandparents is likely to have them waxing nostalgic about the "good old days."

The Untouchables television show continued that classic tradition with archetypal good guys and bad guys. Often there was more complexity given to the gangsters, but basically things were black and white with the occasional shades of gray.

FACT

The Internet is rife with *Sopranos*-related sites, from the official site to numerous unofficial domains and many shrines to the stars of the HBO megahit and message boards for people desperately seeking fellow *Soprano*-philes.

The *Godfather* movies offered more blurring of the black and white with a great deal more subtlety than the old gangster movies. The Corleones did terrible things, but in a way we could identify with. Anyone with a family could see familiar aspects and elements in the trials and tribulations of the Corleone family. And their scope was operatic and Shakespearean—bigger than life.

In *The Sopranos* we do not see bigger than life. We see a representation of a Mafia in decline that mirrors the culture as a whole on the decline. Tony Soprano laments the loss of the "good old days" of the Mafia. He presides over a Mafia family whose glory days are long gone and are never going to return.

There is much culture shock comedy as old mobsters have difficulty adapting to the changing world. One aging Mafioso laments that the mob did not get in on the Starbucks bandwagon, because that is where the real money is these days. Tony Soprano reads self-help books to deal with his many problems. We see a Mafioso picking up tips, tools, and techniques from current trends like pop psychology and applying them to the often grisly business of the Mafia.

Hero Worship

The Sopranos constantly refers to the Mafia epic of all time, *The Godfather*. In a humorous recurring theme, all the members of the Soprano crime family grew up on the *Godfather* movies and regularly quote them. The fictional Corleones are the gods and goddesses on Mount Olympus for these less epic, less empathetic, and less inspired hoodlums.

One area where the Sopranos differ from the Corleones is in the desire for legitimacy. While the Corleones suffered great angst over their lifestyle and career choices, and always claimed that they sought to emerge from the shadows and into the light of respectability, no such beliefs are expressed by Tony Soprano. He likes his job, and probably would not mind seeing his son go into the "family business." Don Corleone wept when he learned that his son Michael killed two men and thus entered the Mafia life. Tony Soprano does not sweat such things.

ALERT!

The Sopranos has generated much ancillary merchandise, including the books *The Psychology of the Sopranos* and *The Sopranos Family Cookbook*. With these you can figure out why you are fascinated by these criminals while enjoying the vicarious culinary thrill of sharing their gastronomic delectables.

Just as *The Untouchables* made many people angry, *The Sopranos* is no stranger to controversy. Italian-American groups have complained that it presents negative stereotypes. One New Jersey congressman wanted to pass legislation to have it banned. There was concern that it would create controversy when it first aired on Italian television, but it was a ratings hit in the birthplace of the Mafia.

The Sopranos is an enormous hit that is one of cable television's "water cooler" shows. You can be guaranteed that the day after a show airs, there will be much chatter at the workplace as people discuss the previous night's show with each other.

Chapter 20

The Mafia in the Movies

Gangsters have been boffo box office in the movies since the Golden Age of Hollywood. From *Public Enemy* and *Little Caesar* to the *Godfather* films and beyond, the criminal element has been portrayed as misunderstood Robin Hoods, tragedians of Shakespearean scope, lovable goombahs, and as nasty and ruthless killers that continue to fascinate us.

When Stars Shone Brightly

From the 1930s and '40s, Warner Brothers produced classic gangster movies starring the likes of James Cagney, Humphrey Bogart, and Edward G. Robinson. These films and their antiheroes differ dramatically from the more realistic cinematic portrayals of gangsters in later years. Rarely were the mobsters overtly identified as being of Italian ancestry. James Cagney had the map of Ireland on his pugnacious puss. Bogart and Robinson were not particularly "ethnic." George Raft, lesser known to modern audiences, was a big star of the day and of Italian ancestry. He was also a good friend of Bugsy Siegel. Siegel visited Raft on movie sets and Raft even helped arrange a screen test for the handsome gangster.

Robin in the 'Hood

James Cagney usually played a basically good guy who grew up on the mean streets and inadvertently stumbled into a life of crime. These films were made during the Great Depression and thus it was often the lack of opportunity for the immigrant underclass to break out of their station that led the prototypical Cagney hero to a life of crime.

The gangster was not a total victim, however. Most movies had a character, usually the hero's friend or brother, who chose the straight and narrow and did not fall into a life of crime. In *Public Enemy*, it is Cagney's brother who remains crime-free. In *Angels With Dirty Faces*, it's Cagney's boyhood friend who becomes a Catholic priest while Cagney's character becomes a hoodlum.

FACT

Despite the repetition by impressionists for decades, James Cagney never actually said, "You dirty rat," in a movie. Similarly, Humphrey Bogart never said "Play it again, Sam," in the movie *Casablanca*. He said something similar, but not that now-famous misquote.

The Cagney persona was guilty of romanticizing the urban outlaw, making him into a kind of metropolitan Robin Hood. In *White Heat*, a film that Freudians surely love, Cagney broke his own mold with a powerful and unsympathetic performance as Cody Jarrett, a psychotic killer with an Oedipus complex. Cold blooded yet perversely pathetic, he is a murderous mama's boy who yells "Made it, ma! Top of the world," before blowing himself sky-high rather than be taken alive.

From *Public Enemy* to *White Heat*, and beyond (he played yet another gangster opposite Doris Day in the musical drama *Love Me or Leave Me*), James Cagney was one of the screen's first and greatest gangsters.

Play It Again, Bogie

The other legendary screen gangster of the Golden Age was Humphrey Bogart. He started out playing secondary villains but eventually became an A-list star and often played the good guy, particularly later in his distinguished career.

Bogart achieved stardom with the part of the vicious gangster in *The Petrified Forest*. It has the now-familiar theme of a group of gangsters holding a collection of characters from "central casting" hostage. Almost twenty years later, Bogart played a suspiciously similar role in the movie *Desperate Hours*. In between he played a variety of good and bad guys. His most famous gangster roles were opposite Cagney in *The Roaring Twenties, Angels With Dirty Faces,* and his very moving portrait of an aging and tired gangster on the run in *High Sierra*.

End of an Era

Bogart teamed with another famous gangster icon, Edward G. Robinson, in John Huston's classic *Key Largo*. Again a group of gangsters hide out and harass the locals, this time in the Florida Keys as a hurricane looms offshore. This time, however, Bogart is the hero and shoots it out with Robinson's evil and froglike hood, Rocco. This film, along with Cagney's *White Heat*, were elegiac swan songs to Hollywood's Golden Age of gangster movies. The world was less innocent, and in keeping with the zeitgeist, the gangsters of the screen were more realistic.

 **ESSENTIAL**

Hollywood tough guy Humphrey Bogart was the original founding member of the "Rat Pack." It was a group of movie star pals who would get together and party hearty. Frank Sinatra was a mere satellite in the cavalcade of stars. After Bogie's death, the Rat Pack was dormant for a couple of years before morphing into its more famous all-guy network of Frank Sinatra, Dean Martin, Sammy Davis, Jr., Peter Lawford, and Joey Bishop.

The *Godfather* Trilogy

In the 1960s, Mario Puzo's novel *The Godfather,* one of the most talked about bestsellers of the time, introduced millions of voracious readers into the world of La Cosa Nostra. The film version was inevitable. It and its two sequels became an American epic. Some thought it glorified the mob and portrayed them as too sympathetic. There is no denying, however, that they are popular entertainment of the highest order, perhaps a classier treatment that the wiseguys deserved.

Dramatis Personae

The Godfather may have been an entirely different experience if other actors considered for the roles had been cast. Imagine Frank Sinatra as Don Corleone. Often linked to the mob and the basis for the notorious "horse's head" scene in the film, Sinatra physically attacked novelist Puzo in a restaurant after the novel was published. Apparently he got over it, because a few years later he expressed interest in playing the titular don. Laurence Olivier and George C. Scott were also considered. Of course the coveted role went to Marlon Brando, who mumbled his way to an Academy Award he ostentatiously refused to accept.

The Godfather made Al Pacino a star. He went on the play numerous other gangster roles, including non-Italian hoodlums in *Scarface* and *Carlito's Way.* But can you imagine Robert Redford or Ryan O'Neal as Michael Corleone? Strange indeed, but they were the producer's choices. Fortunately, director Francis Ford Coppola insisted on Pacino, and the rest, as they say, is Hollywood history.

Dysfunctional Family

The *Godfather* films tell the story of the Corleones, an immigrant family that achieves the American Dream yet loses its soul. Crime does not pay even if it amasses you millions of dollars and the mob version of "respect." And the sins of the father are visited upon the sons and daughters.

FACT

Director Sergio Leone was offered the job of directing *The Godfather*, but he turned it down because he preferred to make his own mob movie. He eventually came out with the movie *Once Upon a Time in America*, released in 1984.

The main character through the three-film epic is Michael Corleone. We first meet him as a returning war hero who loves his family but has no interest in the family business. Life does not always unfold as per our plans, and by the last scene of the last movie, Michael Corleone has lived and died a very different life than he planned.

Part One

In *The Godfather*, we first meet the Corleones. The movie is as much about an American family as it is a gangster movie. It eloquently chronicles the dark side of the immigrant experience and the American Dream. The old don is a powerful crime lord who made his fortune in the criminal underworld yet craves respectability, if not for himself then certainly for his children. The fates have other plans for him. Though he dies rather benignly of a heart attack in his garden, one son dies in a hail of gunfire, and the other becomes the new Don Corleone. He could have been Senator Corleone, Governor Corleone, but there wasn't enough time.

Several famous scenes in *The Godfather* are inspired by real incidents in mob lore, including the shooting of Don Corleone at a fruit stand and the brutal garroting of the galootish goombah Luca Brasi. True, too, is the message sent to notify the Corleones of Brasi's murder—a fish wrapped in newspaper. "Luca Brasi sleeps with the fishes," has entered the pop culture vernacular.

Michael Corleone's fate is sealed when he assassinates the men who attempted to kill his father. From then on he is corrupted, and his destiny is an inexorable juggernaut deeper and deeper into the underworld of the Mafia and a Hades-like underworld of his own tortured soul. Even though he does evil things, such as orchestrating the murder of the heads of the five families and his own brother-in-law, he is an oddly sympathetic character. However, his behavior only gets worse in the second movie.

Part Two

The Godfather, Part II tells the parallel stories of the young Don Corleone, played by Robert De Niro, and Michael Corleone at the height of his power. The story follows the orphaned Vito Corleone's arrival in America at the turn of the twentieth century and his immersion into a life of crime. It counterpoints Michael Corleone's gradual descent into material and spiritual corruption.

FACT

The town of Corleone, Sicily, was too developed by the time the first *Godfather* movie was filmed, so instead filmmakers shot the Sicilian scenes in the countryside town of Savoca.

Real events also inspired elements of the script. The mob's involvement in Cuba before Castro took over is a major element of the plot, as is the mob's involvement in Las Vegas. The colorful Jewish gangster Hyman Roth is based on the less colorful but chillingly competent real hoodlum Meyer Lansky.

Michael, who was somewhat sympathetic in the first film, becomes colder and more ruthless, finally ordering the execution of his own brother, the simple and harmless Fredo. Rival gangsters used Fredo as a dupe and Michael finds it hard to forgive. This is a sin of a Biblical scale and Michael seems beyond redemption.

Part Three

Most fans and critics consider the third installment to be the weakest in the series, but it is not as bad as all that. It is a compelling final installment in the saga of a man who took the wrong path and spent the rest of his life trying (and failing) to get back on track. The old and ill Michael Corleone is still trying go legit, but just when he thinks he's out, they pull him back in. And just as the sins of Don Vito Corleone were visited on his offspring, Michael Corleone watches his sweet and innocent daughter murdered in front of his eyes.

The Godfather, Part III brings closure to a family saga that tapped into the collective unconscious and captured the imagination of filmgoers.

There had been talk of a fourth *Godfather* film, but it looks like it isn't going to happen. Just as *Godfather, Part II* told the parallel stories of the young Don Corleone and son Michael, the fourth film would have counterpointed the lives of the young Sonny Corleone (played by Leonardo DiCaprio) and his illegitimate son Vincent.

Assessment

While the *Godfather* movies are almost universally regarded as great entertainment, those in the know suggest they are unrealistic as Mafia movies. The underworld is more of a vehicle to tell the story of an American family in the twentieth century. Real gangsters are not as sympathetic; their lives are not deserving of a grand operatic treatment. They are not flawed heroes. They are ruthless, nasty, petty, cold-blooded killers with no redeeming qualities. The two filmmakers discussed next are credited for bursting the balloon of Mafia mythology and showing these scoundrels as they really are.

De Niro and Scorsese

One of the most successful actor-director collaborations in the movies is that of Robert De Niro and Martin Scorsese. Among their many joint efforts are some of the best mob movies. Different than the *Godfather* movies, they reveal the mafia mentality in all its nasty and brutish squalor. There are no Macbeth-like flawed heroes here, no noble men gone wrong. These foul-mouthed, colorful, yet creepy characters are more representative of the true mob than the Shakespearean Corleone family.

Martin Scorsese and Robert De Niro are one of the great actor-director teams in the history of film, rivaling John Ford and John Wayne and Akira Kurosawa and Toshiro Mifune. Their collaborations include *New York, New York, Taxi Driver, Cape Fear, The King of Comedy*, and *Raging Bull*. And of course the mob classics *Mean Streets, Goodfellas*, and *Casino*.

ALERT!

Even John Gotti got a movie made about him. Armand Assante played the Dapper Don in a made-for-cable flick. As creditable an actor as Assante is, the subject matter paled by comparison to the classic gangster films and Coppola's masterpiece. John Gotti was more punk than tragic hero.

Badfellas

Goodfellas is based on the book *Wiseguy: Life in a Mafia Family* by crime reporter Nicholas Pileggi. It is the story of Henry Hill, an ex-wiseguy turned "rat," who entered the Witness Protection Program to save his skin. The story chronicles the unsavory activities of the Lucchese crime family from the 1950s through the early 1980s, though the names have been changed to protect the innocent and the guilty.

We see the Mafia in all its sleazy splendor. We meet a cast of characters that bear no resemblance to the Corleones. Low-life hoods and dangerous psychos populate the landscape of New York City and its suburbs. We see how absolute power corrupts absolutely.

In *Goodfellas* we learn the inner workings of mob life. Henry Hill can only go so far in "the family," because he is only half-Italian. His Irish half prevents him from gaining full entry into the inner sanctum. We also get a glimpse of how the mob treats their women. The men all have girlfriends on the side while their wives turn a blind eye. It is a given that a Mafioso has a mistress. She is the one he squires about town and lavishes with gifts while the wife stays home with the kids and becomes no longer an object of desire but rather a maternal figure.

Loose Cannon

The most outrageous character in the movie is the deranged and volatile weasel played by Joe Pesci. He is disarmingly affable at one moment and he viciously kicks a man to death the next. He is exchanging quips with a doofus kid, but when the kid doesn't get him his drink quickly enough, he shoots him. He is too much of a loose cannon even for his handlers, and he is eventually killed by some made guys as vengeance for killing another made guy without permission (and without being a made guy himself). This character is based on a real person, and one wonders how he would have fared in the Corleone family.

Henry Hill

Courtesy of AP/Wide World Photos/Bill Achatz

▲ Former mobster Henry Hill smiles during an interview at the Essex County Jail in Newark, New Jersey, Friday, May 9, 1997. Hill's autobiography inspired the movie *Goodfellas*.

Sigmund Freud wrote of the "Madonna-Whore Syndrome." He maintained that men divide women into two camps: the exalted ideal of purity and the wanton sexual plaything. The Mafia men take this to heart. Most have a girlfriend on the side and come to regard their wives as maternal and therefore not sexual after the children are born.

In *Goodfellas* we see the inherent hypocrisy of the Mafia. The men are Old World traditionalists who claim to treasure family values, but they all have girlfriends on the side that they shower with opulent baubles, bangles, and beads. Yet heaven help the wife who may indulge in extramarital dalliances. Mafiosi are notorious male chauvinists in addition to their many other vices.

Henry Hill, played by Ray Liotta, eventually gets in over his head and begins to use the drugs that he has been selling and finally does the unforgivable. He goes to the feds and turns traitor on his former friends and associates. The real-life Henry Hill is still in hiding, but can be found in cyberspace. He brazenly started a Web site *www.goodfellahenry.com*.

Casino

Another great Martin Scorsese/Robert De Niro/Joe Pesci collaboration is *Casino*. It is the story of Las Vegas in the waning days of the Mafia's control of Sin City. De Niro plays a Jewish gambler who runs a casino for the mob, and Pesci plays another of his patented frenetic psychos who meets an even more grisly fate than he did in *Goodfellas*.

FACT

James Cagney always thought of himself as a "song and dance man." In fact, he won his only Academy Award for the musical *Yankee Doodle Dandy*. Most film fans, however, remember him for his rogue's gallery of classic gangster roles.

This movie details the Mafia's practice of "skimming." The audience sees how it is taken off the top before being reported as income and how much of it is sent back to the bosses back East. We see the ruthless way that card cheats are dealt with. As in medieval times, the hand that cheats is crushed in punishment. We see an embittered Mafioso assigned to kitchen duty spit in the soup of a customer he does not like. The Corleones, one suspects, would never do such a thing. As with *Goodfellas*, *Casino* keeps the audience riveted, yet disgusted with the behavior of the Mafia. They are nothing more than sleazy and despicable punks in Scorsese's films.

Dumbfellas

There have been many mob comedies over the years. There have even been a few musicals about gangsters. Mafia men are usually portrayed in these films as either lovable rascals or "dumbfellas" who function as comic relief. Interestingly, most of the actors who appeared in the great gangster movies of the 1970s and 1980s went on to poke fun at themselves and their images in gangster comedies.

Funnyfellas

In *Analyze This*, Robert De Niro lampoons his tough guy gangster image as Paul Vitti, a New York mob boss who is suffering from panic attacks and crying jags. He solicits the reluctant services of a psychiatrist played by Billy Crystal who helps him get in touch with good stuff in therapy and have a major breakthrough that leads him to going straight. This comedy relies on the audience's decades of familiarity with De Niro and his roles in the Scorsese films and *Godfather, Part II*. The stars teamed for a sequel appropriately called *Analyze That*.

James Caan (Sonny Corleone in *The Godfather*) also played it for laughs in the less successful gangster comedy *Mickey Blue Eyes*. Hugh Grant plays his usual uptight Brit who falls for mobster Caan's daughter. The image of Caan trying to teach Grant to say "Fuggedaboutit," is one of the few highlights of this movie.

Al Pacino played grotesque mobster "Big Boy" in Warren Beatty's live action version of the comic strip *Dick Tracy*. And even the mighty Brando poked fun at his Don Corleone image in a lightweight comedy called *The*

Freshman costarring Matthew Broderick. In a clever conceit, Brando is essentially doing his rasping, mumbling Corleone act, and the characters in the film constantly remark that he reminds them of *The Godfather*. Paramount Pictures was less than amused by the good-natured satire.

Mob Hit Parade

Singing and dancing gangsters were also popular in the movies. The most famous example is of course *Guys and Dolls*. Based on the colorful short stories of Damon Runyon, the 1954 film version of the Broadway show stars a young and slim Marlon Brando and Frank Sinatra as his sidekick. As his 1960s recording of "Luck Be a Lady" clearly reveals, Sinatra should have played Sky Masterson. Brando's bizarre warbling of the tune is, to say the least, unique.

You don't have to be Italian to be in the Mafia. The excellent 2002 movie *Road to Perdition,* starring Tom Hanks and Paul Newman as members of an Irish subsidiary of the Capone mob, is a deeply moving and tragic family drama of fathers and sons.

Toward the end of James Cagney's illustrious career, he played a tap dancing hood in the 1959 musical *Never Steal Anything Small*. The love theme from *The Godfather*, "Speak Softly, Love" was a big hit and was recorded by Al Martino, who played the Frank Sinatra-esque character of Johnny Fontane in all three *Godfather* movies.

And the Rat Pack got into the act in 1964's *Robin and the Seven Hoods*. These lovable hoods sing and dance and machine-gun their way into your hearts. It includes a Sinatra standard, "My Kind of Town (Chicago Is)." It was a favorite of many, including mobster Sam Giancana.

The Brotherhood

A forgotten Mafia movie that presages many elements of *The Godfather* is called *The Brotherhood*. It was released in 1968 and stars Kirk Douglas as a middle-aged Mafia don who is steeped in the old ways. The Mafia has matured around him and he has not changed with the times. Unlike Don Corleone, who did not want his youngest son Michael to be part of the family business, Kirk Douglas's character Frank Ginnetti happily brings his younger brother into the family. He is a proud Mafioso and unapologetic of his lifestyle or his business practices, which involve murder.

The brother, like Michael Corleone, is just back from military service and a lavish wedding occurs, just as in the opening scene of *he Godfather*. The wedding, though not as lavish as the affair in *The Godfather*, also shows the contradictory nature of the Mafia. Lavish pomp and spectacle and putative family values abound, yet violence lurks close to the surface. In *The Godfather*, Don Corleone is conducting business that involves corruption and violence. In the wedding scene from *The Brotherhood*, Kirk Douglas receives a report from two of his goons that they have successfully murdered an informant. *The Brotherhood* depicts a tradition not seen in *The Godfather*. The "canary" has a dead canary stuffed in his mouth after his murder to indicate that he was an informant.

The movie has an interesting take on the role of the Mustache Petes. There are a group of ancient old dons who were friends of Frank Ginnetti's father. They are survivors of the massacres of the Mustache Petes. They have not forgotten and they are eager to get Frank Ginnetti to hit the man who betrayed the old dons to Lucky Luciano.

FACT

The Rat Pack was filming a cemetery scene in the mob musical *Robin and the Seven Hoods* when they got the word that JFK had just been assassinated. His death changed the face of the nation, and the shots that rang out were also a death knell for the defiantly decadent Rat Pack mystique. What was once the epitome of hip was soon seen as passé middle-aged hedonism.

Vinny, the younger brother, is a businessman at heart and is interested in diversifying and expanding into legitimate business. So are the other members of the Commission, depicted in this film as a group of five men of both Italian and Jewish extraction. This reflects the changing face of the Mafia that actually began in the early 1930s.

Frank is so entrenched in the old ways that he rankles the Commission by refusing to go along with the deal. Frank, the Kirk Douglas character, will not vote for a business deal that will bring the mob into more legitimate enterprises. And he is determined to exact a vendetta on the man who betrayed the Mustache Petes, who also turns out to be his dear old friend and the father of his brother's wife.

Without any more spoilers, this movie is an interesting and well-acted pre-*Godfather* depiction of the Mafia. It lacks *The Godfather's* epic quality, but for Mafia movie junkies who have never seen it, it is definitely worth a look.

The Untouchables on the Big Screen

Brian De Palma's *The Untouchables* movie does not have much in common with the TV series of the same name, other than the setting and the antagonists. A young Kevin Costner played a less assured Eliot Ness, tutored by Sean Connery in an Academy Award–winning performance as tough Irish cop Jimmy Malone. Perennial gangster movie star Robert De Niro gained a few pounds for a cameo performance as Al Capone.

Sean Connery won an Academy Award for his moving performance as Jimmy Malone, the Irish cop who serves as a mentor to Kevin Costner's Eliot Ness. The character was a purely fictitious addition to the story. Ness had many brave men on his team, but giving him an elder mentor was purely a dramatic device.

The Chicago Way

Award-winning playwright David Mamet's screenplay does not adhere to the historical facts any more than the television show did. Novice treasury agent Ness arrives in Chicago, and his gung-ho naïveté is mocked by basically the whole Chicago police force and political machinery. He finds "the one good cop in a bad town" in the person of Connery, and together they assemble their version of the Untouchables.

Connery plays a more rough-hewn Obi-Wan Kenobi to Costner's Luke Skywalker as he tutors him in the ways of "the Force," Chicago-style. He delivers the famous advice, "He pulls a knife, you pull a gun. They send one of yours to the hospital, you send one of theirs to the morgue. That's the Chicago way. And that's how you get Capone."

Three Strikes and You're Out

Perhaps the most famous scene in *The Untouchables* movie is the De Niro/Capone baseball bat scene. Capone lectures his tuxedo-clad associates about the importance of teamwork as they are enjoying a fine meal and cigars in an elegant setting. He circles the table comparing their business to a baseball team, before savagely bashing the skull of one of the henchmen who allowed a valuable stash of bootleg booze to be impounded by Ness and company. In real life, Capone is alleged to have personally murdered at least three men with a baseball bat.

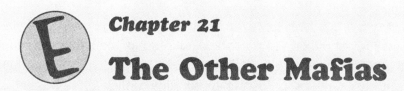

Chapter 21

The Other Mafias

Y ou don't have to be Italian to be in a Mafia, though theirs is the most famous. Many ethnic groups have formed organized crime communities over the centuries. In this chapter we will look at some of the more noteworthy and notorious "other Mafias."

The Russian Mafia

After the collapse of the former Soviet Union in 1991, the organized crime community in Russia came into its own. The underworld went above ground and flourished and thrived as it never did in the era of the Comrades and Commissars. Not content to do business in Mother Russia, they quickly came to America's shores in a form of gangster *glasnost*.

Like the crime families of the American Mafia, the Russian Mafia is not a monolith, but rather a loose confederation of crime outfits from the many republics that once formed the Soviet Union. It is believed that 80 percent of businesses in Russia pay extortion money to the Russian Mafia.

Nuclear Threat

Their threat is more than merely the traditional criminal conduct associated with any Mafia group. Since the Soviet Union fell, it has been a primary concern of both Russia and the United States to keep an eye on Russia's nuclear stockpile. There is a great fear that the Russian mob would not hesitate to get their hands on nuclear materials, maybe even one of the frightening "nuclear suitcases" that we hear about in the news, and sell it to the highest bidder.

This unthinkable horror is no longer the farfetched plot of a James Bond movie. In the post–September 11, 2001, world in which we live, it is a very real possibility. Say what we might about the American Mafia, it is unlikely that they would ever involve themselves in such an enterprise.

Once Americans became aware of the Russian Mafia, it became fodder for the pop culture mill. They showed up as villains in television shows, novels, and movies. Even James Bond, who for years waged the Cold War against the Soviets, battled the Russian Mafia in the 007 movie *Goldeneye*.

Yearning to Breathe Free

In the 1980s, when the Cold War between the United States and the Soviet Union was at its most frigid, it would appear that the sneaky

Soviets played a nasty trick on America. Anti-Semitism was rampant in Russia, and as part of the many negotiations that went on during the Cold War, the communist government agreed to let many Russian-Jewish refugees leave the country. They also used it as an excuse to open their jails and rid themselves of their worst criminals by shipping them off to the United States under the guise of a liberal and compassionate policy.

Fidel Castro did the same thing with the Mariel boat people in 1980. Soviet Russia and communist Cuba simultaneously got rid of the lowlifes in their society and inflicted them upon the United States. Hundreds of thousands of criminals came to America to continue their criminal activities in the New World.

Brighton Beach Memoirs

Initially, the Russian Mafia operating in America preyed mostly on their own people, the other Russian immigrants who had settled in the United States. Shakedowns and extortion were common crimes inflicted on the decent hardworking Russians. They also engaged in the usual crimes such as thievery and prostitution.

The Brighton Beach section of Brooklyn, New York, was a hotbed of activity for the Russian Mafia in the 1970s. It even formed an uneasy alliance with the Italian boys who had been in place for decades. The homegrown Mafia was not about to let these newcomers start muscling in on their territory. The Italians let the Russians operate, but at a price that must have stunned those raised in a communist regime. They had to pay a hefty "tribute" to the Italian Mafia for the privilege of operating in New York. La Cosa Nostra's aggressive capitalism was a rude awakening for the Russian Mafia.

Mafia Family, Russian-Style

The Russian Mafia equivalent of the don is called the *Pakhan*. This boss controls four operating "cells" through his second in command. This number two man is called the *Brigadier*. Given that this crime family structure originated in Russia, where secret police once ruled with terror and fostered a paranoid environment, the Pakhan employs spies to keep an eye on the Brigadier. The cells are made up of the usual suspects—soldiers who deal in drugs, prostitution, extortion, bribery, and all manner of criminality.

FACT

The Russian Mafia is causing trouble in America, but its influence in the United States pales in comparison to the power it wields in Mother Russia. Dozens of political assassinations have been linked to the Russian mob.

The members of the individual cells do not know members of the other cells, though they all report to the Pakhan. This is a crime family of the Eastern European variety. Just as the American Mafia mirrors the legitimate capitalist world, the Russian Mafia reflects the communist regime where it was spawned.

The Code

The Russian Mafia, like its American counterpart, has a code that all members follow. There are eighteen rules to live by, and breaking the rules is punishable by death.

1. The crime family is your new family. Distance yourself from your real family.
2. Do not have a family of your own. No wives or children allowed. Girlfriends are okay.
3. Have another source of income. A real job.
4. Help other members with support. Material and otherwise.
5. Never reveal anything about your cohorts and associates.
6. If necessary, take the rap for a fellow thief.
7. Hold meetings to settle disputes.
8. Freely participate in these meetings.
9. Punish the guilty parties as determined at these meetings.
10. Do not flinch from performing these unpleasant duties even though the convicted party may be a friend.
11. Learn the "Fehnay," or Russian Mafia slang.

12. Never get in over your head with gambling debts.
13. Coach and mentor younger hoodlums-in-training.
14. Always maintain a network of informants among the lower echelon of criminals.
15. Be able to handle your liquor. Nobody likes a sloppy gangster.
16. Do not mingle with the police in social situations or join any social or community clubs. The Elks Club is verboten.
17. Avoid military service. Stay out of the draft.
18. Always keep your word to another member of the Russian Mafia.

The Illustrated Men

One thing that separates the Russian Mafia from the American Mafia is their penchant for tattoos. These are more than mere vanity etchings. They are an illustrated record of their criminal life. The more crimes they have committed, the more tattoos they have. We have all seen police melodramas where a cop discussing a suspect says, "He has a rap sheet as long as your arm." In the Russian Mafia, this is quite literal, though it is not limited to the arm.

ALERT!

Nothing is sacred, not even the Olympics. Russian gangster Alimzhan Tokhtakhounov is accused of putting the fix on the 2002 Winter Olympics in Salt Lake City, compelling judges to vote for the Russian figure skating team in exchange for votes for the French ice dancing team.

Russian criminals take their tattoos very seriously. It has been reported that if a criminal has himself tattooed with markings that show a more impressive history than he actually has, his braggadocio can get him killed. Law enforcement officials who know what the various tattoos mean have it easy in making a case against Russian Mafia members. Despite their denials, their bodies are evidence against them, since the tattoos are a pictorial record of the gangster's crimes and misdemeanors.

California Schemin'

The Odessa Mafia is believed to be the largest Russian Mafia family currently operating in the United States. This is the gang that settled in Brighton Beach, Brooklyn. Members came to New York City in the mid-1970s. They have since sent emissaries out to the West Coast and established a foothold in San Francisco and Los Angeles. There is a steady stream of Russian Mafiosi heading across country to the sun and fun of California. Authorities believe this is happening because the American Mafia is least powerful on the West Coast. La Cosa Nostra's strongholds are in the Northeast and Midwest. The Russian Mafia has to pay a heavy "tax" to the American Mafia when doing business in its territories. California represents more freedom and higher profits for them.

G-Men on Alert

The DEA (Drug Enforcement Agency) is well aware of the growing Russian Mafia. Special Agent Harold D. Wankel, the DEA chief of operations, testified before Congress about the activities. The following is an excerpt from his testimony:

Over the past several years there has been an increase in drug trafficking by organized crime elements in Russia. The country has emerged as a transit route for heroin from Southwest and Southeast Asia to Europe and the United States, as well as for cocaine from South America to Europe. There is an increased threat of international drug money laundering by criminal elements in Russia as well as by criminal elements among Russian emigres located in such areas as Europe and the United States.

The enormous amount of money associated with the drug trade has attracted Russian organized crime elements who now are involved in all aspects of the opium and hashish industries, including cultivation, production, distribution, and money laundering operations. Criminal groups in Russia are exploiting the open access to the West and the lack of regulations in the banking, financial, and commercial sectors of their country.

FACT

A group known by the police as the "Red Mafia" is based in Budapest, Hungary, and is run by mob boss Semion Mogilevich, also known as the "Brainy Don." According to the FBI, he is involved in a vast array of criminal activities, including art fraud.

The Colombian Drug Cartels

The DEA has also had its hands full with the Colombian drug cartels, especially in the 1980s and 1990s. These crime families are responsible for most of the cocaine that finds it way into the United States. Another DEA agent, Michael T. Horn, testifying before the Senate Foreign Relations Committee, compared the American Mafia with these vicious new interlopers:

In the twentieth century, "traditional organized crime" in America rose to what was then considered unparalleled heights. These organizations were built around a hierarchy of leaders and members. This form of organized crime, although of immigrant background, was rooted on American soil. From our earliest exposure to traditional organized crime, a common thread has been and continues to be the violence with which these organizations are operated, expanded, and controlled.

One example of the ruthlessness and violence which has long been a trademark of organized crime is the rise and fall of Carmine Galante. While working as an "underboss" for the notorious mobster Joseph Bonanno, Galante steered the Bonanno family into narcotics. He built their heroin trafficking operations and later expanded them, from New York into Montreal, Canada. As a result of his successful operations, Galante became the successor to Joseph Bonanno upon his death and attempted to gain control of territory dominated by other American crime bosses. His lust for power and control of profits generated by narcotics, pornography, loan-sharking, and labor racketeering ultimately led to his gangland-style slaying. His thirst for notoriety and profit, and his intentions to expand his operations, resulted in his public murder in Brooklyn, New York, in July 1979. As we see today, this threat of encroaching upon other competitors' territory and profits, within the traditional organized crime family, is often met with fierce resistance.

Although Colombian traffickers still control and facilitate significant portions of the drug trafficking in the Western hemisphere, the sophisticated, organized criminal groups from Mexico have eclipsed the drug trafficking criminals from Cali and Medellin, Colombia, as the greatest law enforcement threat facing the United States today. The leaders of these groups—the Rodriguez-Orejuela brothers in Colombia, Juan Garcia-Abrego, Miguel Caro-Quintero, the Arrellano-Felix brothers, and recently deceased Amado Carrillo-Fuentes in Mexico—are simply the 1990s versions of the traditional organized crime leaders that United States law enforcement has fought to dismantle since the turn of the century. But the influence of American organized crime pales in comparison to the violence, corruption, and power that is exhibited by today's criminal group leaders.

DEA's mission is to target the powerful international drug syndicates which operate around the world, supplying drugs to American communities, employing thousands of individuals to transport and distribute drugs. The most significant international drug syndicates operating today are far more powerful and violent than any organized criminal groups that we have experienced in American law enforcement. Today's major international organized crime drug syndicates are simply the 1990s versions of traditional organized crime mobsters United States law enforcement officials have fought since the beginning of this century.

ALERT!

Like the Russian Mafia, the Colombian drug lords became the bad guys of the moment in television shows and movies in the 1980s and early 1990s. Tom Clancy's intrepid hero Jack Ryan took them on in the novel *Clear and Present Danger*.

Ruthless People

The DEA agent speaking above minimizes the brutality of the Colombian drug cartels. Unlike the Mafia, who for the most part only killed their own, the drug cartels were notorious for slaughtering the entire families of their enemies in particularly nasty ways, including women and children. This would have horrified many of the older Mafia dons had they lived to see the horrors that the drug traffic wrought on the innocent.

Colombia produces coca, which is the plant from which cocaine is produced. The nation is geographically ideal for a brisk drug traffic industry. It is at the tip of the South American continent with hundreds of miles of coastline on both the Caribbean and the Pacific Ocean and a little over two hours as the plane flies from the United States.

The Colombian drug cartels also worked with Mexican drug smugglers to transport cocaine into America across the United States/Mexico border. There is rampant corruption in the Mexican government and military, and it is not uncommon for military armored vehicles to accompany drug smugglers across the border and even fire upon the American border patrol officers. The heyday of the Colombian cartels was over, but the Mexican drug traffic remains profitable and violent.

Cartel Organization

The DEA assessed the structure and effectiveness of the Colombian drug cartel operations within the United States in one of its reports to Congress:

Members of international groups headquartered in Colombia and Mexico today have at their disposal sophisticated technology—encrypted phones, faxes, and other communications equipment. Additionally, they have in their arsenal aircraft, radar-equipped aircraft, weapons, and an army of workers who oversee the drug business from its raw beginnings in South American jungles to the urban areas within the United States. All of this modern technology and these vast resources enable the leaders of international criminal groups to build organizations which reach into the heartland of America, while they themselves try to remain beyond the reach of American justice. The traffickers also have the financial resources necessary to corrupt enough law enforcement, military, and political officials to create a relatively safe haven for themselves in the countries in which they make their headquarters.

Colombian cocaine trafficking groups in the United States—consisting of mid-level traffickers answering to the bosses in Colombia—continue to be organized around "cells" that operate within a given geographic area. Some cells specialize in a particular facet of the drug trade, such as cocaine transport, storage, wholesale distribution, or money laundering. Each cell, which may be comprised of ten or more employees, operates with little or no knowledge about the membership in, or drug operations of, other cells.

The head of each cell reports to a regional director who is responsible for the overall management of several cells. The regional director, in turn, reports directly to one of the drug lords of a particular organization or their designee based in Colombia. A rigid top-down command-and-control structure is characteristic of these groups. Trusted lieutenants of the organization in the United States have discretion in the day-to-day operations, but ultimate authority rests with the leadership in Colombia.

Upper echelon and management levels of these cells are normally comprised of family members or long-time close associates who can be trusted by the Colombian drug lords—

because their family members remain in Colombia as hostages to the cell members' good behavior—to handle their day-to-day drug operations in the United States. The trusted personal nature of these organizations makes it that much harder to penetrate the organizations with confidential sources. That difficulty with penetration makes intercepting criminal telephone calls all the more vital. They report back to Colombia via cell phone, fax, and other sophisticated communications methods. Colombian drug traffickers continually employ a variety of counter-surveillance techniques and tactics, such as fake drug transactions, using telephones they suspect are monitored, limited-time use of cloned cell phones (frequently a week or less), limited use of pagers (from two to four weeks), and use of calling cards. The top-level managers of these Colombian organizations increasingly use sophisticated communications and encryption technology, posing a severe challenge to law enforcement's ability to conduct effective investigations.

Medellin Cartel

The first of the major drug operations, called cartels, was the Medellin Cartel. The DEA told the Senate what it knew about them:

During the 1980s, the Medellin Cartel held the citizens of Colombia hostage during a reign of terror that threatened to destroy the country, their way of life, and their institutions. Pablo Escobar, operating with virtual impunity, went so far as to place bounties on the heads of Colombian National Police officers in the amount of $1,000–$3,000 per murder. The ruthlessness of the Colombian traffickers was imported to the United States as they traveled north to meet the growing demand for cocaine. The violence was first manifested in South Florida, where the violence escalated to such a point that the media began describing the Colombian drug traffickers as the "Cocaine Cowboys." The ability of these powerful organized criminal groups to transport this level of vengeful violence to the United States was like nothing that law enforcement had ever experienced before. Failure to perform duties as directed, suspicion of betrayal, or merely the need to set an example were the rationales for dispensing violence at unprecedented levels.

Griselda Blanco, currently incarcerated on cocaine trafficking charges and awaiting trial in Dade County, Florida, has been tied to as many as forty homicides in the United States, primarily in South Florida. She was considered the matriarch of a sophisticated drug ring headquartered in Medellin and Miami, and later in Los Angeles. The organization that she directed made the term "Cocaine Cowboys" a household word, after Blanco ordered the infamous massacre at Dadeland Mall on July 11, 1979, in which two men were left dead and four innocent bystanders were wounded. To foster her reputation as the "Godmother" of cocaine, she named her fourth son Michael Corleone, after the fictional mob character portrayed in the movie "The Godfather".

The Cali Cartel

The heads of the Medellin cartel were gradually murdered and arrested in the 1980s, and the drug outfit that achieved prominence in the lucrative cocaine trade was the Cali cartel. This organization had a little more finesse than its predecessor. Gone were the routine massacres and rampant violence. It was not eliminated entirely, but the Cali cartel was more adept at using legitimate businesses as fronts.

The Cali cartel has extensive operations in the United States. In upstate New York, the state police and the DEA raided a laboratory that had the equipment to produce more than $700 million worth of cocaine a year. And that was just one of their many facilities. It is estimated that the cartel made billions of dollars a year in a period from the late 1980s through the early 1990s.

Like the Medellin cartel, the Cali group had an elaborate network of cells in the United States. Each cell handled a particular aspect of the drug trade, from traffic to storage to bookkeeping. The Cali leadership insisted upon the names of family members of their employees. This was a form of blackmail. As stated earlier, the Colombians would murder entire families of their enemies and employees who fell out of favor either through incompetence or corruption.

When the Colombian drug cartels became known in America, much was written about their tendency to slaughter the whole families of their enemies, including women and children. This is something the American Mafia did not do. It is something that the Sicilian Mafia did. In the Old World, if they killed a man they also killed his sons lest they grow up and exact vengeance.

Colombia does not have an extradition treaty with the United States. As a result it was illegal for the United States to bring Colombian drug lords to justice in the American justice system. Eventually, the combined efforts of the DEA and the Colombian National Police finally produced results after many years of failures. By 1996, the Cali cartel collapsed and its leaders were either in jail or dead. The Mexican problem continues, however.

Mule Train

Heroin is also produced and shipped from Colombia. Poppies, the flower from which opium is produced, grows freely in Colombia and Peru. It goes from the poppy fields to laboratories to be converted into heroin. It is smuggled into the United States via many means, one of which is sure to give the smuggler a tummy ache. People who are called "mules" swallow condoms filled with heroin, fly into the United States, and pass through customs. One would not want to be around when the "mule" discharges the heroin for delivery to the local drug dealer.

In a shrewd business move, Colombian heroin is often sold in the street at a deep discount and in some instances even given away freely in order to build a solid customer base. As a result, more than 98 percent of the heroin consumed in the United States comes from Colombia.

The Yakuza

This Japanese crime organization is much older than the American Mafia, and its members are the outcasts of Japanese society. The name derives from a Japanese card game called Oicho-Kabu. The name is a combination of three numbered cards, which is a losing hand in the game. Hence the yakuza are regarded as losers in the austere and rigid Japanese culture. For losers, they have enjoyed great success in the underworld of crime.

Note that this refers to yakuza with a small *y*. The crime family that grew out of this motley band of outcasts became a well-organized and infamous criminal organization. For our purposes we will deal with the Yakuza with a capital *Y*.

FACT

From 1958 to 1963, membership in the Yakuza grew an astonishing 150 percent, to more than 184,000 members. The average membership of a Mafia crime family during the Mafia's glory days was never more than a few hundred per family.

The Yakuza tradition maintains that they were once proud citizens of medieval times who defended their cities and towns against marauding bandits that were terrorizing the countryside. The tradition paints them as heroic Robin Hood types. This is not entirely accurate. The modern Yakuza really originated in the seventeenth century, when professional gamblers and other miscreants joined forces.

East Meets West

When Japan began to interact and trade with Western culture, it began to experience its version of the Industrial Revolution. Like its American criminal counterpart, the Yakuza began to worm its way into the docks. They also began the age-old practice of bribing politicians.

While Al Capone was in effect the mayor of Chicago, halfway around the world the Yakuza were terrorizing Japan. Yakuza hit men assassinated numerous politicians who refused to play ball, including two prime ministers.

The Modern Yakuza

After World War II the American forces occupied Japan and established a military government led by General Douglas MacArthur. The lower classes of the defeated nation were living in poverty, and a black market developed for the necessities and amenities that people had come to expect. Just as people in America had to pay through the nose for a shot of booze during Prohibition, the Japanese had to pay inflated prices to the Yakuza for the little things we take for granted.

The uniform of the Yakuza changed after World War II, when America began to rule the world not through military might but through consumerism and Hollywood. The Yakuza were influenced by gangster movies and turned in their swords for guns and began to wear dark suits and sunglasses. These Nipponese hoods looked like the Blues Brothers. Their criminal activities became more eclectic as well. They began picking on the average citizen, intimidating and shaking down not just the rich and powerful but the simple shopkeepers as well.

The Yakuza fared well under the American occupation. The American military disarmed the citizenry but weren't able to disarm the criminal underworld. As a result the Yakuza ran roughshod over the law-abiding populace.

The Japanese Godfather

In the 1950s and 1960s the Yakuza increased in membership and power. They had their share of gangland wars just like the American Mafia and were eventually united under a gangster named Yoshiro Kodama. He is considered the godfather of the modern Yakuza.

Kodama was a nationalist who believed in Japan's ethnic and cultural superiority. He served as a spy during World War II. After the war the Americans locked him up. He eventually struck a deal with his jailers and began to spy for the Americans. He was also an intermediary between the Americans and the Yakuza. This was the beginning of the Cold War between the United States and Russia. The Yakuza, like the American Mafia, were staunch anticommunists. Now a free man, Kodama set about unifying the warring Yakuza clans.

Clan Structure

There is a great deal of similarity between the typical Yakuza clan and the American and Sicilian Mafia families. In fact, the titles that the various officers hold make them sound like more of a family than any of New York's big five families.

The head of the Yakuza family is called *Oyabun*, which means father. Subordinates are called *Kyodai* (brothers) and *Wakashu* (children). The equivalent of the consigliere is called the *saiko komon*. He also controls numerous subgangs, the Yakuza version of a mafia crew. Below this rank is the *so-honbucho*, meaning chief, who also controls many subgangs. His second in command is the *wakagashira*. There are many other levels down the Yakuza food chain including assistants (*fuku-honbucho*), advisers (*komon*), counselors (*shingiin*), secretaries (*kumicho hisho*), accountants (*kaikei*), "younger brothers" (*shate*), and "young men" (*wakashu*).

Check out the 1975 movie *The Yakuza* starring Robert Mitchum. It's an entertaining thriller that will give the viewer insight into the Japanese criminal organization, its ruthlessness, and its codes of honor that hark back to Japan's samurai past.

Modern Yakuza are divided into two types—"clan Yakuza" and "freelance Yakuza." A freelancer lives a more precarious existence. They are usually the small-time and petty hoodlums. Without a clan to back him up, the freelance Yakuza has a hardscrabble existence to scrape together a criminal living. Clan Yakuza always have their eye on freelancers. If the freelancer is too successful or discovered to be active in a clan's territory, he is likely to be executed.

Going Straight

Japan began to crack down on the Yakuza in the early 1990s with surprising success. A series of laws were passed (and actually enforced) that diminished the Yakuza's ability to conduct business. Yakuza actually began calling the authorities and inquiring about how they could get real jobs. Japanese companies even began to hire reformed Yakuza in an effort to encourage more and more of them to go straight.

The Yakuza is not defunct as an organization, however. Like many other groups and individuals before it, the Yakuza looks to the "decadent" West as a source of income and base of operations. They are doing business in America, the land of opportunity for people of all races, colors, creeds, and criminal persuasions.

West Side Story

There is a neighborhood on the West Side of Manhattan that was once known as "Hell's Kitchen." This was meant to indicate that it was the toughest of the tough parts of town and the denizens were the toughest guys. This was the 'hood that the Irish gangsters called home. They never achieved the stature of the Italian Mafia. There were many pitched battles, and the Irish lost. They are still around on a small scale, Irish born and Irish-Americans who call themselves "the Westies." Here is a brief history of the Irish Mafia.

Hell's Kitchen, the New York City neighborhood that spawned the Irish gang called the Westies, took its name from a similarly tough neighborhood across the Atlantic in London, England.

At the turn of the twentieth century, the Irish mob in New York City called themselves the Gophers. They were the most powerful of the Irish up until the advent of Prohibition. A disorganized band of hooligans, their crimes never rose above the level of burglaries and waterfront heists. They served as muscle for local politicians, exerting their powers of persuasion at the polling places on election day. They never hit the big time, and faded into gangland obscurity during the Roaring Twenties.

McKiller

The most successful and ruthless of the New York Irish gangsters in the 1930s was a tough mug called Owney "Killer" Madden. He was a dapper dude who partied in the high society of the day. He had interests in the bootleg racket and was the owner of the legendary Harlem nightclub called the Cotton Club. He was treated with respect by Lucky Luciano, and they did business amicably.

Not so amicable was his relationship with a fellow Irishman with the menacing moniker Vincent "Mad Dog" Coll. Mad Dog was the epitome of the loose cannon. He killed his first man when he was only nineteen. He broke all the rules and codes of the Mafia. He worked for Dutch Schultz but eventually bristled in the role of second banana and started his own gang. In a particularly vicious shootout in the street he was responsible for something the Mafia tried to avoid at all costs. An innocent civilian was killed and four others were wounded. Not just any civilian. The victim was a five-year-old boy. This brought unwanted media attention and public outcry directed at the Mafia. Mad Dog was about to be put out of his misery.

ALERT!

Martin Scorsese, known for his classic Mafia movies, looked back at the Irish mobsters of the mid-nineteenth century in his 2002 movie *Gangs of New York*, starring Leonardo DiCaprio and Daniel Day-Lewis.

Mad Dog wanted to muscle in on the Killer's turf, and with names like theirs you know it could only end one way. Owney Madden won the bout. Mad Dog was shot the way one would a mad dog. Madden did a year in the slammer and then retired to Hot Springs, Arkansas. This was a Mafia resort town discovered by Al Capone, and it is famed for its natural and restorative mineral baths. Gangsters put it on the map, and now ordinary citizens still flock there to "take in the waters" and gamble at the world-famous racetrack, Oaklawn Park.

Other Notable Westies

Eddie McGrath was the predominant Irish hoodlum from the 1940s through the late 1950s. He was a bootlegger in the Killer Madden era and became involved with corrupt unions in later years. His two henchmen were called John "Cockeye" Dunn and Andrew "Squint" Sheridan. Clearly McGrath was not averse to hiring the visually impaired. After Squint was sent up the river of no return and Cockeye was whacked, McGrath left the Big Apple for the sun and fun of Florida, and did not look back.

One way to drive out the gangster element is through gentrification. Most low-level Westies can no longer afford to live in Hell's Kitchen, as Manhattan Island becomes inhabitable only by the very rich or the very poor. This does not affect the kingpins, of course, just the working stiffs.

Mickey Spillane, not to be confused with the hardboiled mystery writer of the same name, took over from McGrath. Spillane had a combative relationship with the Italian Mafia. He did not much care for Italians in general and resented the fact that he had to pay them a percentage of his action in order to operate on the West Side. He would occasionally kidnap a Mafioso and hold him for ransom. He faced a Young Turk from his own ranks named Jimmy Coonan. Coonan was jailed for seven years, but the battle resumed when he was released. By then Coonan was a hoodlum in decline. "Fat Tony" Salerno had whacked Spillane's top guys over the years. The Mafia was determined to build the Jacob Javits Convention Center on Manhattan's West Side. Mickey Spillane was killed on March 13, 1977.

Jimmy Coonan's tenure as head of the Westies was one of violence and brutality. He lacked the finesse of his elders. His gang was more like a crew of out-of-control street punks than a sophisticated organized crime family. They drank too much and also indulged in the drugs they pushed. Coonan made an allegiance with Gambino family leader, Paul Castellano. But he was no fan of Fat Tony Salerno. He tried many times to whack him, but without success.

Coonan had a penchant for chopping the hands off those he murdered. No fingerprints to identify the body that way. One assumes he was too loaded and stoned to consider that the cops might use dental records to get the deceased's identity. He was certainly on the right track, however. There were more than thirty unsolved murders in Hell's Kitchen in the 1970s through the mid-1980s that had the mark of the Westies. Coonan was ultimately convicted under the RICO Act and sentenced to seventy-five years.

Kevin Kelley took over after Coonan. He expanded the Westies' jurisdiction over to the East Side, where they supplied cocaine for the Yuppies and other affluent influentials in the so-called decade of greed. Kelley and his sidekick Kenny Shannon could not take the heat, so they turned themselves in. The man who took over was a fellow named Bosco "The Yugo" Rodonovich. One thing is certain from that name—the reign of the Irish was over. The Yugo fled the country to avoid jail in the 1990s and is believed to be alive and well in his native land.

Appendices

Appendix A
The Hit List

Appendix B
Glossary of Terms

Appendix C
Mafia Timeline

The Hit List

Albert Anastasia

Albert Anastasia was also known as "The Mad Hatter" and the "Lord High Executioner" of Murder Incorporated, the assassination wing of the Commission. Anastasia was a natural for the job. He was a sociopathic sadist who thoroughly enjoyed his work. When he rose in the ranks, he was less successful. He did not have what it took to be the don of a family, and he was eventually murdered in a barbershop and succeeded by his second in command, Carlo Gambino.

Joseph Bonanno

The head of the Bonanno crime family who lived to the ripe old age of ninety-seven. He hated his nickname with good reason—it was "Joe Bananas." His life was the subject of the book *Honor Thy Father*, by Gay Talese, and he did something no Mafia boss would have ever considered in the old days. He wrote his memoirs and was interviewed by Mike Wallace on *60 Minutes*. He told Wallace in his thick Italian accent that Al Capone was "a jolly fellow," and also defended his memoir by saying that "nobody can tell the story of Joe Bonanno but Joe Bonanno." Of course, Joe Bonanno, like most autobiographers, told the story of his life that he wanted you to hear. For example, he always denied he was in the drug trade, yet the Bonanno family did a brisk business in the narcotics industry.

Salvatore "Bill" Bonanno

Joe Bonanno's son. Father wanted son to follow in his criminal footsteps, something that almost never happened in Mafia machinations. This prompted what was whimsically known as "the Banana War." It was a protracted mob war that left many dead. Like his father, who in later life went public with his life story, Bill Bonanno consulted with author Gay

Talese on the book about his family, *Honor Thy Father,* and is interviewed on the A&E biography about his famous father.

Alphonse "Scarface" Capone

Al Capone is perhaps the most famous gangster in the long and bloody history of the Mafia. He got his start on the mean streets of New York City but eventually ventured out to the windy city of Chicago. There he became the Kingpin of Crime during the Roaring Twenties. His battle with treasury agent Eliot Ness and his band of Untouchables has become the stuff of American legend, and the subject of both TV and big screen renditions. Capone was a ruthless killer who personally killed many men and ordered the deaths of many more, but what finally brought him down was a conviction and jail sentence for income tax evasion.

Frank Capone

An older brother of Al Capone. His career in crime was cut short when he died in the proverbial hail of bullets. He allegedly pulled his pistol when surrounded by a group of cops and paid heavily for this error in judgment. The cops called it self-defense and were exonerated of any wrongdoing. This was in Cicero, Illinois, during Al Capone's attempt to take total control of the city. Capone got his wish, but it cost his brother his life.

Ralph Capone

Another brother of Al Capone. He lived the longest and remained a fixture in the Mafia. He never achieved the prominence and success of his brother, but traded on his name to stay in the game. The name Capone was a legendary one in Mafia circles, so his name gave him respect, but he did not have the charisma nor did he exert the influence of his brother Al.

Two-Gun Hart (née Capone)

In a fascinating case of divergent family paths, Al Capone had a long-lost brother who left New York City and his Italian immigrant roots, and went to the American heartland long before Al Capone ever made it to Chicago. He changed his name to Richard Hart. It was common for immigrants with very ethnic sounding names to "Americanize" their names in an effort to better fit into society. Richard Hart went on to become a hero in World War I, a frontier lawman in the early twentieth century West, and ironically, a Prohibition agent with an impressive record for shutting down bootleg operations in Nebraska. He was reunited with his gangster siblings late in their lives, after Al Capone had been released from prison. He had kept his origins secret from his own family, and his wife and children were stunned to learn that their stalwart lawman husband and father was the older brother of the most infamous gangster of the era.

Paul Castellano

The mob boss whose assassination in 1985 prompted the ascendancy of John Gotti to power and prominence. The hit was an easy one, something a shrewd Mafia don should have seen coming. He was not above using the traditional Mafia business practices of murder and mayhem, but he brought the Gambino crime family into more legitimate businesses. But he did not have the survival instincts to save his life. John Gotti was the man who arranged the hit, and he became the head of the Gambino family afterward.

Roy Cohn

This high-powered New York attorney was an intimate of Senator Joseph McCarthy and Francis Cardinal Spellman, Archbishop of New York, and was also an attorney for Mafiosi Fat Tony Salerno, Carmine Galante,

Tommy and Joe Gambino, Carmine Fatico, Angelo Ruggiero, and John Gotti. He was the embodiment of the "strange bedfellows" syndrome that has often linked the political world and the underworld over the decades. He bridged both worlds and had a secret world of his own. He kept his private life private, but like J. Edgar Hoover there were plenty of rumors. He eventually died of AIDS.

Joseph Colombo, Sr.

The mob boss who died in a very public manner. He had the audacity to found the Italian-American Civil Rights League. This organization, founded by a Mafioso, was meant to combat the negative stereotypes that Italian-Americans all have some connection to the Mafia. The other more shrewd Mafia dons did not like the light of publicity on them in any way, as this would do more damage than good. Colombo was shot at his own rally in New York's Columbus Circle. He did not die outright but tragically lingered, living as essentially a vegetable for seven years.

Frank Costello

Long before the movies *Analyze This* and *Analyze That* and the TV series *The Sopranos*, Frank Costello was a rare bird among members of the Commission—he was the patient of a psychiatrist. He was also one of the most politically connected members of the syndicate. He had numerous elected officials and judges in his pocket. They were paid well and deeply indebted to Costello. He is credited with keeping J. Edgar Hoover off the Mafia's case by giving him tips on the horses. And when Frank Costello gave you a tip, you could be sure it was a sure thing. He was nicknamed "Prime Minister of the Underworld" because of his skills as a politician and diplomat. He preferred to use nonviolent means to achieve his ends, but like all Mafiosi, violence was part of his arsenal. He was shot in the head but survived the botched hit and lived to enjoy a comfortable retirement.

Aniello Dellacroce

An underboss of the Gambino crime family who was one of the Mafia's more sadistic killers who really enjoyed his work and did not rationalize it as "strictly business." In a perverse irony, he often masqueraded as a Catholic priest when traveling the country on Mafia business. He was John Gotti's mentor and was passed over as don in favor of Paul Castellano. This led to John Gotti's power grab and rise to national prominence as the "Dapper Don."

Thomas E. Dewey

The crusading New York district attorney and special prosecutor who made war against the Mafia, in particular Lucky Luciano. He was also a politically ambitious man who used his mob convictions to further his political career. He eventually became the governor of New York state. One of his duties, ironically, was to pardon Lucky Luciano on the condition he be deported to Italy. He was also the Republican presidential candidate in 1948, against Harry S Truman. His name is perhaps known best from a still photograph from that era. The winner of the election, Truman, is shown beaming as he holds up a somewhat premature newspaper with the headline: "DEWEY DEFEATS TRUMAN."

Carmine Galante

Nicknamed "the Cigar" because of the ubiquitous stogie in his mouth, he was by all accounts one of the scariest of a very scary fraternity. He was head of the Bonanno crime family for a while, but he was a dangerous and unstable loose cannon. The Commission unanimously voted to whack him. When he was shot to death in a New York City restaurant, his cigar stayed fixed in his mouth during the shooting and remained between his lifeless lips.

Carlo Gambino

Gambino was the deceptively docile don who became the Boss of Bosses after Lucky Luciano was deported back to Italy. He was originally thought of as a timid and cowardly man. He endured much humiliation from the hot-tempered Albert Anastasia, but he was working behind the scenes to whack his volatile boss and seize control. And when he did, he elevated his crime family into an efficient and profitable enterprise. He was a successful don and died of natural causes in 1976. The power plays that followed his death led to the rise of John Gotti and his reign during the 1980s and early 1990s.

Vito Genovese

Head of the Genovese crime family and another ambitious killer who sought to be the Boss of Bosses. His dubious contribution was to keep the Mafia in the drug business. This was a controversial issue. There was "a lot of money in that white powder," as Sonny Corleone said in *The Godfather*. But the old-timers from the old school thought it was a nasty business, dangerous and destructive compared to gambling and prostitution. It was his drug trafficking that got him in trouble with the law, and he died in the slammer, one of the rare instances where a power-seeking don did not find himself whacked by rivals.

Sam "Momo" Giancana

He was a friend of Frank Sinatra and he also shared a girlfriend with President John Fitzgerald Kennedy. He was instrumental in using Mafia influence in hopes of helping John F. Kennedy become president, but came to quickly regret it when Attorney General Robert Kennedy began an aggressive campaign against the mob. He was also a violent-tempered murderous hoodlum who was a high-level member of the Chicago crime family. According to one of Shirley MacLaine's many volumes of memoirs, she was at a party with Giancana and his date, who Shirley described as a "dominatrix." This is an interesting insight into the psychology of a powerful Mafioso. Giancana was a man who inspired fear in the world of the Mafia but behind closed doors he may have explored his submissive side. Conspiracy theories also link Sam Giancana with the JFK assassination. He was murdered in 1975.

Vincent "The Chin" Gigante

Nicknamed "The Oddfather" by the media, this Mafia don had a unique strategy to avoid prosecution. He wandered around his New York City neighborhood in a bathrobe chattering away to himself. He had hoped his reputation as mentally ill would enable him to plead insanity in the event he was ever brought to trial. But FBI wiretaps recorded a sane and lucid Gigante on tape. In his youth he was known as the man who shot Frank Costello in the head but did not kill him. The gangster that could not shoot straight tried to convince the feds that he was a don that could not think straight. As of this writing he is in jail.

John Gotti

The Dapper Don was the last of the great flamboyant folk hero Mafiosi. He became the Capone of modern times, but the "Teflon Don" who had successfully avoided prosecution for many years became the "Velcro Don" who ended up in the slammer. He became head of the Gambino crime family after orchestrating the murder of Paul Castellano and became a media darling during his years in power. His celebrity status went to his head and he left himself open for prosecution by his arrogant attitude. He was ultimately betrayed by his underboss Sammy "The Bull" Gravano, but most agree that it was Gotti's hubris and recklessness that did him in. He was sent away for life in 1992. He developed terminal cancer while in prison and died in 2002 at the age of sixty-one.

Sammy "The Bull" Gravano

John Gotti's underboss and one of the "rats" who decided to save his hide and sing to the feds. He confessed to murdering nineteen people over a twenty-year period, an average of about one whack per year. The state thought he would be an invaluable asset in nailing the Teflon Don. His testimony brought down several members of the Gambino, Colombo, and Genovese crime families, including the seemingly indestructible John Gotti. The Bull was granted immunity and entered the Witness Protection Program. He had an active criminal life under his alias while living in Arizona. As of this writing he is in trouble again and facing serious jail time.

Jake Guzik

Al Capone's best friend and the financial brain behind his empire. Even after Capone was jailed and spent his last years in a degenerative state in Florida, Guzik continued to be a powerful and revered Chicago mob figure. Capone's friendship with Guzik was part of the younger generation's willingness to mingle with men from other ethnic groups. The Old World Sicilian Mafia did not deal with other crime outfits, and their lack of tolerance led to their decline and the rise of the Young Turks, who eventually became the venerable elder statesmen of the Americanized Mafia.

James R. Hoffa

Jimmy Hoffa's disappearance in 1975 made him one of the most famous missing persons in American history. Though his fate is not known, you can bet the bank that he was the victim of a Mafia hit. Hoffa was head of the Teamsters Union for many years and spent most of that time as the target of federal investigations into corruption in his union. His primary antagonist was Robert F. Kennedy, who went after Hoffa as a counsel to the McClellan Committee and later as attorney general. But it was the Mafia who eventually terminated the Teamster. Legend has it that he is under the goal post in Giants Stadium in the Meadowlands, New Jersey. Jack Nicholson portrayed Hoffa in a movie of the same name that is a surprisingly sympathetic portrait and paints Robert Kennedy as an overweening little weasel.

J. Edgar Hoover

The all-powerful figure who headed the Federal Bureau of Investigation for almost fifty years. He had dirt on just about everyone, but remained curiously disinterested in the Mafia. In fact, he denied its very existence for decades as the mob grew in size, power, and influence. The Apalachin conference brought the Mafia out from the underworld and onto the pages of *Life* magazine. Hoover looked very bad as a result for having denied their existence and belatedly began to crack down on the Mafia. Rumor has it he had a penchant for cross-dressing, but this has never been confirmed.

Robert F. Kennedy

The former attorney general and senator who spearheaded numerous campaigns against the mob, despite the fact that the Mafia allegedly helped his brother become president of the United States. He took on Jimmy Hoffa and sent him to jail. He also created big headaches for Sam Giancana, Johnny Roselli, and others. He was struck down in a suspicious assassination in 1968. Conspiracy theories abound about both Kennedy assassinations, and many link the Mafia to the murders. There is no doubt that the Mafia had the motive, but did they have the means to orchestrate so elaborate a conspiracy and the cover up? We may never know for sure.

Meyer Lansky

He was the genius behind the National Crime Syndicate, also known as the Commission. He was also the man behind the Mafia's great success with casino gambling and other business ventures on the island of Cuba under the corrupt Batista regime. The famous quote "We're bigger than U.S. Steel" is attributed to him. He was close friends with Lucky Luciano and Bugsy Siegel, but not averse to ordering the hit on Siegel when the volatile hoodlum became out of control and megalomaniacal in his quest to build an empire in the desert town of Las Vegas. Lansky saw that none of his children followed in the "family business." In fact, he arranged for one of his sons to attend the military academy at West Point. Lansky died of old age in Israel after a low-key but highly successful criminal career.

Charles "Lucky" Luciano

The man who, along with Meyer Lansky and others, formed the National Syndicate, also known as the Commission. He came out on top in the aftermath of the Castellemmarese War, when the old and conservative Mustache Petes were completely ousted from power. He turned the Mafia into a well-organized and profitable corporate-like entity. He was ultimately arrested, only to get an early release because of his contributions to the "war effort" during World War II. He was exiled to his native Italy where he died in 1962. He did not live a quiet life when deported. He organized an efficient and massive drug empire that smuggled heroin into the United States and created hundreds of thousands of addicts.

Frank Nitti

This Capone mob lieutenant was given more credit than he deserved when his character became a regular on the television version of *The Untouchables* and the thoroughly despicable villain in the 1987 movie version. Neither version is accurate. He was not respected by the East Coast Commission, and he did not wield power as a criminal mastermind. Nor was he thrown off the roof of the courthouse by Eliot Ness as depicted in the movie, however viscerally appealing that event would have been. In fact he committed suicide rather than face the prospect of a stretch in the slammer.

Dion O'Banion

Al Capone's main rival in the Chicago bootleg wars of the 1920s. Capone won and O'Banion was killed, but his friends and associates waged a vengeful campaign that made Chicago's reputation as a slaughterhouse extend beyond its famous stockyard district.

Joseph Profaci

This crime boss lived lavishly but was generally regarded as a cheap-skate. He compelled members of his family to pay $25 a month in what were essentially union dues. He was also a devout Catholic who sought salvation through generous gifts to the church. The church accepted with a blind eye what was essentially blood money, as tainted as the thirty pieces of silver paid to Judas Iscariot. He was a rarity as far as dons go—he died of natural causes (cancer) while still head of his crime family.

Arnold Rothstein

His claim to fame is the apocryphal tale that he masterminded the fix of the 1919 World Series. Today it is believed that he learned about the scam and profited from it, but was not in on the fix. He was not a flamboyant gun-toting gangster, but rather a shadowy figure pulling strings behind the scenes. Even a low-profile moneyman was not immune to getting whacked, which is the fate that befell Rothstein.

Benjamin "Bugsy" Siegel

Bugsy Siegel was a colorful gangster with leading man looks and a way with the ladies. He was also aptly nicknamed. "Bugsy" referred not to the animated "screwy rabbit" but to Siegel's unbalanced mental state. Best buddies with Meyer Lansky since childhood, the two little rascals formed the Bugs and Meyer mob, an assassination bureau that preceded Murder Incorporated. Their friendship was tested when Siegel went to Las Vegas and had a vision to turn the desert town into a gambling mecca. He went about making the dream a reality with messianic zeal. Unfortunately, his volatile temper and titanic ego got the better of him. His inflated budget and inability to take orders led to his murder, probably on the orders of his boyhood chum Lansky. Bugsy was a good-looking guy who had dreams of being a movie star, and even had movie star pal George Raft arrange a screen test. He never got his wish, but another movie star, Warren Beatty, played Siegel in the 1991 movie *Bugsy*.

Frank Sinatra

One of the greatest entertainers of the century, he also had a naïve and adolescent hero worship of tough guy Mafiosi. Framed more positively, he was a loyal man, and when he was down and out, it was the Mafia who employed him at their many saloons and nightclubs. And when Sinatra was back on top, he did not forget the guys who helped him out when he was at his lowest point. He introduced both John Kennedy and Sam Giancana to party girl Judy Campbell, creating the ultimate "strange bedfellows" in American politics. Say what you want about Old Blue Eyes, he was a great singer, a very good actor, a philanthropist, and more much more than that, he did it his way.

John Torrio

One of Al Capone's two mentors, he instructed Little Al in the ways of the criminal underworld. He was a lesser-known founding member of what became the Commission, and he was upstaged in Mafia lore by the unassuming Meyer Lansky. After a nearly successful attempt on his life, he soured on the whole mob milieu. He eventually retired from the "business" and bequeathed his holdings and his influence to Capone.

Joseph Valachi

He was the most famous of the "rats" that began telling tales out of school to the government about the inner workings of the Mafia. The stories he told, while certainly interesting, were not groundbreaking, nor did they result in any major arrests or convictions. Much of Valachi's testimony should be taken with more than a few grains of salt. Nevertheless he made for "must-see" television when the Senate subcommittee headed by Senator John L. McClellan aired in 1963. Peter Maas wrote the best-selling book *The Valachi Papers,* and Charles Bronson played him in a movie.

Glossary of Terms

Mafia Lingo

action: Gambling that is done through a bookie or other illegal means. The Mafia always demands "a piece of the action."

administration: In the corporate hierarchy, this is the top echelon of a Mafia family. It includes the boss, underboss, and consigliere. Like the top officers in any legitimate corporation, these are the men who make the decisions, though in the underworld, termination has more finality than a pink slip.

agita: The Italian expression for a tummy ache. It is also used to convey a general state of free-floating anxiety.

airing: If a Mafioso says this to you he is not inviting you to join him to savor the gentle evening breeze. It means that he is going to kill you.

alkali: Whiskey, especially of the bootleg variety. It is a slang for the word "alcohol."

alky cooker: Prohibition language for a still, a makeshift distillery to make moonshine alcohol.

alky racket: Prohibition expression for the bootleg business. Alky is a slang expression for alcohol and sometimes for an alcoholic.

American way: This is not a patriotic slogan or part of Superman's super-mandate of fighting for "truth, justice, and the American way." It is the Mafia's phrase for the peaceful coexistence of rival crime families.

amico: A friend or associate of a crime family who is not a member of the family.

amico nostro: The Italian phrase for "friend of ours." It is how a member of a crime family introduces a stranger who is also a made man.

Apache Indian job: Attack by firebomb that kills the victim and destroys the building they were in with such efficiency that identification of the body is difficult.

area man: An organized crime official who has jurisdiction over a particular area within a crime family's turf.

the arm: Another name for an organized crime family. Perhaps also the basis for the slang expression "to put the arm on someone," meaning to intimidate them.

assassin's special: The preferred weapon of choice for many a Mafia hit man. A .22-caliber handgun with a silencer.

associate: The Mafia equivalent of an office temp. He works for a crime family but is not a wiseguy or a made man.

attaché casing: Making the rounds and collecting bribes of such volume that they have to be lugged home to the don in a briefcase.

away: When a Mafioso is doing jail time, he is simply said to be "away." Another euphemism is the ironic "away at college."

babania: The drug traffic, especially heroin. Forbidden for many years, but eventually the old dons looked the other way because of the big profits made in the narcotics business.

babbo: A doofus and dummy in Mafia lingo. The antithesis of a man of respect.

baby sister: A police or federal bodyguard for a "rat" who is under witness protection.

bag man: A low-level hood who is sent on errands. He is usually either picking up or delivering money.

banana race: A horse race that has a "sure thing" winner. In other words, the race has been fixed.

B-and-A racket: Standing for beer and alcohol, it is another expression for Prohibition.

Bangkok Connection: The path that illegal drugs travel from Southeast Asia to the United States. The narcotics industry, long eschewed by the Mafia, eventually became one of its biggest moneymaking rackets.

barracuda: A politically incorrect expression for an unattractive woman.

barrel murder: The instance when a murder victim is stuffed into a barrel and left there to decompose, or sometimes weighted down and dumped in the river or at sea.

beauty doctor: A steel-tipped club. This particularly nasty weapon is designed to maim and mutilate the victim.

beef: A disagreement with or grievance against someone.

beefer: A person who has "a beef" with someone else.

big earner: The Mafia equivalent of Salesman of the Year. A member of a crime family whose activities made a lot of money for the team.

big papa: A slang word for the Thompson machine gun, the weapon of choice for many mobsters in the 1930s.

black robe: The slang expression for a judge, who of course wears a black robe during court proceedings.

the books: Those ironic Mafiosi! Since nothing is committed to paper, they call their activities "the books." When there is an opening to join a family,

the books are open.

boosters: Small-time street thieves.

borgata: Another name for a Mafia crime family.

boss: Another name for the head of a Mafia family. See also *don*.

Boss of Bosses: The Mafia don who was the de facto head of the Commission. Outsiders assume that the Alpha Mafioso among the heads of the five families is the Boss of Bosses, but internally the term is not used, since the other four family heads would disagree with the fifth don's claim to the title.

break an egg: To kill someone.

broken: The same meaning as in the military. To be demoted in rank for an offense against the family.

brugad: Another name for a crime family. See also *borgata*.

buckwheats: A particularly nasty murder where the victim is tortured at length before being put out of his misery. This was used in revenge killings of men who had done something especially bad in the eyes of the Mafia.

buon' anima: This Italian phrase is translated as "rest his soul." It is obviously uttered in reference to one of the dearly departed. Or with mordant irony about someone who has just been whacked.

burn: To kill someone.

bust out: Bankruptcy the hard way. Not through abusing credit cards, but through theft and corruption by the mob. It was used as a method to destroy an enemy's livelihood.

buttlegging: It refers to another form of

bootlegging—the buying and selling of untaxed cigarettes.

button: Another name for a Mafioso who has become a "made" man.

cafone: A disreputable character, or as Shakespeare would say "a slight, unmeritable man."

canary: A "stool pigeon." Someone who "sings" to the law, betraying fellow members of the Mafia.

cane corn: A type of bootleg alcohol made from corn and cane sugar.

capo: The Italian word for "captain." A middle-management Mafioso, usually in charge of a crew or two.

capodecina: A supervisor in a crime family who manages ten "soldiers."

Capo di tutti Capi: The Italian expression meaning "Boss of Bosses."

caporegime: A lieutenant in a crime family. Unlike the military, where a captain is the superior officer to a lieutenant, the caporegime outranks the capo.

captains of industry: An early name for the Commission, or National Syndicate. Perhaps used as an ironic term, comparing themselves with the Carnegies, Vanderbilts, and other legitimate businessmen whom the Mafia believed to be, in their own way, as ruthless and corrupt as themselves.

carpet: Another phrase for a meeting held between two or more Mafia families to settle disputes. Perhaps a variation of the slang expression "called on the carpet."

case: Checking out a site of a planned robbery or hit, as in "casing the joint."

cement coffin: This is when a murder victim is stuffed into a tub or barrel that is filled with cement and dumped in whatever body of water is most convenient.

cement overcoat: Similar to *cement coffin.*

cement shoes: In this instance, only the feet are encased in cement till it hardens, then the victim is buried at sea, sometimes while still alive.

chairman: A consultant or adviser to the Commission.

chairman of the board: Another term for don, boss, or head of a crime family. Also a nickname given to Old Blue Eyes himself, Frank Sinatra.

chased: To be outcast by the Mafia. A harsh sentence, but there is no doubt that those who are "chased" prefer it to being "whacked."

che bruta: An Italian phrase that means "how ugly you are."

che peccato: An Italian phrase that means "what a pity, what a shame."

chiacchierone: An Italian phrase that means "chatterbox."

chief corrupter: The member of a crime family whose job it is to corrupt police, judges, elected officials, and others.

cleaning: The efforts that a mobster takes to avoid being followed by any enemy or the law. It involves eluding a tail, or someone following the mobster in a car or on foot or by other means.

clip: To steal from someone. Also, to kill someone.

clock: To monitor someone's activities; keeping an eye on a person.

code of silence: See *Omerta.*

col tempo la foglia di gelso diventa seta: An

Italian phrase that means "Time and patience change the mulberry leaf to satin."

comare: A Mafia girlfriend. A term of endearment.

The Combination: A 1930s name for the Mafia.

come heavy: To arrive on the scene carrying a gun. If a Mafioso is told to "come heavy," he knows that there is likely to be gunplay.

come in: An audience with the don when he requests your presence. This is an invitation you can't refuse.

The Commission: The Mafia leadership made up of the bosses of the five New York families—Gambino, Genovese, Lucchese, Colombo, and Bonanno.

compare: A pal, chum, or a buddy in Mafia lingo.

connected: A person who regularly does business with the Mafia but is not a member of a family.

consigliere: The counselor or adviser to the don, often but not always an attorney.

contract: When a hit is ordered on a person and a Mafioso assumes the role of "whacker," it is called a contract.

Cosa Nostra: The Italian phrase literally meaning "Our Thing," which is what the Mafia calls itself. The phrase came to national attention during the Valachi hearings. For years J. Edgar Hoover denied the existence of La Cosa Nostra. A bad thing for the nation's "top cop" to be in denial about.

crew: A band of Mafia soldiers that reports to a capo. Crews engage in all manner of mischief, including heists and hijacking.

cugine: An ambitious and youthful Mafioso whose goal is to be "made." Though he is valuable, he is also regarded with a wary eye by the elder gangsters, since he may also be a threat sometime down the line. See also *Young Turks*.

CW: An FBI term that stands for "cooperating witness." It does sound a little nicer than "rat."

deadbeat: Someone who does not pay his debts.

deli: Abbreviated version of the word "delegate," as in union delegate.

dime: The slang expression for $1,000.

district man: A crime family officer whose turf covers a small section of a city or suburban area.

do a piece of work: To kill someone.

dollar: Another slang expression for $1,000.

don: The title for the boss of a Mafia family. An Italian term of respect.

double-decker coffin: A coffin with a false bottom that accommodates two bodies. The paying customer is in the top tier, and the victim of a mob hit whom the Mafia would like to secretly bury is secreted below. One of the Mafia's many interests is the funeral home business.

drop man: A low-level hood who picks up the bets from the numbers runner.

earner: A moneymaker for a crime family. See also *big earner*.

eat alone: To be a greedy gangster and keep the loot for yourself, not allowing others to "wet their beaks."

elder statesman: Another name for the boss of a crime family.

empty suit: A Mafioso wannabe, a hanger on who is regarded with contempt by the members of the family.

enforcer: A tough guy who uses violence to send a message from his Mafia superiors. See also *muscle*.

envelope: Money paid for protection or bribery, handed over in an envelope.

executioner: An unusually direct Mafia phrase meaning hit man.

***facia bruta*:** An Italian expression that means "ugly face."

The feds: The federal government, specifically its law enforcement wing. It has been the longtime bane of the Mafia's existence.

fence: A person who takes stolen merchandise and is able to sell it without attracting the attention of the authorities.

field man: A mobster-manager who supervises a group of numbers runners.

fifth estate: Another name for organized crime.

finger: To inform on a person and report them to the Mafia. This could be for a lesser offense or for a hit.

The five families: The Bonanno, Colombo, Gambino, Genovese, and Lucchese crime families, located in New York City. These are the most powerful organized crime units in the country. There are crime families all across the country, but it is believed they report to the big bosses in New York and Chicago. It is also believed that the New Orleans crime family is independent of the rest.

five times .38: To be shot five times with a .38 caliber revolver. Mafia hit men often almost empty their guns into their target. Better safe than sorry.

forbidden fruit: Like Eve and the apple, this refers to a "good" Italian girl who attracts the attention of an amorous Mafioso.

***fratellanza*:** The Italian word for "brotherhood," another name for the Mafia.

friend of mine: The expression for someone who is not a member of the crime family but is deemed trustworthy.

friend of ours: What one "made" man says when introducing another "made" man to the family.

fugazi: A slang expression for anything that is counterfeit, including counterfeit currency.

G: Shorthand for the government. FBI agents were called "G-Men" in the Golden Age of Mafia misbehavior.

gaff: A crooked person and unrepentant con man and thief.

gangbuster: A law enforcement officer at the federal, state, or local level whose mandate is to battle organized crime. Eliot Ness and Thomas E. Dewey were two famous gangbusters. So was Rudy Giuliani before he became mayor of New York City.

gangland: A generic name for organized crime. It was also the nickname for Chicago during the Al Capone years.

get a place ready: A nice way of saying that a place should be prepared to dispose of a person who is soon to be whacked.

gift: A euphemism for a bribe.

***gira diment*:** An Italian phrase that means "going crazy."

give a pass: This is something that a Mafioso would be happy to hear. It means that he has been granted a stay of execution. In other words, he is not going to be whacked.

giveup: The percentage of a mobster's ill-gotten earnings that he must hand over to his bosses. Just like any business, the bosses in the boardroom make the big money while the working stiffs get the scraps from the table.

godfather: Another name for don that entered the vernacular through Mario Puzo's novel and Francis Ford Coppola's trilogy of the same name.

going: This refers to a person who has been targeted to be murdered.

going south: When a mobster goes "on the lam" to avoid the feds.

goner: A person who had been marked for murder by the Mafia.

goodfellas: Another name for wiseguys. Also the title of one of the most realistic Mafia movies.

good people: The term that mobsters use for someone who is easy to deal with, i.e., someone that will not have to be whacked anytime soon.

goombah, sometimes **gumba:** A Sicilian slang word for buddy.

goon: Another term for *leg breaker* and *muscle*.

graft: Money paid to corrupt politicians, policemen, and judges for favors and to look the other way.

guests of the state: A euphemism for being in jail.

gumod/gumar: A term of endearment for the girlfriend or mistress of a gangster. Most Mafiosi have a kept woman on the side.

hack: Mafia slang for a prison guard, not an underpaid freelance writer.

half-assed wiseguy: A wannabe who seeks entry into a crime family.

ham-and-cheese sandwich: Graft paid to a union official.

handbook: The mobster who sponsors a bookie's gambling operation.

head crusher: Yet another colorful name for *leg breaker, muscle,* and *goon.*

headhunter: A gun for hire. A contract killer; hit man.

heat: Pressure and scrutiny from the law.

hijack: To steal goods and products, usually from a vehicle. Hijacking stuff from airports before it gets to its final destination is a common Mafia enterprise.

hit: To kill someone.

hit man: The assassin who does the hit.

hitmobile: The vehicle the hit man drives, always a nondescript car to avoid attention.

The Honored Society: A reverential name for the Sicilian Mafia.

hot place: A location that the Mafia suspects or knows is being targeted by the feds and is probably under surveillance by camera and wiretaps.

ice: Another of the many synonyms for murder.

ice pick kill: Just what it sounds like. An ice pick is jammed into the ear and enters the brain.

independent: A bookie that is not a Mafioso, but pays a tribute to be allowed to stay in business. Kind of like a 7-11 franchise operation.

in the wind: A person who has disappeared into the Witness Protection Program. They are "gone with the wind."

Italian rope trick: Not as charming as it sounds. Strangulation by a rope.

jamook: An insulting expression. A jamook is basically a dope.

joint: A slang expression for prison.

juice: The interest in a loan from a loan shark, which is invariably higher than your worst credit card company. Anything over 25 percent interest is illegal, which is why some credit card companies stop at 24.99 percent.

kickback: Payoff given to the law to look the other way and to avoid the inconvenience of raids.

kiss of death: A mobster kisses another in a public place. This is not an expression of affection. It means that the Mafioso being kissed is in danger of getting whacked if he doesn't play ball.

lammest: A person who has gone "on the lam," meaning they have gone on the run or into hiding to avoid arrest by the police or the wrath of the Mafia.

large: Slang expression for $1,000.

LCN: The acronym for La Cosa Nostra.

Little Joe: This is an assassination technique reserved for compulsive gamblers in over their heads to the loan shark. They are shot four times in the head in two rows of two shots.

loan shark: A person who loans money with a higher interest rate than your friendly neighborhood credit card company.

made guy: A hoodlum who is made an official and trusted member of a crime family. The prerequisite for admission is usually to kill someone.

madonn': Not the pop star. This an expression of surprise.

mafie: Sicilian gangs that terrorized the peasants and townsfolk back in the Old Country. This was the genesis of the modern Mafia.

make a marriage: When two mobsters are brought together for family business.

make one's bones: Making a killing, quite literally, in order to become a "made" man in the Mafia.

mannagge: This means going to the mattresses in a mob war.

mattresses, going to: Gang war, which is usually a long and bloody affair.

the meets: When the Mafia families get together to discuss business.

mercy room: Mafia slang for the emergency room of a hospital.

message job: This means to shoot someone in a particular body part to send a message to his buddies as to why he was killed.

mezza morta: An Italian phrase that means "half-dead."

middle: In gambling parlance, this is a "sure thing." This is a bet you cannot lose.

middling: Reselling stolen merchandise that "fell off the back of a truck."

mobbed up: Someone who is "connected" to the Mafia.

Moe Green Special: Moe Green was a character in *The Godfather* who was shot in the eye. The character gave the name to this type of Mafia hit.

mortadella: Another Mafia insult, it literally means an Italian sausage.

motorcade murders: Drive-by shootings are not a modern phenomenon. During the 1920s there were numerous celebrated drive-bys.

muscle: Low-level Mafiosi who are the bodyguards, enforcers. Those who are called upon by their superiors to use violence to get the point across.

Mustache Petes: An old-fashioned or conservative Mafioso. They were wiped out in gangland wars in the late 1920s and early 1930s.

nickel: The Mafia denomination that means $500.

OC: The acronym for organized crime.

off: Another synonym for murdering someone.

off the record: Doing something that is not sanctioned by the family.

The Office: The nickname for the New England Mafia.

old man: An affectionate name for the don.

Omerta: The code of silence that a Mafioso takes when he is initiated into a crime family. Breaking the vow is punishable by death.

on the record: Doing something that has the approval of the family.

oobatz: u'pazzu: An Italian expression meaning "crazy."

The Outfit: The name for the Chicago Mafia branch.

parakeet: A not very politically correct term for a good-looking woman.

payola: Another word for graft. Payoffs to corrupt officials to ensure their cooperation.

pazzo: The Italian word meaning "crazy" or "nuts."

piacere: An Italian phrase that means "Pleasure to meet you."

piece: Slang for a gun, as in "packing a piece."

piece of work: A contract to assassinate a person.

pigeon: As in stool pigeon, an informant who betrays the Mafia by going to the feds.

pinched: Meaning to be arrested.

pop: Another word for murder.

pre-hits: Ancillary targets in a major hit. It is wise to whack the associates of a bigwig, lest they try to seek vengeance when their don is killed.

problem: An expression for someone who has caused a problem and is worthy of being whacked.

The Program: Shorthand for the Witness Protection Program.

put the X on: To mark for murder. See *finger*.

put to sleep: The Mafia probably has more euphemisms than any other organization for murder. This is another.

racket: Any illegal business. There was the bootleg racket, gambling racket, prostitution racket, etc.

rat: A made Mafioso who violates the sacred code of Omerta.

respect: Something demanded by all Mafiosi. The Mafia brand of respect is of course based on fear of getting whacked.

RICO: Passed into law in 1970, the Racketeer Influenced and Corrupt Organizations Act gives prosecutors latitude to get tougher sentences for criminals if it is proven that they are members of an organized crime family.

right arm: See *underboss*.

rub out: Another in the lengthy litany of Mafia synonyms for murder.

screw: Mafia name for a prison guard.

serious headache: Mafiosi have an ironic penchant for understatement. Advil won't help this kind of headache. It means a bullet in the head.

serious trouble: If you are in the Mafia's definition of serious trouble, you will not get away with corner time in the social club. If you are in serious trouble you are likely to get a serious headache. See above.

shills: The characters you see in a gambling situation who are winning and making it look easy. They are plants to lure in unsuspecting gamblers.

shiv: Mafia slang for a knife.

shylock: Another term for loan shark. Shylock is a character in William Shakespeare's play *The Merchant of Venice.*

Sicilian necktie: Piano wire that is not used to play Beethoven's Fifth. It is used to strangle the Mafioso's target.

sit-down: A meeting among high-level Mafiosi to settle disputes and grievances before violence ensues.

skim: Just what it sounds like. Taking money off the top, usually from gambling profits, so it is not reported to the IRS as taxable income.

skipper: Not Gilligan's big buddy; it is another name for a capo.

snitch: Another word for someone who is revealing things they shouldn't.

soldier: An infantryman in a Mafia crime family. He is a low-level member of the organization and reports to the capo.

sottocapo: The Italian name for underboss, the second in command in the Mafia family.

spring cleaning: This refers to getting rid of the evidence after a crime has been committed.

stand-up guy: Someone who is eminently trustworthy and will not "rat out" other mobsters under any circumstances.

stone killer: An especially sadistic and ruthless professional assassin.

stoolie: See *pigeon.*

straightened out: To become a "made man." Inducted into a Mafia family.

swag: This expression means the booty lifted during a heist; stolen property.

take for a ride: Your mother warned you not to get in a car with a stranger. The same applies to Mafiosi. If you are taken for a ride, chances are you won't be coming back.

tax: A euphemism for taking a cut of another's Mafioso's booty.

telephone solicitor: A bookmaker, or bookie, who takes bets over the phone.

through the eye: As in a bullet in the eye.

through the mouth: As in a bullet in the mouth. This is a form of execution administered to turncoats and stoolies.

trunk music: This would not be music to your ears. This is the Mafia euphemism for the decomposing flesh of a murder victim stuffed in the trunk of a car.

turban: To bash someone on the head, compelling the medical community to apply a large cast, or "turban," in whimsical mob slang. It is not designed to kill. See also *whack.*

Uncle Sugar: This is not the latest children's cereal. It is Mafia slang for the Federal Bureau of Investigation.

underboss: Second in command in a Mafia family.

underworld: Not the Hades of Greek mythology. This is a generic expression for the world of organized crime.

usury: Lending money and collecting interest. It was once banned by the Catholic Church but is a common practice by your credit card company and the corner loan shark. And the interest rate is not all that's different between the two.

va fa napole: An Italian expression that literally means "Go to Naples" but is used to convey the sentiment "Go to hell."

vig: The excessive interest of a loan shark.

walking book: A bookmaker who does not have an office. He makes the rounds to visit his clients.

walk-talk, take a walk: To have a discussion in a public place, such as a golf course, to avoid the possibility that listening devices might pick up the conversation.

waste management business: A slang expression for organized crime.

wearing it: Flashy Mafia strut their stuff like peacocks by wearing the accoutrements of the well-dressed Mafioso, including fancy threads and a pinky ring.

whack: To commit murder.

wiseguys: Mafiosi who are not "made men," hence not admitted to the inner sanctum.

Young Turks: Aggressive and ambitious young Mafiosi who are a threat to the older established dons.

zips: An insulting expression for the Sicilian Mafia used by the American Mafia.

Rat Pack Slang

bag: Interests and hobbies.

barn burner: A very attractive woman.

beard: A man who escorts a woman who is really the date of another, usually married, man on the scene. Peter Lawford reportedly often acted as the beard for John F. Kennedy.

beetle: A woman who has a penchant for gaudy attire.

big-leaguer: A guy who is at the top of his game.

bird: A euphemism for the genitals.

bombsville: A failure, either in business or social affairs.

broad: This term for a woman is considered an insult nowadays, but it was meant as a compliment by the Rat Pack.

bum: A person held in contempt. In Sinatra's case it often referred to members of the press.

Charley: If they forgot a guy's name, the Rat Pack simply called him Charley or sometimes Sam.

chick: An attractive woman.

clyde: An all-purpose expression that can mean any number of things in any given situation. For example, a person might be called a "clyde." Adding the suffix "ville," as in Clydesville, refers to a situation.

creep: Someone who is disliked and held in contempt.

crumb: See *creep.*

dame: A woman that the Rat Pack deemed unattractive.

dig: To enjoy or appreciate something or someone.

end: Means that a person, thing, or event is the last word on the subject, the best.

endsville: the opposite of *end*. A talented or attractive person would be "the end," i.e., the last word on the subject, but endsville would be an unpleasant event or situation.

fink: Similar to *rat* and *stoolie* in Mafia slang.

fracture: To find something funny. Something funny "fractured" a Rat Packer.

gas: Something or someone that is great fun, also called a "gasser."

gasoline: A slang expression for alcohol.

gofer: This has entered the larger vernacular. It means someone who performs menial tasks, who you would send to "go for" something.

good night all: Frank Sinatra would say this when he wanted the topic of conversation to be immediately changed.

Harvey: A derisive expression for someone the Rat Pack did not like. Sometimes shortened to "Harve."

hello!: This is blurted out when an attractive woman strolls by. It is not said to anyone in particular. The character who does this in contemporary pop culture is Austin Powers.

hunker: Another expression for "gofer."

let's lose Charley: The desire to get away from a dull person in their presence.

mouse: A petite young woman whom the Rat Pack could not decide whether to buy an ice cream cone or invite to their dressing room.

nowhere: Someone whom the Rat Pack deemed a loser.

player: another expression that is still in use today. A club hopper and ladies' man who puts his own pleasures first. The Rat Pack thought these were admirable qualities.

rain: No need to look out the window if Frank said this. It meant he was bored and wanted to leave the party.

ring-a-ding: Something that was a good thing. An expression of appreciation.

scramsville: To make a hasty retreat; split the scene.

smashed: Drunk.

square: A provincial and conservative bore.

tomato: An extremely desirable woman.

twirl: A young woman who liked to dance.

twist: See *twirl*.

witch doctor: An expression for any man of the cloth.

Mafia Timeline

1890–1891:	New Orleans Police Chief David is murdered, allegedly by members of the Mafia. The subsequent trial and mob vigilantism makes international headlines.
1919:	Al Capone arrives in Chicago.
1920:	The Volstead Act becomes law, beginning Prohibition.
1927–1931:	The Castellemmarese War occurs.
1929:	St. Valentine's Day Massacre.
1931:	Lucky Luciano orchestrates the assassination of the Mustache Petes, Masseria and Maranzano.
	Al Capone is sentenced to 11 years for income tax evasion.
1933:	Prohibition is repealed.
1935:	Dutch Schultz is killed.
1936:	Lucky Luciano is convicted and sentenced to 30 to 50 years.
1944:	Murder Inc.'s founder Louis "Lepke" Buchalter gets the electric chair.
1945:	Lucky Luciano is released from prison and deported to Italy.
1947:	Bugsy Siegel is murdered.
1957:	Frank Costello survives a botched hit.
	Albert Anastasia is not so lucky. He is murdered in the barbershop of New York's Park Sheraton Hotel.
	The raid on the Mafia conference on Apalachin, New York gives the gangsters unwanted publicity.
	Carlo Gambino becomes the Boss of Bosses.
1971:	Joe Colombo is shot at the Italian-American Unity Day he organized. He lingers in a vegetative state for years before dying.
1976:	Carlo Gambino dies and is succeeded by Paul Castellano.
1985:	Paul Castellano is hit, most likely on the order of John Gotti, who becomes head of the Gambino crime family.
1992:	John Gotti is sentenced to life for racketeering and murder.
2002:	John Gotti dies in prison.

Index

Omerta requirement of, 208
Sammy Davis, Jr. and, 95, 96, 105
Extortion
American beginnings, 22
Black Hand, 12, 15, 22
"protection money", 22
Sicilian Mafia and, 12, 15, 22

F

Favara, John, 135–36
FBI. *See* Federal Bureau of Investigation (FBI)
Federal agents, 46. *See also* Hoover, J. Edgar; Law enforcement; Ness, Eliot
Federal Bureau of Investigation (FBI)
Al Capone and, 48
Mafia denial by, 53–54, 128
movies/TV programs, 52, 53
Top Hoodlum Program, 127, 128
See also Hoover, J. Edgar; Law enforcement
Ferrigno, Steve, 122
Ferro, Vito Cascio, 60, 63
Feudal system, 13–14
Field man, 192
Five families, 65, 111–28
Five times .38, 206
Flamingo Hotel, 92–93
Flegenheimer, Arthur. *See* Schultz, Dutch
"Frankenslang", 210–12
Fratianno, Jimmy "The Weasel", 97, 150
Freedom fighters, 2–4
Free trade, 196–97
Friel, Tom, 46
Fusco, Richard "Nerves", 97

G

Gagliana, Gaetano, 124
Gagliano, Tom, 65
Galante, Carmine "The Cigar", 114–15, 262
Gallo, "Crazy Joe", 116, 118
Gallo brothers, 116
Gallo Wars, 116
Gambino, Carlo, 263
Anastasia hit and, 87, 119
Castellemmarese War and, 65
death of, 123, 132
as family head, 87, 122–23
Joe Columbo and, 116–17
John Gotti and, 131–32
photograph, 97
Vito Genovese and, 87, 119, 120

Gambino family, 122–23
Gambling
skimming, 94, 148–49, 178–79, 230–31
slang, 210
"Gangsterism", 18
Gardner, Bill, 46
Genovese, Vito, 65, 69, 263
Anastasia hit and, 119
Apalachin meeting and, 127
Carlo Gambino and, 87
Frank Costello and, 118–20
Gaetano Reina hit by, 124
Joe Valachi and, 120, 170–73
prison time, 120, 127
Genovese family, 118–21, 180
Get a place ready, 206
Giancana, Sam, x, 263–64
Frank Sinatra and, 57, 92, 104, 105, 107, 270
John Kennedy and, 57, 104, 105, 107, 263, 270
Judy Campbell and, 57, 105, 270
Las Vegas interests of, 94
Robert Kennedy and, 105, 107, 263
Giannola, Vito, 149
Gianolla, Gaetano, 147
Gigante, Vincent "the Chin", 121, 264
Giordano, Anthony, 149
Giovane D'Honore, 191
Glick, Allen, 178
G-Men. *See* Federal agents; Federal Bureau of Investigation (FBI); Hoover, J. Edgar; Law enforcement; Ness, Eliot
Godfather. *See* Don
Godfather, The
The Brotherhood and, 232–34
inspiration for, 113
leadership lessons from, 196–202
reality and, 11, 224–27
The Sopranos and, 219, 220
Goodfellas, 124, 125, 173, 174, 175, 228–30
Goon, 192
Gotti, John "Dapper Don", x, 122, 129–41, 264
Aniello Dellacroce and, 131, 262
death of, 134, 141
death of son, 135–36
downfall of, 128, 138–40
drug trafficking by, 133
early years, 130–31

as family head, 123, 134
Mafia 'justice' of, 135–36
marriage of, 130
Paul Castellano and, 123, 132, 133–34, 260
photograph, 136
prison time, 131, 132, 140
public fascination with, 136–37
as "Teflon Don", 137
Gotti, John "Junior", 138
Gravano, Sammy "The Bull", 138–40, 141, 184, 185, 265
Guardalabene, Vito, 148
Guys and Dolls, 232
Guzik, Jake, 37, 70, 265

H

Hammurabi, Code of, 7–8
Hart, Richard, 43, 260
Head crusher, 192
Hennessey, David Peter, 24–26
Heroin. *See* Drug trafficking
Hill, Henry, x, 124–25, 145, 173–75, 228–30
Hill, Virginia, 92–93
Hoff, Maxie "Boo Boo", 32–33
Hoffa, Jimmy, 94, 107, 147, 156, 265–66
Hoover, J. Edgar, 266
betting tips, 54–55, 261
Clyde Tolson and, 51–52, 53
communists and, 51, 54, 55
death of, 57
Eliot Ness and, 50, 53
FBI and, 51–52
files amassed by, 51, 53, 57
jealousy of, 50, 52–53, 214
Kennedys and, 55–57
Mafia acknowledgement by, 55, 128
Mafia denial by, 53–54, 128, 261
Melvin Purvis and, 52–53
personal life, 51–52, 53
photographs, 56, 108
Hughes, Howard, 97–98
Humor, sense of, 204–5

I

Iannuzzi, Joseph "Joe Dogs", 181–82
Ice pick kill, 206
Independents, 192
Informants, 169–85
Angelo Lonardo, 175–81
Henry Hill, x, 124–25, 145, 173–75,

THE EVERYTHING TALL TALES BOOK

By Nat Segaloff

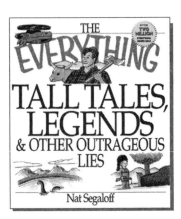

Everyone has heard a story too outrageous to be true. *The Everything® Tall Tales, Legends, & Outrageous Lies Book* debunks these legendary fabrications and explains how each one got started. You'll learn the truth behind some truly bizarre stories, including many of the most infamous scams and Hollywood hoaxes. From the real-life inspirations for mythic heroes like Paul Bunyan, to urban legends that have shocked the world, you'll be amazed to find out what is real and what is just hype.

Trade paperback,
$12.95 ($19.95 CAN)
1-58062-514-2, 288 pages

OTHER *EVERYTHING*® BOOKS BY ADAMS MEDIA CORPORATION

BUSINESS

Everything® **Business Planning Book**
Everything® **Coaching & Mentoring Book**
Everything® **Home-Based Business Book**
Everything® **Leadership Book**
Everything® **Managing People Book**
Everything® **Network Marketing Book**
Everything® **Online Business Book**
Everything® **Project Management Book**
Everything® **Selling Book**
Everything® **Start Your Own Business Book**
Everything® **Time Management Book**

COMPUTERS

Everything® **Build Your Own Home Page Book**
Everything® **Computer Book**

Everything® **Internet Book**
Everything® **Microsoft® Word 2000 Book**

COOKING

Everything® **Bartender's Book, $9.95**
Everything® **Barbecue Cookbook**
Everything® **Chocolate Cookbook**
Everything® **Cookbook**
Everything® **Dessert Cookbook**
Everything® **Diabetes Cookbook**
Everything® **Low-Carb Cookbook**
Everything® **Low-Fat High-Flavor Cookbook**
Everything® **Mediterranean Cookbook**
Everything® **One-Pot Cookbook**
Everything® **Pasta Book**
Everything® **Quick Meals Cookbook**
Everything® **Slow Cooker Cookbook**

Everything® **Soup Cookbook**
Everything® **Thai Cookbook**
Everything® **Vegetarian Cookbook**
Everything® **Wine Book**

HEALTH

Everything® **Anti-Aging Book**
Everything® **Dieting Book**
Everything® **Herbal Remedies Book**
Everything® **Hypnosis Book**
Everything® **Menopause Book**
Everything® **Stress Management Book**
Everything®**Vitamins, Minerals, and Nutritional Supplements Book**
Everything® **Nutrition Book**

HISTORY

Everything® **American History Book**

All Everything® books are priced at $12.95 or $14.95, unless otherwise stated. Prices subject to change without notice.
Canadian prices range from $11.95–$22.95 and are subject to change without notice.

Everything® **Civil War Book**
Everything® **World War II Book**

HOBBIES

Everything® **Bridge Book**
Everything® **Candlemaking Book**
Everything® **Casino Gambling Book**
Everything® **Chess Basics Book**
Everything® **Collectibles Book**
Everything® **Crossword and Puzzle Book**
Everything® **Digital Photography Book**
Everything® **Drums Book (with CD),**
    $19.95, ($31.95 CAN)
Everything® **Family Tree Book**
Everything® **Games Book**
Everything® **Guitar Book**
Everything® **Knitting Book**
Everything® **Magic Book**
Everything® **Motorcycle Book**
Everything® **Online Genealogy Book**
Everything® **Playing Piano and**
    Keyboards Book
Everything® **Rock & Blues Guitar**
    Book (with CD), $19.95,
    ($31.95 CAN)
Everything® **Scrapbooking Book**

HOME IMPROVEMENT

Everything® **Feng Shui Book**
Everything® **Gardening Book**
Everything® **Home Decorating Book**
Everything® **Landscaping Book**
Everything® **Lawn Care Book**
Everything® **Organize Your Home Book**

KIDS' STORY BOOKS

Everything® **Bedtime Story Book**
Everything® **Bible Stories Book**
Everything® **Fairy Tales Book**
Everything® **Mother Goose Book**

NEW AGE

Everything® **Astrology Book**

Everything® **Divining the Future Book**
Everything® **Dreams Book**
Everything® **Ghost Book**
Everything® **Meditation Book**
Everything® **Numerology Book**
Everything® **Palmistry Book**
Everything® **Spells and Charms Book**
Everything® **Tarot Book**
Everything® **Wicca and Witchcraft Book**

PARENTING

Everything® **Baby Names Book**
Everything® **Baby Shower Book**
Everything® **Baby's First Food Book**
Everything® **Baby's First Year Book**
Everything® **Breastfeeding Book**
Everything® **Get Ready for Baby Book**
Everything® **Homeschooling Book**
Everything® **Potty Training Book,**
    $9.95, ($15.95 CAN)
Everything® **Pregnancy Book**
Everything® **Pregnancy Organizer,**
    $15.00, ($22.95 CAN)
Everything® **Toddler Book**
Everything® **Tween Book**

PERSONAL FINANCE

Everything® **Budgeting Book**
Everything® **Get Out of Debt Book**
Everything® **Get Rich Book**
Everything® **Investing Book**
Everything® **Homebuying Book, 2nd Ed.**
Everything® **Homeselling Book**
Everything® **Money Book**
Everything® **Mutual Funds Book**
Everything® **Online Investing Book**
Everything® **Personal Finance Book**

PETS

Everything® **Cat Book**
Everything® **Dog Book**
Everything® **Dog Training and Tricks**
Everything® **Horse Book**
Everything® **Puppy Book**
Everything® **Tropical Fish Book**

REFERENCE

Everything® **Astronomy Book**
Everything® **Car Care Book**
Everything® **Christmas Book, $15.00,**
    ($21.95 CAN)
Everything® **Classical Mythology Book**
Everything® **Divorce Book**
Everything® **Etiquette Book**
Everything® **Great Thinkers Book**
Everything® **Learning French Book**
Everything® **Learning German Book**
Everything® **Learning Italian Book**
Everything® **Learning Latin Book**
Everything® **Learning Spanish Book**
Everything® **Mafia Book**
Everything® **Philosophy Book**
Everything® **Shakespeare Book**
Everything® **Tall Tales, Legends, &**
    Other Outrageous Lies Book
Everything® **Toasts Book**
Everything® **Trivia Book**
Everything® **Weather Book**
Everything® **Wills & Estate Planning**
    Book

RELIGION

Everything® **Angels Book**
Everything® **Buddhism Book**
Everything® **Catholicism Book**
Everything® **Judaism Book**
Everything® **Saints Book**
Everything® **World's Religions Book**
Everything® **Understanding Islam Book**

SCHOOL & CAREERS

Everything® **After College Book**
Everything® **College Survival Book**
Everything® **Cover Letter Book**
Everything® **Get-a-Job Book**
Everything® **Hot Careers Book**
Everything® **Job Interview Book**
Everything® **Online Job Search Book**
Everything® **Resume Book, 2nd Ed.**
Everything® **Study Book**

All Everything® books are priced at $12.95 or $14.95, unless otherwise stated. Prices subject to change without notice.
Canadian prices range from $11.95–$22.95 and are subject to change without notice.

WE HAVE EVERYTHING . . . .

SPORTS/FITNESS

Everything® **Bicycle Book**
Everything® **Fishing Book**
Everything® **Fly-Fishing Book**
Everything® **Golf Book**
Everything® **Golf Instruction Book**
Everything® **Pilates Book**
Everything® **Running Book**
Everything® **Sailing Book, 2nd Ed.**
Everything® **T'ai Chi and QiGong Book**
Everything® **Total Fitness Book**
Everything® **Weight Training Book**
Everything® **Yoga Book**

TRAVEL

Everything® **Guide to Las Vegas**
Everything® **Guide to New England**
Everything® **Guide to New York City**
Everything® **Guide to Washington D.C.**

Everything® **Travel Guide to The Disneyland Resort®, California Adventure®, Universal Studios®, and the Anaheim Area**
Everything® **Travel Guide to the Walt Disney World® Resort, Universal Studios®, and Greater Orlando, 3rd Ed.**

WEDDINGS & ROMANCE

Everything® **Creative Wedding Ideas Book**
Everything® **Dating Book**
Everything® **Jewish Wedding Book**
Everything® **Romance Book**
Everything® **Wedding Book, 2nd Ed.**
Everything® **Wedding Organizer, $15.00** ($22.95 CAN)

Everything® **Wedding Checklist, $7.95** ($11.95 CAN)
Everything® **Wedding Etiquette Book, $7.95** ($11.95 CAN)
Everything® **Wedding Shower Book, $7.95** ($12.95 CAN)
Everything® **Wedding Vows Book, $7.95** ($11.95 CAN)
Everything® **Weddings on a Budget Book, $9.95** ($15.95 CAN)

WRITING

Everything® **Creative Writing Book**
Everything® **Get Published Book**
Everything® **Grammar and Style Book**
Everything® **Grant Writing Book**
Everything® **Guide to Writing Children's Books**
Everything® **Writing Well Book**

ALSO AVAILABLE:
THE EVERYTHING®  KIDS' SERIES!

Each book is 8" x 9¼", 144 pages, and two-color throughout.

Everything® **Kids' Baseball Book, 2nd Edition, $6.95** ($11.95 CAN)
Everything® **Kids' Bugs Book, $6.95** ($10.95 CAN)
Everything® **Kids' Cookbook, $6.95** ($10.95 CAN)
Everything® **Kids' Joke Book, $6.95** ($10.95 CAN)
Everything® **Kids' Math Puzzles Book, $6.95** ($10.95 CAN)
Everything® **Kids' Mazes Book, $6.95** ($10.95 CAN)
Everything® **Kids' Money Book, $6.95** ($11.95 CAN)

Everything® **Kids' Monsters Book, $6.95** ($10.95 CAN)
Everything® **Kids' Nature Book, $6.95** ($11.95 CAN)
Everything® **Kids' Puzzle Book $6.95,** ($10.95 CAN)
Everything® **Kids' Science Experiments Book, $6.95** ($10.95 CAN)
Everything® **Kids' Soccer Book, $6.95** ($11.95 CAN)
Everything® **Kids' Travel Activity Book, $6.95** ($10.95 CAN)

Available wherever books are sold!
To order, call 800-872-5627, or visit us at everything.com

Everything® is a registered trademark of Adams Media Corporation.